THE JEWISH MYSTICAL TRADITION

Ben Zion Bokser

THE PILGRIM PRESS/NEW YORK

Library of Congress Cataloging in Publication Data
Main entry under title:

The Jewish mystical tradition.

Bibliography: p. 275
1. Mysticism—Judaism—History—Sources.
2. Cabala—History—Sources. 3. Hasidism—History—Sources. I. Bokser, Ben Zion, 1907–
BM723.J485 296.7′1 80-27627
ISBN 0-8298-0435-8
ISBN 0-8298-0451-X (pbk.)

The Pilgrim Press, 132 West 31 Street, New York, New York 10001

Dedicated to the loving memory
of Rabbi Ephraim Zalman Halpern

Contents

THE WORLD OF THE KABBALAH

THE RISE OF ḤASIDISM

LATTER DAY MYSTICS

AFTERWORD

People are wrong to be frightened by the word 'mystical.' . . . We must tear it out of its obsolete and mouldy appearance and take it in its pure, sublime and perfected form. . . . But without mysticism would one great picture, one great poem or even one important social movement come into being?

from "Chagall and the Fantasy of the Shtetl," by Nadine and Henri Kaspi in *Forum,* Winter 1979, p. 90

Preface

The mystical dimension in Jewish experience represents a rich treasure of wisdom of special interest to modern man. Mystical wisdom focuses on the inner man, the spiritual dimension of his nature, and the deeper hungers of his spirit that cannot be satisfied on the material or sociological planes alone. And it is in the Jewish mystical tradition that these insights are exemplified with special richness.

The material assembled in this volume offers representative selections from the most significant writings of the Jewish mystics from the earliest times to our own day. As will be explained in the introductory chapter, I find the earliest expression of Jewish mysticism in the Bible, and the most significant of the latter day Jewish mystics in Rabbi Kook. The introductory chapter characterizes the general nature of mysticism, and the distinctiveness of its Jewish component. Each of the figures whose writings are quoted is introduced briefly, in the context of his times, with an assessment of his general philosophy. The texts quoted are also introduced briefly, with an indication of their general nature, and the circumstances of their original publication. All the translations are my own, including those of biblical passages which may differ, in some cases, from the conventional translations. The numbers which head individual paragraphs are for the purposes of this book only and often bear no relationship to the divisions of the original works.

The work as a whole is an outgrowth of a course in Hasidism and Jewish mysticism which I have taught at Queens College. While its format will make it especially useful as a text for students studying this subject in a formal manner, it is also intended to serve the interests of the general reader.

I am grateful to students, colleagues and friends who extended to me assistance and stimulation in dealing with various problems touched on in my work. I acknowledge the help extended to me by my wife, whose insightful comments stimulated me to a deeper understanding of the subject. I acknowledge the help extended by my son, Professor Baruch Micah Bokser, who assisted me with some problems in research, and by my daughter and son-in-law, Miriam and Dov Caravella, who stimulated my sensitivity to the phenomenon of mysticism in the course of our many discussions on the subject. I am indebted to my secretary, Mrs. Shirley Tendler, who typed the manuscript in the varying stages of its development.

I acknowledge with thanks the permission granted to me by Dr. Yitzhak Rafael to quote materials from several of the publications of Mosad Harav Kook.

B.Z.B.

EXPANSES, EXPANSES

Expanses, expanses,
Expanses divine my soul craves.
Confine me not in cages,
Of substance or of spirit.
My soul soars the expanses of the heavens,
Walls of heart and walls of deed
Will not contain it.
Morality, logic, custom—
My soul soars above these,
Above all that bears a name,
Above delight,
Above every delight and beauty,
Above all that is exalted and ethereal.
I am love-sick—
I thirst, I thirst for God,
As a deer for water brooks.
Alas, who can describe my pain,
Who will be a violin to express the songs of my grief,
Who will voice my bitterness,
The pain of seeking utterance?
I thirst for truth, not for a conception of truth,
For I ride on its heights,
I am wholly absorbed by truth,
I am wholly pained by the anguish of expression.
How can I utter the great truth
That fills my whole heart?
Who will disclose to the multitude,
To the world, to all creatures,
To nations and individuals alike,
The sparks abounding in treasures
Of light and warmth
Stored within my soul?
I see the flames rise upward
Piercing the heavens,
But who feels, who can express their might?
I am bound to the world,
All creatures, all people are my friends,
Many parts of my soul
Are intertwined with them,

But how can I share with them my light?
Whatever I say
Only covers my vision,
Dulls my light.
Great is my pain and great my anguish,
O, my God, my God, be a help in my trouble,
Find for me the graces of expression,
Grant me language and the gift of utterance,
I shall declare before the multitudes
My fragments of Your truth, O my God.

—*Abraham Kook*

GENERAL INTRODUCTION

Mysticism and Judaism

Mysticism is the quest for the ultimate meaning of life. The mystic looks at the world, with all its glamor and allurement, and finds it wanting. Empirical existence appears to him fragmented, beset by endless conflicts and contradictions between individuals and groups; the values on which it tends to focus are material things. The mystic is a sensitive spirit who rebels against such an orientation of life. By delving deeper he claims to have found another reality, in which all life is linked with God in a harmonious unity, in which the spiritual essence supersedes all material concerns.

The term mystic derives from the Greek *mystes,* a name given to an initiate to the Greek mystery religions. The initiate possessed the secrets of the cult, which were tantamount to the secrets of life itself. The mystic's discovery of a reality behind the empirical world was regarded similarly as the uncovering of a secret, because empirical existence tended to obscure the divine reality. As a rule the mystic's quest occurred in the context of some religious tradition, and all religious systems include some elements of mysticism.

The goal of the mystic is not to gain conceptual knowledge, to find confirmation that a higher reality exists; it is rather to establish an emotional bond with it. It is to embrace the vibrations of this higher reality which pulsate through existence. It is to establish *devekut,* union with, or, as Jewish mystics prefer to define it, cleaving to God. The fruits of this experience are a reconciliation to life as something noble and exalted, a surge of creative energy that enables a person to pursue tasks hitherto deemed too arduous, and an inner illumination which reveals a wisdom beyond the reach of dialectical reason. As Rufus Jones put it: "The essential characteristic of the mystical experience is the attainment of personal conviction by an individual that the human spirit and the divine spirit have met, have found each other, and are in mutual and reciprocal correspondence as spirit with Spirit. In short, mystical devotion means direct, first-hand fellowship with God, and the deepened life-results which emerge.[1]

The mystic does not see himself as venturing into a realm unknown when he orients his life to God. On the contrary, his encounter is a kind of homecoming. The ultimate reality resides in his own heart; it is the soul, or the spiritual dimension of his nature. It is the image of God we all bear on us as part of our humanity. In the routine of life we are often alienated from it; its claims are ignored. The rewards of worldly or surface existence allure us, and we are content to live on that plane. But some are stirred by a higher sensibility, and they find such rewards trivial and unsatisfying. During times of crisis especially, the rewards on that level are often thrust out of our hands, and we face tragic aspects of life. Then many of us seek a firmer anchor for our existence; and then we discover the inner light and follow the path to which it points. Abraham J. Heschel described this with striking phraseology: "Man's walled mind has no access to a ladder upon which he can, on his own initiative, rise to a knowledge of God. Yet his soul is endowed with translucent windows that open to the beyond. And if he wishes to reach up to Him it is a reflection of the divine light in him that gives him the power for such yearning . . . For God is not always silent and man is not always blind."[2]

Not only religious mystics have testified to the existence of a transcendent, inner world, beyond the experiences of the senses. Artists brooding on the sources of their vision have often credited an illumination or inspiration from a transcendent realm. Mozart, confessing his bafflement at the profusion of musical ideas which con-

---

1. *Rufus Jones Speaks to Our Time,* ed. Harry Emerson Fosdick (Macmillan, New York 1951), p. 12.

2. *God in Search of Man* (Farrar, Strauss & Cudahy, New York 1955), p. 138.

tinually flowed in his mind, put it thus: "Whence and how they come I know not; nor can I force them ... This is perhaps the best gift I have my Divine Maker to thank for.[3] Walt Whitman, in his *Leaves of Grass*, declared: "The hand of God is the elder hand of my own ... the spirit of God is the elder brother of my own." Marc Chagall has put it more generally: "Our whole inner world is reality, perhaps even more real than the apparent world."[4] Prophets and reformers of all kinds have invariably claimed that a "call" from a divine source has sent them to undertake their mission. Evelyn Underhill has summed it up in these words: "As we watch life, we realize how deeply this double fact of God's inciting movement and the response it evokes from us, enters into all great action; and not only that which we recognize as religious. In all heroic achievements, and all accomplishment that passes beyond the useful to seek the perfect, we are conscious of two factors which cannot be separated ... There is ever a genuine and costly personal effort ... and there is inciting, supporting and using this devoted thrust of the creature, this energetic love, a mighty invading and enveloping Power."[5]

The mystical experience itself has an objective component, but the shape it assumes allows for a wide play of subjectivity. The poet or the musician shapes his inspiration according to subjective patterns of style and value judgments, and so does the mystic. The uniqueness of persons, the distinctiveness of religious and cultural expressions, the mood of the times—all will influence the interpretation he gives to his own experience. As Gerschom Scholem has stated: "Mystical experience is fundamentally amorphous. The more intensely and profoundly the contact with God is experienced, the less susceptible it is of objective definition ... Because mystical experience as such is formless there is in principle no limit to the forms it can assume."[6]

There is a school of thought that regards the mystical experience and the pursuit of reason as antithetical, but there is a long tradition in the history of mysticism which regards the two as complementary. This, for instance, was the position of Plotinus, who stressed rational as well as moral requirements in the life of the true mystic. As summarized by E.R. Dodds: "The habit of analytical thought is to Plotinus a necessary and valuable discipline ... Mystical union is not a substitute for intellectual effort but its crown and goal. Nor is it a substitute for moral effort ... 'Without true virtue,' he says, 'all talk of

---

3. Cited by Brewster Chiselin, *The Creative Process* (New American Library, New York 1955), pp. 44f.

4. Quoted in *American Artist* (May, 1961), p. 3.

5. Cited by Rufus Jones, *The Testimony of the Soul* (Macmillan, New York 1937), p. 209.

6. *On the Kabbalah and its Symbolism* (Schocken, New York 1965), p. 8; cf. Edwyn Bewan, *Symbolism and Belief* (Beacon Press, Boston 1938), pp. 353f.

God is but words.' He who would attain to the experience must be an artist in morals."[7] Maimonides, too, belonged to this tradition. Generally looked upon as the exponent of rationalism in Jewish tradition, there was, in fact, a pronounced mystical strain in his thought. As J. Abelson put it, "Maimonides is rationalist and mystic at the same time. While striving to strip the Hebrew scriptures of the supernatural and the miraculous, he exhibits his strong belief in a world impregnated with traces and symptoms of a Divine life."[8] It is to be noted also that Maimonides listed intellectual and moral perfection among the pre-requisites of prophecy, which for him was a higher kind of mystical illumination.[9]

Mystics were the initial creators of every religious system. Their souls were lit with a vision which they sought to share with other men, and religions were born to cultivate this vision and enshrine it as an abiding treasure for generations to come. Mystics functioned as devotees of organized religion and as rebels who challenged its authority, seeking to make room for fresh illumination which they had experienced. Some mystics were identified with their particular national or ethnic group and sought to redress its wrongs, while others were universalists who dissolved their people's earthly problems in a withdrawal to spirituality. Some mystics sought to deepen the levels of spirituality of their own established religious community, and others appeared as masters seeking to enlighten men across all the boundaries of formal religious traditions. They sometimes envisioned the ultimate reality as a personal God patterned after the imagery of traditional religion, and sometimes they were close to pantheism and pictured the ultimate reality as the spirit immanent in the universe.

Some mystics renounced the world and withdrew into contemplative solitude; some renounced marriage and the family as a yielding to the claims of the flesh; some even renounced speech in order to break their links with the worldly. But this process of withdrawal at times led to a blunting of the ethical component of religion, for ethics is the blueprint of a lifestyle *within* the world, and a projection of goals for redressing its inequities. A definition of perfection as a vertical ascent toward the divine has at times carried with it a dissociation from the world and its problems as the trivialized preoccupation of those who are not yet liberated from worldliness. Not all mystics follow this path, of course. But otherworldliness has in many instances been the characteristic of the mystical quest, and it

---

7. *Pagan and Christian in an Age of Anxiety* (W.W. Norton & Co., New York 1970), pp. 87f.

8. J. Abelson, *Jewish Mysticism* (Hermon Press, New York 1969), pp. 65f.

9. *Guide* II 36, 45.

has borne with it an alienation from the world of temporal existence and from all efforts to cope with its problems.

As Albert Schweitzer has noted: "Every philosophy has its mystical aspects, and every profound thought is mystical. But mysticism has always stopped with the passive, on an insufficient basis, as regards ethics. Indian, Stoical, medieval, all great mysticisms, have aimed at achieving union through passivity."[10] Rivka Schatz has called attention to a similar passivity in Ḥasidism.[11]

Sometimes mystics have brought with them the problem of sectarian fragmentation. Those who adhere to a religious tradition hallow it in all its institutional forms, and the visionary who has experienced a new illumination and seeks to proclaim it seems like an intruder, a disturber of the familiar way of faith. Those mystically inclined, for their own security and for the more effective cultivation of their treasured new spiritual discoveries, will often form separatist groups which may develop into sects or cults of their own. This problem has appeared in every religious community.

The gravest problem posed by mysticism has been the apotheosizing of the master. Mystically inclined people usually rally around a central figure, a charismatic individual, who experienced the divine illumination, and by whose light they see light. Sometimes they idolize the master as a semi-divine or divine figure, and his teachings are invested with absolute authority. The master himself, under the spell of his illumination, may forget his own finitude, and support this idolization by his followers. The attempt to order life after the blueprint projected by these "prophets" has often been costly to humanity. The Bible calls for careful scrutiny of every new claimant to prophecy (Deut. 13:2–4). According to Rabbi Kook, who was undoubtedly influenced by Maimonides in this respect, every mystical illumination must go through a process of ethical and rational refinement if it is to yield its great spiritual potential for the advancement of civilization. "A profound moral and rational refinement," Rabbi Kook states, "must precede the illumination of a psychic force from the higher autonomous realm of the spiritual . . . One unrefined element in the area where the light from the source of existence is acting can create a world of confusion and inflict immense damage upon great multitudes for generations to come."[12]

Jewish mysticism seeks the same goal as all mysticism but it speaks in an idiom of its own. In addition to the subjective factors, Jewish

---

10. *The Ethical Mysticism of Albert Schweitzer,* ed. Henry Clark (Beacon Press, Boston 1962), p. 189.

11. See her *Ḥasidut keMistikah* (Magnes Press, Jerusalem 1968), ch. 1–5.

12. *Abraham Isaac Kook,* ed. Ben Zion Bokser (Paulist Press, New York 1978), p. 290.

mystics also reflect the uniqueness of the cultural ethos of their Jewish experience. They seek an answer not only to personal sufferings, but to the sufferings of their people. They seek to reconcile God's choosing of Israel with the circumstances of Israel's tribulation in the dark night of exile. They seek God's face not only in the vicissitudes of the world, but they also seek Him in the reality of Jewish tradition itself, which they were taught to regard as a divine revelation. They seek a place in the mystical way for the Torah and the commandments. Formalism, outer conformity, the sharpening of the mind through study—these do not satisfy them. They seek in all things the added dimension of the invisible inner light in which alone they find satisfaction to still the hunger of the spirit.

II

The earliest traces of Jewish mysticism are to be found in the Bible. Scholem regards mysticism as a post-biblical phenomenon, but he notes that the medieval Jewish philosophers, Maimonides included, in effect identified prophecy with the mystical experience. Scholem writes: "Can we and should we identify prophetic revelation and mystical experience? It is an old question, that has led to endless controversy. Personally I reject such an identification . . . In the medieval philosophy of both the Arabs and the Jews there developed a theory of prophecy which amounts to an identification of the prophet with the mystic."[13] Indeed, Scholem himself, in defining the nature of mysticism, cites a verse from the Bible (Ps. 34:9): "Taste, and see that the Lord is good."[14]

It is true that the prophet is primarily concerned with serving the world rather than with the quest for illumination as such. But this only illustrates the diverse expressions of mysticism; it does not argue for the exclusion of the prophet from the category of the mystic. As Sidney Spencer has stated: "The most widely differing views have been held as regards the relation of the religion of the Old Testament to the attitude and experience of the mystic . . . It is true that there is a certain distinction between the experience of the prophets and that of the mystics generally . . . But if the prophet's union with the divine is a functional union, if (as he believes) he is made one with God as His messenger for a particular end, his experience has nonetheless an essentially mystical quality . . . And the Psalmists are not only moved by a mystical passion for a reawakening of God-consciousness; they

13. *On the Kabbala and its Symbolism*, pp. 9f.
14. *Major Trends in Jewish Mysticism* (Schocken, New York 1946), p. 4.

give evidence again and again of an abiding communion . . . which links them with God in an enduring unity."[15] Abelson takes the same position: "Jewish mysticism is as old as the Old Testament . . . The Old Testament scintillates with sublime examples of men whose communion with God was a thing of intense reality to them . . . The sudden and unexpected inrushes of Divine inspiration which seized the Old Testament prophets . . . all these represent a stage of first-hand, living religion to which the name of mysticism is rightly and properly applied."[16]

Biblical mysticism is generally direct and uncomplicated by esoteric teachings. It expresses deep yearning for God as the all-good, beyond the sordidness of the mundane world. This motif is especially pronounced in the Book of Psalms, which is a veritable collection of love songs between man and God. "My soul yearns for God, for the living God," the Psalmist cries out (42:3), and this yearning is his constant mood and emotion. He cites the wondrous panorama of nature, and the beneficence of divine providence, but these hold no spell for him in themselves. It is the God who transcends them and of whom they serve as a constant reminder who is the object of his adoration. There is a strong moral tone in these songs, the Psalmist knows that he must be worthy of God's love, and the one measure by which he can be purified from life's dross is a sincere faith and, above all, the deeds of love for God's creatures. He senses one problem which appears to obscure God's reign, the problem of evil, but he is confident that the triumphs of evil are only a temporary frustration and that soon the wicked will inherit the full measure of divine retribution.

In the writings of the prophets the vision of the illumined spirit is translated into other tones. The prophets are also stirred by their faith in and love for God, and they have also experienced His presence in their lives. Sometimes they, too, sing of the glories of God, but the divine touch has turned them in more realistic directions, to offer guidance to their people in times of stress. They are champions of justice who denounce the greed and selfishness of society; they expose and denounce religious formalism which is devoid of depth and sincerity; they predict doom for their people because of its straying; and when their people have suffered exile the prophets encourage them to the faith in future redemption.

The mystical illumination proceeds directly from its divine source to its mortal recipient. All it needs is a perceptive human sensibility to receive the light, and the encounter can be effected. But the

---

15. *Mysticism and World Religion* (A.S. Barnes and Co., New York 1963), pp. 170, 173, 175.

16. *Jewish Mysticism*, pp. 7, 17.

imagination of the mystic will sometimes elaborate on his experience and project physical channels for the movement between the human and the divine realm. The ladder and the chariot have appeared frequently in this role. We find them in the testimonies of mystics in non-Jewish as well as Jewish mystical literature.[17] It is especially when the mystic's vision is intense, when it occurs while asleep or while in a trance, that the imaginative projection of a physical channel for communication between the earthly and the heavenly is added to the mystical experience itself.

The fusion of the core experience of the mystic with its imaginative elaboration is well illustrated in the Bible. Jacob's dream included a ladder which linked heaven and earth (Gen. 28:12). Elijah is described as having been taken to heaven in a fiery chariot (II Kings 2). Ezekiel's vision (Ezekiel I) glimpsed the divine throne as set on a chariot which was moved by a group of strange angelic beings. Isaiah's call came to him in a vision (Isaiah 6) in the Temple in which he saw God on His divine throne, and heard His voice charging him with his mission. But be it noted that in both Ezekiel and Isaiah the point of the vision is not to disclose heavenly mysteries; it is rather to describe the context in which the prophets first felt themselves called to lead their people, to reprove them for their wrongdoing and to chart for them the way to go.

This is the distinctive character of prophetic mysticism. It is not a retreat from the world to God; it is the return to the world after an encounter with God, to seek its transformation toward divine ideals, to make it worthy of the Creator who graced it with His concern by calling it into being.

III

Mystical interests in talmudic times were often directed toward the esoteric. There were some who sought to break out of the bounds of the finite world and to draw nearer to the special realm where God's presence was centered. The biblical allusion to a chariot that apparently links heaven and earth was seized on by mystics eager to draw ever closer to God, and they developed the notion that, through proper preparation, the mystic might in a trance or in an ascent of soul after death ride on this chariot to the divine realm, at least to the chamber where the divine throne was set.

We have several writings of mystics, the so-called *Hekhalot* literature (also known as Merkabah mysticism), which describes this

---

17. See Franz Cumont, *Astrology and Religion Among the Greeks and Romans* (Dover, New York 1960), p. 101.

ascent of soul, and the glories which those chosen spirits experienced. They were able to join the heavenly chorus in singing praises to God; they saw the judgment meted out to the enemies of their people; they learned secrets about the destinies of individuals and of the world; they became impregnated with all kinds of potency usually denied to mortals. We have some allusions to this and other types of mysticism in talmudic literature. Some rabbis clearly cultivated it, and sought to gain its ineffable rewards. Others, however, discouraged it, and in some cases even sought to suppress it. The throne mysticism had in it too much of the other-worldly and the esoteric; it was a disruptive influence working against the stability of life. It was a secret avocation for the chosen few, but the general public could have no share in it.

Another type of esoteric mysticism pursued in talmudic times centered on the pronunciation of God's proper name, which may be approximated by the consonants YHWH. There was an ancient belief that a name bears with it the essence of the thing or being which the name represents. This invested God's proper name with a special association for the mystic. The pronunciation of the name was believed to conjure up God's very presence and to invoke the full play of His hidden potency. In the words of Ernst Cassirer: "It is most of all the proper name that is bound up by mysterious ties to the individuality of an *essence*. Even today we often feel this peculiar awe of the proper name—this feeling that it is not outwardly appended to a man, but is in some way part of him . . . But for mythical thinking the name . . . expresses what is innermost and essential in the man, and it practically is this innermost essence—Name and personality merge . . . The name of a god, above all, constitutes a real part of his essence and efficacy. It designates the sphere of energies within which each deity is and acts."[18]

Sheldon H. Blank has traced various allusions in the Bible to the divine potency which is associated with the pronunciation of God's proper name.[19] This tendency became more evident in talmudic times. Miraculous events recorded in the Bible were accounted for by reference to the potency released through the pronunciation of God's proper name. A natural by-product of this belief was "name magic"—the conviction that through the right pronunciation of God's name one could command the divine potency to carry out his bidding. The rabbis reacted by banning the pronunciation of God's proper name and replacing it by various appelations. Even in writing replacements were substituted. The only exception made was in the priestly blessing

18. *The Philosophy of Symbolic Forms* (Yale University Press, New Haven 1955), pp. 40f.

19. "Some Observations Concerning Biblical Prayer," *Hebrew Union College Annual* XXXII (1961), pp. 76f.

in the Temple during the High Holy Day service. We have a graphic description in the Mishnah (Yoma 6:2) of the awe which pervaded the congregation as they heard the High Priest pronounce God's proper name. The people fell on their faces and prostrated themselves, and responded with the exclamation: "Praised be the name of His glorious sovereignty forever and ever." Ten times did the High Priest pronounce the divine name during the Day of Atonement service, and each time there followed the response of the people by prostration and exclamation. This procedure came to an end some time during the second century B.C.E., following the death of the High Priest Simeon the Just, when the ban against the pronunciation of God's proper name was extended to the priests in the Temple as well.[20]

The interdict on the pronunciation of the divine name in official religious life did not dislodge it from common use. Hananiah ben Teradyon, a sage who died a martyr's death during the Hadrianic persecutions in 130 C.E., was alleged to have uttered God's name. The term used in the Talmud to designate his practice is *hagah,* which has a variety of meanings, one of them to "mutter" as in pronouncing a spell. It may well be that this was really the nature of his act, that he performed mystic or magic rites by means of the divine name. The rabbis were scandalized by his action and they held that his eventual martyrdom was a merited punishment for his transgression. They also justified the tragic fate which befell his wife on the ground that she had not protested his offense against the divine name. Abba Saul, who was an older colleague of Hananiah and who survived the persecutions under Hadrian, felt constrained to declare that "anyone who mutters the divine name will have no share in the world-to-come.[21] A passage in the Avot de-Rabbi Nathan (ch. 12, end) speaks of "anyone who *uses* (*hamishtamesh*) the divine name will have no share in the world to come." The term "use," when applied to the divine name YHWH, clearly implies a theurgic use or an invocation for purposes of magic, according to Scholem.[22]

The interest in God's proper name continued in mystical circles, and it is still with us, especially in various practices related to magic. But many masters of the Talmud were clearly opposed to it.

There was another focus of mystical belief in talmudic times which the rabbis seem to have discouraged, namely the color blue. Apart from its intrinsic aesthetic appeal, blue carries an added interest: it resembles the color of the sea, from which terrestrial life began, and of the sky, generally looked upon as the abode of the deity. In Exodus 24:10 the "nobles of the children of Israel" are described as having

20. Yoma 39b.
21. Avodah Zarah 18a; Mishnah Sanhedrin 10:1.
22. *Major Trends,* p. 358, n. 17.

seen a vision of God. They are said to have beheld that "under His feet there was, as it were, a sapphire pavement, as the substance of the heavens for purity." In Ezekiel 1:26 the divine throne is described as a work of sapphire. The sapphire of antiquity was the *lapis lazuli,* a deep blue stone filled with starlike, goldlike particles.

There was finally another textual contribution to the mystery of the color blue. The Bible (Numbers 15:37–41) calls for the addition of the thread of blue to the fringe on each corner of a garment. The sage Rabbi Meir said, "The verse does not say, 'You shall see them' (the fringes) but 'you shall see him' (*oto*). The verse means to teach us that whoever keeps the law of the fringe, it is as though he had seen the divine Presence, for the blue resembles the sea and the sea resembles the sky, and the sky resembles the throne of the divine glory, as it is written (Ezekiel 1:26), 'And above the firmament over their heads was the likeness of a throne as the appearance of a sapphire stone.' "[23]

The interpretation of Rabbi Meir is quoted with minor variations by many authorities throughout talmudic literature. The color blue was endowed with the mystical potency released by the divine presence, and various miracles recorded in the Bible were ascribed to its power. We have one suggestion that the staff borne by Moses with which he performed the miracles at the Red Sea and in the wilderness was really sapphire, the sparkling blue stone, and as it released its hidden power, the will of Moses was done.[24] Being robed in a *tallit* with the blue thread in its fringes, we are told, endowed a person with this awesome potency. One sage in the Midrash is quoted as saying: "When the children of Israel robe themselves in a fringed garment, let them not think that they robe themselves merely in blue; let the children of Israel look at the fringe as the glory of the *shekhinah* upon them, for it is written, 'that you may look upon him.' Our text does not say, 'that you may look upon them,' but upon him (*oto*) referring, therefore, to the Holy One, praised be He."[25]

A study of the talmudic sources reveals a proliferating stress on the mystical powers of the thread of blue. It also reveals a subtle counter-offensive against it. The first action which had the effect of de-emphasizing the thread of blue is reflected in the Mishnah (*Menahot* 4:1), which ruled the blue and the white as not interdependent and that a fringe of either color entirely was satisfactory. Since the blue was expensive and difficult to obtain, this in effect invited the omission of the blue thread altogether. In one instance, the authorities in Jerusalem issued an interdict against inserting the thread of blue in a

---

23. *Sifrei* on Numbers 15:39.

24. *Mekhilta and Mekhilta deRabbi Simeon ben Yoḥai* on Exodus 17:6.

25. *Midrash Tehillim* on Psalm 90:28. Cf. B.Z. Bokser, "The Thread of Blue," in *Proceedings of the American Academy for Jewish Research* xxxi (1963), pp. 1ff.

garment, and their ruling appears to have won general compliance, for we are told, "Whoever wears a thread of blue in Jerusalem evokes astonishment against himself" (Menahot 40a).

Those inclined to mysticism felt keenly the disappearance of the thread of blue, and there was even an attempt in ḥasidic circles at a later date, to restore it. But it apparently shared the fate that befell other manifestations of the esoteric in talmudic Judaism. Cherished in some circles, revered by some as a precious link with the divine, these expressions also evoked a negative reaction. They remained in the underground of popular religion and continued in their old veneration by some sages, but the major thrust of talmudic opinion was to discourage them.

The Talmud had another way for building links with God: the study of the Torah and the practices of the commandments. Since these reflected God's mind and will, they became a bridge that linked man with God. This was one of the factors which inspired the Jewish zeal for the study of the Torah, and the observance of its precepts—each was a tie that bound man to his Creator. Indeed, even by associating with a master of the Torah, one achieved, indirectly, a link with God. Thus the Talmud states: "Anyone who marries his daughter to a scholar, or who pursues business activities for the benefit of a scholar, or benefits a scholar from his estate, is deemed by the Torah as though he cleaved to the divine presence."[26] There was, of course, a danger that the study of the Torah and the performance of the commandments might become formalized, losing the inner meaning that was crucial for its larger spiritual efficacy. The talmudists were aware of this and therefore they stressed the need for *kavanah,* the right intention which must accompany the deed. They spoke admiringly of pietists who would spend an hour in preparatory meditation before beginning to recite their prayers. The problem posed here is universal: a rite is created to reinforce an inner sensibility but in time the rite takes on a life of its own in detachment from the sensibility, and then we are constrained to awaken the sensibility in order to save the rite from degenerating into a mere habitual gesture. The personal experience of God through the way of piety developed by the talmudists has been described by Max Kadushin as "normal mysticism."[27]

IV

As a philosopher, Moses Maimonides advocated a rational approach to religion but, as we noted earlier, there was a distinct mystical

26. Ketubot 111b.
27. *The Rabbinic Mind* (Jewish Theological Seminary, New York 1952), ch. 6.

dimension in his thought, and his philosophy represents an important contribution to the history of Jewish mysticism. Maimonides was impressed with the role of reason in illuminating many aspects of existence. Since all existence is an exemplification of God's design and purpose in creation, a pursuit of the study of nature serves as an aid in revealing the grandeur and wisdom of God. But reason is not the only path to truth. Maimonides believed that certain spirits, if they are duly qualified, may, by the grace of God, be granted a direct illumination. In essence, the process in which this illumination occurs is a mystical experience, and its highest expression is prophecy.

The Maimonidean contribution to mysticism was two-fold. He helped clarify the phenomenon of the mystical encounter, and he expounded a technique for cultivating closeness with God, which is the highest goal of the mystic. Having placed prophecy within the category of mystical experience, Maimonides felt the need to account for those strange visions seen and voices heard, as reported by the prophets. He regarded these as purely subjective phenomena, which are contrived by the imaginative faculty, when the mystic's experience is intense enough, as when he is in a trance or in a dream. This concretization of the mystic's message is an aid to communication, but it must not be regarded as literally true. Some of the grossest errors in interpreting the prophetic message have resulted from the literalistic reading—and acceptance—of these images seen and voices heard.

Maimonides was concerned that what sometimes poses as a mystical experience and is offered to the world as a prophetic illumination may, in fact, be a hallucination contrived by a sick imagination. He suggested criteria by which it may be possible to detect the spurious "prophecy." If it runs counter to clearly established truths, or, if its claimant, by his life or his teaching, subverts clearly established moral norms, then we have the marks of the illusory. The claimant may be self-deceived, or, he may be an imposter trying to deceive others.

Maimonides was also concerned with guiding people toward the mystical quest of cultivating closeness to God. In this sense, he, too, represents what we may call pietistic mysticism. Only the exceptional person can rise to prophecy or to certain stages of creativity which he calls preliminary to prophecy. But all can seek closeness with God. The technique he recommended is the technique advocated by all mystics: meditation on God's perfection. Religious rites were for him primarily an aid in withdrawing the mind from worldliness and focusing on God. We cannot focus on God directly. We can reach Him by focusing on His work, by meditating on God's perfection as revealed in the fruits of divine revelation—the Torah and the commandments—and as revealed in nature. It was especially the latter which was unique in the thought of Maimonides. It had long been controversial in Jewish religious thought whether the study of nature as pursued in science and philosophy is a legitimate preoccupation for a devout person. Maimonides held it to be not only legitimate, but mandatory. The knowledge of nature is a knowledge of God's work, a disclosure of His perfection. As such it is a vital stepping-stone on the path to the experience of love for, and awe of, God, and the feeling of closeness to him.

V

In all these developments which we have charted, Jewish mysticism remained essentially an experience open to the learned. The common man struggling with the hard realities of everyday living needed the supporting strength of God's closeness, but it was not easily within his reach. He was not a scholar in the dialectics of the Talmud, nor a philosopher who could act on the Maimonidean invitation to seek God's closeness by meditating on God's ways as revealed in the study of nature. In 13th century Germany there arose a movement known as Ḥasidei Ashkenaz, which reached out to the common man. (This movement must not be confused with the ḥasidic movement initiated by Israel Baal Shem Tov in the 18th century in eastern Europe, though the two had many elements in common.)

The Ḥasidei Ashkenaz show the influence of some esoteric ideas emanating from the "throne" mysticism, and from the early Jewish philosophers like Saadia Gaon and Maimonides. They adopted Saadia's concept of a kind of intermediary between God and His world, the so-called *kavod,* or "glory of God," which was seen as the first in the order of creation. Prophetic visions and voices were interpreted as the actions of the *kavod* rather than of God Himself. This idea has affinity with Philo's concept of the *logos,* and the concept of the *sefirot* as developed in the later Kabbalah. The denial of all form and corporeality and emotion in God had tended to make Him distant, and the positing of an intermediary helped bridge the gap. But these and other esoteric ideas were on the periphery of the larger scope of this movement. Its most significant literary legacy is the *Sefer Ḥasidim,* a collection of teachings from many sources, but principally the work of Judah he-Ḥasid. A contribution to the category of pietistic mysticism, it sums up the mystical-pietistic ideas which were prevalent among large sections in the Germanic-Jewish community. The way to God as here advocated is through acts of devotion, beyond the formal call of prescriptive law, in a spirit of outgoing love.

The statement of Maimonides in disparagement of formal piety is quoted, including the demand for the study of God's creation as antecedent to meditating on His perfection, which was to distill an emotional response of love and awe. But the intellectual call of this passage does not express the primary thrust of this book, which asked the common man to approach God directly by fervent prayer, by the detachment from worldliness, from bodily lusts, by solicitousness for all God's creatures, even for the animal. It is significant that though this movement took form in the period which saw the persecutions of Jews during the Crusades, there is little retaliatory hostility to the non-Jewish world. The response to that tragedy was expressed in a deepened piety, in a deepened attachment to God. A strong faith in a heavenly reward for the martyrs after death comes to expression here, and this was a steadying influence which sustained the morale of the Jewish community. And the *Sefer Ḥasidim,* expressing a characteristic sensibility of mystics, declares the devout person as higher in stature than one who has attained mere learning.

VI

The most renowned chapter in Jewish mysticism is that of the Kabbalah, but the Kabbalah is a mysticism of a special kind. Its authenticating source is not a direct encounter with the ultimate reality, nor is its goal to lead its adherents to cleaving or attachment to God. Most kabbalistic texts expound a theosophy, which offers illumination concerning the mysteries of God and the universe. It proceeds through an intricate web of esoteric symbols, and its offering is primarily a *gnosis,* an esoteric knowledge which *in itself* is said to yield man the highest rewards of divine commendation. Scholem has called attention to this special characteristic of the Kabbalah as differentiated from mysticism generally. In his words, "Kabbalah is a unique phenomenon, and should not be considered to be identical with what is known in the history of religion as 'mysticism . . .' In what sense it may be called mysticism depends on the definition of the term, a matter of dispute among scholars. If the term is restricted to the profound yearning for direct human communion with God . . . then only few manifestations of Kabbalah can be designated as such . . . However, Kabbalah may be considered mysticism insofar as it seeks an apprehension of God and creation whose intrinsic elements are beyond the grasp of the intellect . . ."[28]

The Kabbalah was in many respects a radical revision of Jewish religious thought, but its roots go back to earlier layers of Jewish

28. *Kabbalah* (Quadrangle Books, New York 1974), p. 3.

tradition. It drew on the Bible and the Talmud, on the *Hekhalot* literature and on other early mystical texts. It drew on Maimonidean categories of thought, his halakhic as well as his philosophic writings. But its most important precedents were in the *Sefer Yeẓirah* and the *Sefer haBaḥir.* The *Sefer Yeẓirah,* of unknown authorship, has been dated between the third and sixth centuries. The *Sefer haBahir,* also of unknown authorship, made its appearance at the end of the twelfth century and it is in this period that the Kabbalah emerged as a distinct movement in Jewish mysticism. Naḥmanides (Moses ben Naḥman, 1194–1270) was the first to use the term *kabbalah,* which literally means tradition, in a technical sense, as referring specifically to the mystical tradition.

One of the most colorful figures in the early history of the Kabbalah was Abraham ben Samuel Abulafia (1240–1292). Abulafia introduced an ascetic as well as an ecstatic influence into the Kabbalah. His basic concern was to chart a way of liberating man from the "knots" and "seals" that keep him in a kind of imprisonment in the world of sense experience. The way of liberation was to withdraw from mundane affairs, from the world of flux, into the world of the intellect, so that the soul might be free to reunite itself with the Active Intellect, with God who is the ultimate reality behind the phenomenal world. This concept was close to the teaching of Maimonides, and, indeed, Abulafia was an ardent Maimonidean all his life. But while starting with Maimonidean rationalism he went beyond it. True liberation can be attained only by another type of meditation. The contemplation of the conceptual world for Abulafia still left one in the realm of finitude. To go beyond, to reach the eternal flow of divine energy pulsating through the universe and emanating from beyond it, he advocated meditating on the letters of the Hebrew alphabet, in their various permutations and combinations, in their relationship to the names of God. The highest reward that would come to the mystic pursuing this path was the attainment of prophecy.

The most influential work in the Kabbalah is the *Zohar* ("Radiance"). The *Zohar* is a pseudoepigraphic work. It pretends to be a mystical text going back to the talmudic period, with the tanna Rabbi Simeon bar Yohai as its author. But internal evidence points to a much later date of composition. For example, in one passage (II 9b) the *Zohar* notes that twelve hundred years have passed since the destruction of the Temple, which would mean that it was written after 1268! A careful weighing of the internal evidence has led scholars to identify it as the work of a thirteenth century Kabbalist, Moses de Leon. Mystics were often under suspicion as the bearers of unconventional ideas, and a doctrine gained greater credibility if it had behind it the authority of an ancient and highly revered master.

The *Zohar* is concerned with a problem which has confronted all religions, but especially those involved in mysticism. The mystic's quest is to draw near to God, but how can one bridge the gulf that separates the infinite God who abides in eternity from a world of finitude? The answer projected by all mystical theosophies is to posit some form of mediator between God and the world of finite creation. These mediators have included angels, the *logos* or divine "word" of Philo, the *kavod* or "glory" of God of the Ḥasidei Ashkenaz, and the charismatic leader or guru, often invested with semi-divine attributes, posited especially by schools of popular mysticism.

The *Zohar* projected its own conception of mediators between God and the world, which was the realm of the *sefirot*. It draws a distinction between God as He is in Himself, the *En Sof,* the Infinite, to whom we may not ascribe any of the involvements which are ascribed to God in the Bible and in popular religion, and God as He is described in religious tradition and as He is encountered in the world of experience. But the *En Sof* also manifested Himself in a series of ten divine powers or *sefirot.* These *sefirot* are a bridge between the Infinite and the finite. They embody divine potency and, in graded stages, effect the emergence of a material world of particularity and finitude. A father may not be personally on the scene throughout his child's life, but he has released a force of love and prudence which may continue to guide the child, and find materialization in various actions in different stages of his life. In a certain sense, these powers or forces, the *sefirot,* emanating from God, or as is sometimes explained, representing the attributes of God, act similarly, setting in motion a chain of events in the non-material, and eventually, in the material world.

It may be assumed that the number ten into which the *sefirot* are divided is not vital to the role assigned to them; a scheme might have been contrived with a lesser number. But the author of the *Zohar* was no doubt influenced by the affinity for the number ten in Jewish tradition. It has various associations in the Bible. The Talmud (Ḥagigah 12a) speaks of ten mediants through which God created the world: wisdom, discernment, knowledge, strength (physical), rebuke, power (moral), mercy, justice, love and compassion. The *Sefer Yeẓirah* posits ten *sefirot* as the media of creation, but here the term means numbers: "The ten *sefirot* are like the fingers of the hand, ten in number, five corresponding to five. But in the middle of them is the knot of unity" (1:3). The term is also used in the *Sefer haBahir,* but here it seems to mean "radiance." The *Zohar* apparently took the term *sefirot* from those early works of Jewish mysticism.

The first of the *sefirot* listed in the *Zohar* is *keter,* or crown, which is the potency deriving directly from the *En Sof,* and which is so close to the divine source that it defies characterization. Below it are *ḥokhmah,* wisdom, and then *binah,* discernment; the former is wisdom in its comprehensive wholeness, while the latter involves the discernment of varying principles into which *ḥokhmah* may be analyzed. Then follow *ḥesed,* kindness, or love, and *gevurah,* power or sternness, which involves the confinement of love within certain boundaries, lest the abundance proceed endlessly, thus subverting an ordered world. Next is *tiferet,* beauty, which is a balancing principle that brings the other elements into proper proportion, and then *nezaḥ,* endurance, which invests creation with the element of perseverence or stability. Then comes *hod,* majesty, followed by *yesod,* foundation, a synthesis of all the above, which turns itself to the seed of life or what we commonly call the life force. The last *sefirah, malkhut,* sovereignty, is the final point where the divine potency is clothed with finitude and materiality. Every artist puts something of himself into his handiwork, and God put something of himself, the *sefirot,* into each of His creations.

Another concept basic to the Kabbalah which was introduced by Rabbi Isaac Luria (the Ari; 1534–1572) was *ẓimẓum,* or "withdrawal." To make room for a finite world which was to emerge in the act of creation, Luria pictured a kind of contraction in the divine realm. Only in a zone from which God had, so to say, withdrawn, could there be the possibility for a finite and imperfect world to exist. But the withdrawal was not total, a *reshimu,* a residue of divine potency remained in the vacuum formed by God's withdrawal and this divine residue functions as a prodding agent stirring the finite world to relate itself to God. Direct influences, too, continue to emanate from the divine realm, which work subtly on the realm of finitude to direct it toward its divinely appointed goals. Here Luria introduced another concept of bold dimension. Into the realm of "emptiness" formed by the withdrawal of the *En Sof,* the divine light which was to engender creation began to stream in great profusion. But the "vessels" that were to effectuate the particularization of finite existence could not contain that light, and they broke, begetting a state of disorder in which "holy sparks" were everywhere surrounded by *kelipot,* husks of gross substance of a lower order which impeded the light. This cosmic disorder is the root of all human problems. The exile of the Jewish people is a phase of this disorder. But it is not only they who are in exile. God Himself, the holy sparks of divine light, are also in exile. It is the vocation of the Jew, by his withdrawal from worldliness and submission to the disciplines of mystical piety, to redress this condition, to effect restoration, or *tikkun,* perfection. The messiah will come when this process of *tikkun* has been completed.

Luria envisioned groups of *sefirot* as having separate identities. The *sefirah keter,* in which there is the initial stirring of divine activity, in which there is as yet no differentiation in aspects of potency and in which no severity whatever is discernible, was called *Atika Kadisha,* the Holy Ancient One, or *Arikh Anpin,* the patient one. The *sefirot ḥokhmah* and *binah,* because they are the generating potencies for the other *sefirot,* were called *abba* and *imma,* father and mother. The next six *sefirot,* which include the potency of *gevurah* that releases sternness and judgment, were called *Zeir Anpin,* the impatient one. The last *sefirah, malkhut,* identified with the *ṣhekhinah,* which was conceived as a feminine element, and with the *keneset yisrael,* the congregation of Israel, was called Rachel. These groupings of the *sefirot* were called *parẓufim,* "faces." Sometimes erotic similies were introduced into the interactions among the *sefirot.* While Luria was especially active in these elaborations of the sefiraitic symbolism, his disciple Ḥayim Vital cautioned the student against taking these terms literally. They represented a kind of mythology. They were metaphors to make more vivid an esoteric universe of discourse. In the words of Vital: "Know that the sages of the *Zohar* and the Ari (Isaac Luria) felt constrained to make use of these images and these characterizations drawn from bodily life in order to explain wondrous mysteries that cannot be explained except through such designations and analogies from the bodily life."[29]

The transition from the immaterial world of the *sefirot* to our material world was also elaborated on by the kabbalists. They interposed three other worlds between the *En Sof* and the world of material existence. There was the world of *aẓilut,* emanation, the realm of the *sefirot;* then came the world of *beriah,* creation, the realm of the Throne and the Chariot; this is followed by the world of *yeẓirah,* formation, where the angels abide; the last is the world of *assiah,* making, which finally yields the terrestrial realm. The ten *sefirot* were active in all the four worlds, in accordance with their receptiveness to the supernal light. There are references to these four realms in the *Tikkunei Zohar,* but this concept received its fullest elaboration among the Safed mystics in the 16th century, especially in the circle of Isaac Luria.

The Safed kabbalists lived as a closely knit circle. Many were masters of talmudic study and had made their mark in halakhic scholarship. But their primary interest was the pursuit of the "mysteries" of the Torah. This often went beyond pure speculation. It embraced, as well, an effort to establish direct links with the heavenly realm. Like ecstatics in other mystical traditions, some of the kab-

---

29. *Sha'arei Kedushah,* 3, end.

balists claimed para-normal experiences that yielded them divine revelations. The best known among these was Joseph Karo, the celebrated author of the *Shulḥan Arukh,* who claimed regular visitations by a *maggid,* a spirit personifying the Mishnah, who brought him celestial messages in audible speech. R.J.Z. Werblowsky, in his study of Karo's *maggid,* put it thus: "Kabbalistic life was not restricted to mystical speculations but also involved regular para-normal experiences and celestial revelations of diverse kinds . . . Automatic writing, automatic speech, induced intuitions, various methods of mystical and magical contemplation were practiced in this remarkable mystical circle."[30]

The kabbalistic teaching, its elaborate and intricate language of symbolism, the involved interpretations by which kabbalists sought to reconcile their theosophy with biblical and rabbinic teaching, made it a forbidding zone to most people. They could find little meaning in it and were discouraged from pursuing it. But some kabbalistic ideas exercised great fascination. The concepts of *tikkun,* and the belief in the power of the kabbalist to influence celestial workings on behalf of human purposes, merged with age-old dreams of messianic redemption, and even many who did not understand kabbalistic theories turned to the Kabbalah as the source from which the good news of the messiah's arrival would finally come. This proved to be the fertile spawning ground for the messiahship of Shabbetai Ẓevi (1625–1676). The debacle of that movement, with Shabbetai's apostasy to Islam, posed a crisis for the Kabbalah. Its prestige suffered decline. Some, who focused on the central core of its theosophy, continued to study it with the usual concentration which this required. But for the multitude it had become a dead-end street. The traditional pattern of Jewish life, which had always been suspicious of mystical adventurism, asserted its claim with new authority.

The Kabbalah may have lost some of its old authority but the epoch of its preeminence left an enduring imprint on the Jewish mentality. For example, the belief in the soul's reincarnation is first encountered in the *Sefer haBahir* but it received fresh emphasis in the later strata of the Kabbalah. It fitted in especially with the Lurianic teaching, which saw in the soul's wandering from incarnation to incarnation another instance of the disorder that followed "the breaking of the vessels" at the time of creation. This belief reappeared in Ḥasidism and we find it in many expressions of popular religion. Many innovations in the Jewish liturgy were inspired by the kabbalists, and some have remained in vogue in many circles to this day: the recitation of a selection from the *Zohar* (*Berikh Shemeh, Zohar* II 206a), on the taking

30. *Joseph Karo* (Oxford University Press, London 1962), p. 287.

of the Torah from the ark; the observance of the eve of the new month as "a minor Day of Atonement" (*Yom Kippur Katan*); the holding of night-long vigils of study and meditation on the nights of *Shavuot, Hoshana Rabba* and the seventh day of Passover; and the welcome of the Sabbath by singing the hymn *Lekhah Dodi,* and the recitation of the Song of Songs and the last chapter of the book of Proverbs ("A woman of valor who can find"). The latter were invoked to celebrate the reunion of God and the *shekhinah,* personalized as God's mystical bride. The Sabbath was a commemoration of that reunion, and as an emulation of the higher realm by the lower, the Sabbath also became the traditionally hallowed time for the conjugal union between husband and wife. Many of these kabbalistically inspired practices entered the mainstream of Jewish religious life, but the Kabbalah itself receded as the primary expression of Jewish mystical piety.

One of the detours of kabbalistic teaching was in the area of magic practices. This stemmed in part from the belief that the kabbalist had access to supernatural potency, that his meditations and incantations wrought effects in the supernal worlds. Since he was able to "unify" the earthly and supernal realms and perfect and mend what was fragmented and broken, why not direct those energies toward the mending of what was broken in the private lives of individuals as well? Another important ingredient in the many notions underlying these practices was the belief in the potency of the divine names. We have noted this belief in the mysticism of the Talmud. It lived on in the Kabbalah with new elaborations that derived from the alleged potency of the *sefirot.* Kabbalistic masters often warned against the profanation of the divine realm by turning it to practical uses, but this did not inhibit the continuing proliferation of magic in a kind of kabbalistic underground. It fascinated the popular mind, which remained its staunchest advocate, as may be seen by the widespread popularity of amulets and incantations, some of which continue to have a following to this day.

We have discussed the role of the Kabbalah in the history of *Jewish* mysticism. But the Kabbalah also won adherents in the Christian community. The father of the Christian Kabbalah was Pico della Mirandola. He pursued his studies under a Jew, Johanan Alemanno. His nine hundred *Theses,* which he published in 1486, at the age of twenty-four, included this bold declaration: "No science yields greater proof of the divinity of Christ than magic and Kabbalah." Pope Sixtus IV was so delighted with his work that he urged him to translate kabbalistic texts into Latin for the use of divinity students. Mirandola translated Menahem di Recanati's commentary on the Bible, Eliezer of Worms' *Ḥokhmat haNefesh* and Shem Tov Falaquera's *Sefer haMa'alot.*

John Reuchlin studied Hebrew and Kabbalah under the Jewish court physician of Frederick III, Rabbi Jacob ben Jehiel Loans. His first kabbalistic treatise, *De Verbo Mirifico,* was published in Basel in 1494. Twenty-two years later he published his *De Arte Cabalistica,* which was a more mature exposition of the same basic ideas. These works made Reuchlin the most talked of man of letters in Europe, whose writings were read avidly in Protestant and Catholic circles alike.

The celebrated sixteenth-century philosopher and alchemist Paracelsus did not write books on the Kabbalah as such, but he applied the insights of the Kabbalah to his own scientific and philosophic studies. His attitude toward the Kabbalah is stated clearly, and it is typical of what the leading intellectual lights of Europe believed: "The art of the Kabbalah is beholden to God, it is in alliance with Him, and it is founded in the words of Christ."

Of course, the Christian Kabbalah differed from the Jewish model which inspired it, but both are essentially similar in conception. The quest for the nearness of God of the Jewish kabbalists motivated their Christian disciples as well. But the Christian Kabbalah had a goal of its own—to validate the distinctive doctrines of the church. Its adherents were particularly interested in a confirmation of the doctrine of the trinity and they were aided in this quest by the kabbalistic doctrine of the *sefirot.* The introduction of a male and female principle in the expression of God's creative self suggested to Christians that it is possible to speak of God as "begetting" and "begotten." Thus, though the Jewish and the Christian Kabbalah employed the same language, they spoke very differently.

VII

The normative basis for Jewish religious life was the Oral Torah, the vast literature of the Talmud, with its commentaries and super-commentaries, and the complex of commandments which governed the day-to-day discipline of the Jew, his piety, his morals, his rules for personal life at home, in the synagogue and in the marketplace. The hierarchy of social status in the Jewish community was determined on the basis of mastery in talmudic knowledge. The problem which this engendered was two-fold. The common people who had to struggle with the commitments of earning a livelihood could not fathom the intricate discussions of the talmudic texts, and they were thus denied the great benefits of a deeper Jewish religiosity. The focus on highly obstruse discussions in the field of law to which the Talmud is largely dedicated tended to make this a preoccupation for the mind, with little recognition of the claims of the heart for inspiration and consolation in the face of life's burdens. And the commandments themselves, with their stress on behavior rather than on underlying spiritual motivations, also tended to be formalistic and devoid of that inwardness which is the true leaven of religious faith.

There had been voices in the Jewish community who protested this development. As we have noted, the *Sefer Ḥasidim* decried formalistic prayer. It asked for inwardness, for devotion, for turning prayer into a vehicle in the quest for God's nearness. Better to pray in the vernacular than in an incomprehensible Hebrew, and better, if one cannot pray with proper intention, to postpone prayer for a more conducive time, this work also argued. And we have here the announcement that a truly God-fearing person is to be regarded as higher than the scholar whose mind is cultivated but whose inner spirit is not. Rabbi Judah Loew of Prague (the Maharal; 1509–1615) had denounced the stress on talmudic dialectics which he felt often made study an end in itself, failing to cultivate the sensibility to God. For him this was the true end of all religious striving. But the state of Jewish piety did not visibly change as a result of these and other pleas, and the Jewish community suffered a condition of religious aridity and stagnation.

The crisis came to a head in the beginning of the 18th century. The massacres of Jews perpetrated by the Russian Cossacks under Chmielnicki decimated Jewish communities throughout Poland. As we have noted earlier, Shabbetai Ẓevi, who quickened the dreams of 17th century Jews by proclaiming himself as the messiah who would lead them to freedom, had embraced Islam, rather than face death at the hands of the Turkish sultan, thus bringing consternation and shock to his erstwhile followers. At the same time, the spokesmen of the religious establishment remained largely insensitive to the inner struggles and frustrations of their people. The answer to these problems was to come from a new movement of religious renewal which is known by the name of Ḥasidism.

Ḥasidism was a unique development in the history of Jewish mysticism. Inaugurated by the teaching of Rabbi Israel Baal Shem Tov (the Besht; 1700–1760), it soon became a mass movement that effected a veritable upheaval in the world of Judaism. The ḥasidim tended to withdraw from the established community organization and formed synagogues of their own. They introduced modifications into the liturgy and developed a different style of worship, which was more fervent and emotionally demonstrative. Ḥasidic worship often included group singing, dancing, clapping of hands, and spontaneous chants of passages in the prayers. At the center of the ḥasidic community was the living master, the Rebbe, who served as a link between the people and higher divine realms.

These and other innovations evoked against Ḥasidism the ire of the established Jewish community just as, in other times, virtually every manifestation of the mystical spirit met with opposition from the communal establishment. This tension derives principally from the fact that the mystic places a high priority on his own experience, while in conventional piety the ultimate authority rests with tradition. As Sidney Spencer put it: "In mystical experience there is implicit a claim to immediate revelation . . . Insofar as authority is externalized and identified with the written words of Scripture . . . while it may be accepted by the mystic, there is always the possibility of conflict between its dictates and his inner vision."[31] There was, as we have seen, resistance to mysticism in the Talmud. There was a similar opposition to the kabbalists. One of the most noted of them, Rabbi Moses Ḥayyim Luzzatto, author of *Paths of the Righteous* and other pietistic works, was made to sign a vow never to write books in the style of the *Zohar,* nor to allude in his writings to any hint of personal revelation through a "mentor-angel," a *maggid,* such as that claimed by Joseph Caro.[32] This was also, no doubt, at the heart of the opposition to Ḥasidism. It was branded as schismatic and heretical; its adherents were vilified and put under the ban, so that other Jews were forbidden to have any dealings with them. Calumnies were spread against the movement before the imperial Russian government, charging that those associated with Ḥasidism were, in truth, a conspiratorial cabal whose true design was to destroy the imperial regime. As a result of these calumnies, Rabbi Shneur Zalman of Lyady (1745–1813), the renowned theoretician of the Ḥabad school in Ḥasidism, spent intermittent periods in Czarist jails. But, despite all opposition, Ḥasidism continued to thrive and ultimately became the dominant force in East European Jewry, eventually extending its sway to other parts of the Jewish world. However, it should be noted that in the process it tended to change its character, losing much of its mystical character, and becoming itself another kind of religious establishment.

Certainly sociological and historical factors conditioned the rise and phenomenal expansion of Ḥasidism. But those historians who see it primarily as a response to social conditions, as a kind of mass revolt against the oppressive oligarchy that ruled Jewish communal life at the time, oversimplify the situation. Ḥasidism is a resurgence of a basic yearning of the human spirit for closeness to God. It is one of the climactic developments in the long history of Jewish mysticism. It is mysticism breaking out from the small circles of devotees to become

31. *Mysticism in World Religion,* p. 337.

32. *Meir Benayahu, Shevu'at Ramḥal Laḥdol Milḥaber Sefarim al pi 'maggid,' Mahuta veToẓa'oteha, Zion,* vol. XL11, 1–2, 1977, pp. 24–48.

the possession of the people as a whole, going through, in the process, certain changes in emphasis, in idiom of communication, and in organizational structure. It is the basic teaching of Ḥasidism, however, which is our primary interest, rather than the historical context which conditioned its emergence.

What are the core elements in the ḥasidic teaching that have endowed it with so much vitality in the face of all the mutations and conditions in the world? The core of ḥasidic thought derives from the Kabbalah, but it is free of the esoterics of kabbalistic symbolism. The teachings of Ḥasidism are expounded in an extensive literature, and each exposition reflects the distinctiveness of the mind from which it flowed. Some texts, like the *Tanya* of Rabbi Shneur Zalman of Lyady, develop a system of mystical theosophy of great subtleness. For the most part, however, because the ḥasidic masters directed their teaching to the common man, the esoteric elements in their thought remained in the background. What comes through in repeated emphasis is the homily that seeks to console and inspire, and that affirms the viability of faith in God and His providence despite the harshness of life. This tends to present the ḥasidic writings with a great degree of parallelism, and permits a common delineation of ḥasidic thought as though it were a comprehensive whole.

Ḥasidism holds that God is present in the world, not merely through the action of His providence, but through His direct involvement in the life of all existence. A divine spark inhabits all that has being; it is a kind of emanation flowing from the divine source and entering the world of finite things to animate them with life and purpose. This divine element is what stirs man toward higher aspirations, toward unity with all other beings and toward unity with its divine source. It is present in other beings as well, but here it is more inchoate and passive. It is only in man that it acts, sending him to yearn toward the goals it points to for his life. The divine sparks of which the ḥasidic masters spoke were in effect the sephiraitic potencies alluded to in the Kabbalah, but Ḥasidism shunned the esoteric vocabulary of the Kabbalah, and spoke in an idiom closer to common understanding.

The world does not generally reflect its divine dimension. It lies fragmented and lost in grosser concerns. This is because these divine elements are imprisoned in the shell of its lower self. The shell, or *kelipah,* is a concomitant of the holy sparks; the two are part of the oneness of life. The need to liberate the sparks from their shell is uniquely the vocation to which man is summoned. He must struggle with himself to break his own *kelipah,* to liberate his own holy sparks, and he must help others struggling toward the same end.

Man's zone of action is not limited, however, to the human plane alone. All existence, all the beings that inhabit this world, the animate and the inanimate alike, are caught in the same predicament. They are pervaded by a divine element, they are inhabited by divine sparks that need to be lifted, liberated. Those sparks are liberated when the beings they inhabit enter into the unity of existence, into the unity that embraces the comprehensive drama of life, and the larger unity of creation and Creator. But the world cannot liberate itself; the beings below man are passive, helpless, doomed to wait—until man performs the holy act and lifts them from their isolation to enter the universal unity of life.

How does man liberate the holy sparks in the world? He does so by the spirit in which he acts in the world, by the direction he gives to the life process in the course of his encounter with it. A person who directs his life toward unification raises all things he touches toward the level of his own aspirations and dedication. The tools he uses, the food he eats, the animal that performs his chores—all are raised if he uses them toward holy ends, if the larger context of his life is dedicated toward the higher quest.

Ḥasidic literature employs three additional technical terms to describe man's goals: *devekut, yiḥud,* and *ayin. Devekut* is attachment or cleaving to God, in which a double process is set into motion: man's life and work, through his intention and thought, flows back to its own divine source, and man in turn becomes the recipient of a fresh influx of divine energy from the divine realm. *Yiḥud* means unification; it refers to the reuniting of all things, transcending their particularity and separatism and achieving the universal relatedness which is the true nature of existence; it also refers to the reunion with God, overcoming the isolation and estrangement of creation from its Creator. The climactic moment in the struggle for *yiḥud* is the realization of God's goal in having created the world. When this is reached, we shall have attained the time of the messiah, the state of true redemption toward which the world moves by slow and faltering steps. *Ayin* means "nothing"; it refers to a state of total self-transcendence, in which all worldly strivings have been overcome and God has become the dominant passion of one's life.

Ḥasidism is confronted with the paradox that this world, struggling to emerge from the shells which imprison the divine splendor, is itself the divine creation. God apparently willed to surround the holy sparks with the *kelipot* that obscure the light and that are responsible for the evils of alienation and estrangement which fracture the unity of existence, and beget the evil that wounds and frustrates existence. Why did God adopt this pattern in creating the world? Why did He not create a world that would automatically reflect its underlying unity, the relatedness of all its particularities to each other and to their divine source? Why did He not create a world to reflect His own perfection?

We have various efforts in Ḥasidism to deal with this paradox, but essentially they all express, in differing formulation, the same basic doctrine, sometimes summed up in the Lurianic doctrine of *ẓimẓum,* "shrinking" or "limiting." A world without *kelipot* would in effect be a world of diffused or extended divinity. The goal of creation was to beget a realm of finitude which was slowly to evolve toward perfection. This could be effected only through the deliberate "shrinking" or "limiting" of the divine. A mortal father will deliberately shrink his paternal care to permit his child to grow toward maturity and self-mastery. Similarly, God withdrew into Himself to release a zone opaque and unillumined, from which His light was obscured, to permit the emergence of finite creatures capable of stumbling and falling, capable of lingering in the imprisonment of the *kelipot.* But compensating for this planned deficiency is the gift with which man was endowed, to wage war against the *kelipot,* to grow in illumination, and slowly to achieve "unification" with his fellow creatures and with the Eternal One whose will has begotten all life.

Indeed, as man achieves the mission with which he has been charged, to liberate the holy sparks from their imprisonment, he rises in stature above the angels. For a perfection that expresses the automatic workings of a scheme ordained from another realm is inferior to a perfection attained through a successful and freely willed journey toward the light. For God, as well as man, the turning of life into an adventure, a struggle to overcome the resisting coarseness of the world in its unredeemed state, confers a boon. For when victory occurs it is a source of infinite delight, and the struggle itself invests life with intense meaning.

So God diminished the light in order to permit the emergence of a world of finitude. The *kelipot* which serve to obstruct the light and form the resistant grossness which clings to all things thus serve a purpose; they are a provisional good, a ladder on which a man climbs higher in his quest for the good. The so-called realm of evil is, in other words, only relatively evil. In the economy of divine providence it also contributes toward the purpose of creation. But even its negative role is only transitional, for as man liberates the holy sparks, the realm of "evil" is conquered, and then it is also won for God; it is included in the higher unity of creation, and of God and creation. This is what is sometimes described as serving God with both passions, the passion for the good, the *yeẓer hatov,* as well as the evil passion, the *yeẓer hara.* In a liberated man the two passions have merged; they have both become channels for the divine service.

Man's struggle for the light, for the redemption of the holy sparks from their imprisonment, is a lonely ordeal; he must wage it within himself and by himself. But God has provided aids to assist him in his quest. The divine element God has planted in all things seeks, by its very nature, to be liberated from its shells. In the world below the human it is doomed to passivity, but in man it exerts its claims. It aspires, it longs for liberation, and it disturbs the person who is insensitive to the higher dimension with restlessness and, at times, with a sense of guilt. It summons him to look deeper into himself and into the world, and to see the divine light shining through. Each person must confront himself, and define the area of his special weaknesses which he must learn to overcome. He must open his eyes and his ears to God's presence which surrounds him on all sides, though in his state of insensitivity he is not aware of it.

One of the great aids in this quest is withdrawal from the distractions of the world, to meditate on the mystery of God and the destiny of man. In such meditation man is encouraged to speak directly to God, to unburden his heart and to speak, as a child speaks to his mortal father. Out of such encounters the bonds linking man and God will be forged ever deeper. Ḥasidism calls this act of withdrawal *hitbodedut,* the cultivation of aloneness. The ideal place where it can be pursued, according to one of the great masters of Ḥasidism, Rabbi Naḥman of Bratslav, is in the stillness of nature, where noises subside and the music of creation can be heard singing in the soul.

In addition, God has placed into the world special sensitizing agents whereby the world is guided in its struggle for perfection. The most important channel of divine sensitivity in the world is the Jewish people. The endowment of distinctiveness in all things is part of the divine mystery. Thus God created certain elements in nature to serve as antidotes to certain diseases, and the Jewish people similarly acts as a therapy for the world's waywardness. The dispersion of the Jewish people among the nations was sometimes explained in ḥasidic writings as divinely willed, so that through contact with the nations of the world the Jewish people might serve to liberate the holy sparks imprisoned among them.

But the Jewish people itself has its own struggle with the *kelipot.* Despite an inherited predisposition for the spiritual, despite the sensitizing impact of the Torah and the commandments, many Jews are estranged from God and from the divine dimension in themselves. God has, therefore, provided a mediant to function within Jewish life as a fountain of divine grace, to direct the people toward the light, and this is the *ẓaddik,* "the righteous man," the living master, the rebbe. His is a superior soul, a soul saturated with holiness; by establishing contact with him the individual is given the helping hand he needs in his efforts to ascend toward God.

The *ḥasid,* the individual disciple, must seek to be continually in touch with the rebbe. He spends certain holy days in his court, within the radius of his direct influence. The rebbe interprets the Torah and commandments in a special way, to bring out their higher meaning which is hidden in the husk of their physical form. The rebbe's prayers rise with immense potency and they bear along with them the less inspired prayers of the adherents who are not altogether liberated from the grossness of the world. The rebbe knows how to descend to the level of life where the people are in order to raise them ever higher. The radiance of the rebbe's influence is elicited especially by being within the range of his vision and the touch of his hands. The contact established conveys a *berakhah,* a blessing, with all its salutary effects on a person's spiritual, and even his physical self. For the sense of God's presence surrounds a person with an insulating wall which shelters him from the vicissitudes of time and circumstance. The rebbe is in a sense a redeemer—a redeemer of the holy sparks imprisoned in the world. He helps effect the reunion between God and His creation. In the words of the Maggid of Mezhirech, Dov Baer, he bears "the holy sparks toward the heavenly realm." Some turned to the rebbe for advice on practical problems, some sought his intervention with the divine powers to help them meet the onslaught of the hardships of life. But behind this idealization of the rebbe and his investment with superhuman powers was the perception of his principal role as a channel of divine influences. He brought the divine influence from the celestial realm and directed it into the lives of people struggling with day to day problems. But it was he who also opened the lives of his adherents to receive the divine influence, and thus they became the beneficiaries of its transforming power.

The rebbe was the center of the ḥasidic community. His adherents enjoyed the measure of godliness which they were able to receive into their lives, thanks to their contact with him, and they felt the thrust of a power turning them ever onward and upward toward a higher quest deriving ultimately from God Himself. The rebbe was the commander-in-chief of an army moving victoriously toward its highest goal—the conquest of the self and of the world—for God.

The adulation of the rebbe sometimes reached the level of hero worship. He was often looked upon by his adherents as a miracle worker who could heal the sick, cause barren women to bear children, or redress a person's failing business fortunes. He was even judged to have the power of speeding the coming of the messiah and bringing on the redemption. He was seen as God's surrogate on earth whom

God had entrusted with vast powers to help direct the destinies of His people. The miracle working powers of the rebbe come to expression especially in many of the ḥasidic tales which reflect the popular conception of the role of the rebbe in God's world. The theosophy of ḥasidic thought receded in the popular conception as the idealization of the rebbe became the dominant factor in the ḥasidic way of life, a price paid by every sophisticated ideology when it opens itself to popular embrace. The focus of popular loyalty is not the abstract idea but the person who personifies it. But the idea abides while the person must succumb to the vulnerabilities of all mortals. It is the legacy of its ideas which makes Ḥasidism an important chapter in the history of the Jewish mystical tradition.

The purpose of man's life, as defined by Ḥasidism, is to reunite himself and his world with God, to raise the holy sparks immanent in mundane existence back to the divine source from which they have been severed in the act of creation. But what happens when man fails to do this? What happens when he sets his life within the realm of the *kelipot,* when he chooses to remain trapped in the lure of worldliness? He delays the world's perfection, he delays the cosmic redemption for which God—and all creation—have been waiting since the beginning of time. He delays the coming of the messiah. And what happens to the person himself? In conventional rabbinic thought, such a person was seen as doomed to retribution in hell. But is not this a harsh and, in some respects, a futile ending for a soul unfortunate enough to have been consigned to a person who resisted its prompting, and thus missed his vocation in life?

There were various efforts in Jewish thought to mitigate the horrors of hell. The Talmud limited the duration of a wicked person's sentence in hell to twelve months (Shabbat 33b), and some Jewish philosophers interpreted the concepts of heaven and hell figuratively. The hereafter was seen as a state of bodiless existence and neither its rewards nor its punishments were physical. Its joys were constant union with God, while its misery was the misery of alienation from God. The fiery, lurid tortures with which hell was pictured were interpreted as a figurative expression for the realm of negation to which a person draws himself when he is alienated from God. But neither of these mitigations resolved the difficulty posed by the frustrated soul that cannot effect its mission, and remains exiled from the divine home which is its endless craving.

Jewish mysticism had another solution to this problem: the belief in reincarnation. This belief is not to be found in the Bible or in the Talmud. It appears to have developed first among the Hindu mystics and it is found among the Pythagoreans and the Platonists. Its earliest expression among Jews is in the writings of Philo. It was embraced by the Kabbalists and it was taken over into Ḥasidism. According to this concept, when a person who has failed to fulfill his life's calling dies, his soul is given a second chance. It is reincarnated in the life of another person who hopefully, in his life, will make good what the previous one failed to accomplish. A soul may be subjected to a series of reincarnations until the person whom it inhabits heeds the soul's call to enlist in the struggle for the liberation of the divine sparks from their imprisonment. The cycle of reincarnations is a kind of exile for the soul, and when it is finally permitted to return to its divine source, then it has found its peace.

Closely related to the belief in reincarnation was the belief in *ibbur,* which asserts that a soul released from a previous incarnation may temporarily enter another person. The purpose of this temporary entry may be two-fold. If the person in whom it was previously incarnated failed to perform some particular commandment, the new person to whom it is joined may be able to redress this omission. But it was also envisioned that some specially righteous soul may enter a deserving person in order to lend his greater inspiration to a life of holiness. The term *ibbur* means "fetus." It is a life within a life; the temporary entry of soul into a person represents a fusion of a soul within another soul. This concept appears in the *Zohar* but it received added elaboration among the Safed mystics, especially in the Lurianic school, and Ḥasidism received this concept from its kabbalistic antecedents.

The soul of a wicked person may also enter another life, sometimes with nefarious objectives, and this was called *dibbuk.* The latter eventuality gave rise to various techniques for exorcising the *dibbuk.* The problem of the *dibbuk* and the practice of exorcism became major concerns in the later Kabbalah and in Hasidism, and exerted a great influence in Jewish folklore and popular literature.

VIII

Ḥasidism was a source of stability in the Jewish community. It gave Jewish life a vitality that enabled the Jew to overcome the hostile forces pressing against him from the outside world and from within the Jewish community itself. But Ḥasidism did not exhaust the Jewish interest in mysticism. Ḥasidism, as it crystallized into an organized popular movement, sometimes lost its original spontaneity. In time it tended to become another tradition-centered religious establishment. The mystical spirit that craves for a direct encounter with God, for a fresh illumination of soul, is not content with pondering a tradition, even a mystical tradition. To gain this boon the mystic must travel the lone road of meditation, of struggling with his own opaque material self, to break the barrier that separates him from God and to enter directly into contact with the divine mystery. There were such mystics in Judaism in the post-ḥasidic world. They drew inspiration from ḥasidism and they were assiduous students of the classic writings of the ḥasidic masters, but they were not part of the ḥasidic movement as such. They saw with a unique light and their testimony is a fresh illumination of the divine mystery.

The most important Jewish mystics in the post-ḥasidic world were Rabbi Ḥayyim of Volozhin (1749–1821) and Rabbi Abraham Isaac Kook (1865–1935). Rabbi Ḥayyim was a disciple of the Gaon of Vilna, and he himself was a celebrated talmudist, serving as the head of the Volozhin Yeshivah, one of the most famous centers of talmudic learning in the East European Jewish world. Rabbi Ḥayyim was a Kabbalist, a student of the *Zohar* and related kabbalistic literature, but he was a critic of Ḥasidism. In his work *Nefesh haḤayyim,* which was published posthumously, he formulated a neo-kabbalistic system, at the same time taking sharp issue with many elements in ḥasidic theology and its way of life. Above all, he was offended by what he regarded as the ḥasidic disparagement of talmudic study and its overemphasis on the study of pietistic and moralistic works. He was also troubled by the ḥasidic stress on God's immanence, which went to the extreme of claiming that God is present in all things, even in what we call evil. If taken literally this would in effect obliterate the distinction between the zones of the holy and the profane.

Rabbi Kook, who served as the chief rabbi of Palestine prior to the rise of the state of Israel, was closer to the world of Ḥasidism, and often bemoaned the failure on the part of his contemporaries to stress the need for studying pietistic and moralistic works. But he complained that Ḥasidism, as exemplified in the ḥasidic communities of his time, had often betrayed the ḥasidic ideal, that it had in effect become a rigid and formal pietism, not much different from the piety of the conventional religious establishment. Kook was not content with asking for a re-establishment of the ḥasidic ideal, however. He favored the study of all cultural disciplines, of literature and art, philosophy and science. Every expression of the human spirit was for him at the same time an added clue for the understanding of the divine mystery, which pervades all existence.

Kook saw a divine dimension in all things, even in the realm of secularity, even in forces ostensibly antithetical to the religious spirit, such as the teachings of atheism. For him, atheism was a divinely inspired, though very much exaggerated, protest against the abuses of religion in its established, institutional forms.

He also considered that Ḥasidism tended to diminish man's initiative, making him depend solely on God to shape the direction of life. Kook stressed the role man was meant to play as a co-worker with God in the "perfecting" of the world. This made him a sympathizer of all movements seeking to redress the abuses in the social and political order. It made him into an ardent sympathizer of the Zionist movement which he saw as an aid in furthering the messianic redemption as God needs human collaboration to effect His purposes in history. The goal of Zionism for Rabbi Kook was not to make the Jews "like the other nations," but to give them the normalizing components of land and nationhood that they might be enabled to cultivate their uniqueness as a "kingdom of priests and a holy nation."

One of his great maxims was to "revitalize the old and hallow the new," and the traditional and the classical speak with a new cogency in Rabbi Kook's thought. At the same time he invested all the latest expressions of the human spirit in its grappling with the mystery of life with a dimension of holiness. Scholem called Rabbi Kook "a splendid type of Jewish mystic." Only a few of the more than thirty-six volumes which he left as his literary legacy to the world have been published, but they reveal him as one of the truly great spirits whose writings make up the exciting story of Jewish mysticism.

IX

Mysticism has been a vital part of the Jewish tradition, but it has not kept pace with the mystical interests of many Jews in our spiritually disoriented world. The writings of Rabbi Kook are largely unknown to the English-reading public. Even in Israel the interest in Rabbi Kook's thought generally centers on his pro-Zionist pronouncements, while his purely religious meditations are virtually ignored. There is considerable interest in Ḥasidism throughout the Jewish world, as is evidenced by the influence of Martin Buber's interpretations of the ḥasidic vision of life, and by the popularity of such evocations of the ḥasidic lifestyle as Elie Wiesel's *Souls on Fire,* and the novels of Chaim Potok.

Ḥasidism, as a popular movement, is represented in several ḥasidic communities, among them the followers of Rabbi Nahman of Bratslav, the Rabbis of Satmar, Ger and Bobov and especially the Rabbi of Lubavitch. The Satmar ḥasidim are largely self-centered, and cherish no aspiration to share the vision with those outside their immediate community. They combine a deep Jewish piety with a sharp hostility to the state of Israel, whose creation they regard as a usurpation of God's initiative to effect the redemption in His own good time and way. The Bratslav and Lubavitch communities have been movingly described in Herbert Weiner's 9 1/2 *Mystics* (Collier Books, New York,

1969). The Lubavitch group is aggressive in spreading its teachings and has succeeded in penetrating many circles in all strata of Jewish society, winning adherents even among those conditioned by secularism and assimilation.

Candor compels one to acknowledge, however, that these movements have failed to channel the interest in mysticism on the part of many Jews seeking a deeper spiritual life. Jews are to be found in large numbers among the adherents of those groups drawing their inspiration from eastern gurus. A small group interested in the mysticism of Sant Mat exists in Tel Aviv, and some of the writings of Charan Singh, the master of this movement, have been translated into Hebrew. The quest for a deepened spirituality has sent some Jews to seek salvation in Christianity.

The failure of mystically inclined Jews to seek a Jewish response to their inner quest is, in part, the result of assimilation. With their Jewish identity of minimal potency, with little background in Jewish education and experience, it is natural that such Jews will enter the mainstream of general culture to seek general answers to their inner problems.

But we must also admit to a certain neglect of mysticism in the normative piety of the established Jewish community. The mystical element is a historical part of the Jewish tradition but it has been greatly minimized in contemporary Judaism, except, of course, for the centers of Ḥasidism which we have mentioned above. Jewish life has long been dominated by the problems of group survival; the concerns of sociology and politics have been paramount in the minds of Jewish thinkers. The Jewish religion itself is dominated to a great extent by the peoplehood of Israel, its origin, its divine calling, its exile and its hoped-for redemption. Personal religion, the search of the individual for answers to the problem of doubt, guilt, suffering, death—these tend to receive lesser attention. The conventional religious establishments, whether Orthodox, Conservative or Reform, are still reacting to the challenge of the Emancipation; they see themselves as alternative formulae for dealing with the conflict between Jewish tradition and modern life and the criteria by which they seek to establish their claims are invariably dialectical and rational.

Jewish spirituality has also suffered because of another circumstance. The focus of conventional Jewish religiosity has generally been on the study of Torahitic texts, especially the Talmud, and on outer conformity to a prescribed code of religious disciplines. The piety of religious inwardness has often been neglected. This has created a state of spiritual impoverishment in Judaism which has alienated some of the most sensitive children of our people.

Rabbi Kook wrote of this often. In one of his most touching pronouncements he spoke directly to the rabbis of his time: "My dear brothers, sages of the Torah . . . We, too, have sinned, we engaged in dialectics and relished new insights in the *halakhah* . . . but we forgot God and His might. We did not heed the admonitions of the prophets of truth, of the best of our sages through the generations, the saints and scholars in the field of ethics and mysticism who insistently warned us that the study of the practical aspects of the Talmud by itself is bound to run dry, unless we add to it from the vast domain of pure faith which stems from within the soul, and emanates from the source of life.

"Now the time has come. When our nation is being revived the call comes to us to heed the claim of the whole man, the claim of the divine soul . . . to illumine it and to revive it."[33]

Rabbi Kook's challenge still waits for an answer.

---

33. *Orot* (Mosad Harav Kook, Jerusalem 1963), p. 101.

THE MYSTICAL DIMENSION IN BIBLE AND TALMUD

1.
The Bible

All Jewish thought, including Jewish mysticism, has its roots in the Bible, the account of God's encounter with the Jewish people. The founders of the Jewish people were seekers of God, and God met their quest by revealing Himself to them and teaching them to become His emissaries to a wayward world. The vision of God as experienced by the teachers of the Bible is sometimes esoteric, involving a crossing of the boundaries of the normal world, but more often it remains within that world. In the tumultuous phenomena of life, the biblical seers discovered a divine dimension, inspiring them to sing of the wonder of life, now seen as transfused with the divine elements; or they heard a divine call charging them to become God's spokesmen to His people or to the world, rebuking the wayward, strengthening the faint-hearted, renewing the faith of those in whom it was eroded by the pressures of the world.

The selections included here are from the bookof Psalms and from the writings of Isaiah, Ezekiel and Daniel.

The book of Psalms is traditionally ascribed to the authorship of King David, but many of the individual psalms bear the names of other authors. The Talmud itself acknowledges that the book is not a unity but a collection of poems by various authors, though the majority are clearly assumed to have been authored by David (Bava Batra 14b).

The prophet Isaiah was active during the last forty years of the eighth century B.C.E., one of the most critical periods in the history of Judea, which enjoyed only a precarious independence after its sister kingdom of Israel in the north had been conquered by the Assyrians. Isaiah's prophecies oscillate between strong rebuke of the people for their moral offenses and their reduction of religion to a rigid, soulless formalism, dire warnings of divine judgment which would follow upon this betrayal, and a glowing portrayal of a reformed new world that will follow the reformation which he believed was due to come in the end of days.

The prophet Ezekiel lived among the exiles in Babylonia who had been settled there after the fall of Judea in 586 B.C.E. Like all prophets, he castigated alienation from God and the betrayal of moral ideals, but speaking to exiles, who were often discouraged and pessimistic about their future, he called on them to trust in God's mercy which would eventually restore those "dead bones" to new life.

The book of Daniel is placed in the Bible among the post-prophetic writings. Daniel lived at the beginning of the Hellenistic period, while the Syrian-Greeks enjoyed hegemony over Judea. This is generally regarded as the time after prophecy had ceased. But in inspiration and pronouncement, Daniel's writings reflect a spirit parallel to that of the classic prophets. Daniel witnessed the persecutions under Antiochus IV in 167-164 B.C.E. His prophecies are a series of visions depicting how Jews who had remained steadfast in loyalty to their faith during earlier persecutions were delivered from their enemies. And he predicts the end of the current reign of evil and the vindication of the faithful in a new consummation to be inaugurated by God's intervention in history. From chapter 2, verse 4b to chapter 7, verse 28 is in Aramaic; the rest is in Hebrew. With much concentration on angelic lore, it is the first book to individualize angels and assign to them specific names and titles.

SONGS ABOUT GOD

Psalm 16

Watch over me, God, for I have taken shelter in You.
I have said to the Lord, You are my God,
I have no other good but You.

All my desire is for the holy and the noble of the earth,
Those who pursue other gods increase their sorrows,
I will not join in their feasts,
I will not bring their names to my lips.

Lord, You are my portion, my cup of joy.
You are the support of my life.
I have been allotted a delightful portion,
I have a goodly inheritance
I will praise the Lord who has counselled me,
In the night my heart corrects me.
I have set the Lord always before me,
He is at my right hand, I shall not stumble.

Therefore does my heart rejoice,
My soul is exultant.
For You will not abandon my soul to death,
You will not assign Your faithful to destruction.

Teach me the way of life,
To find abiding joy in Your presence,
Endless delight at Your right hand.

Psalm 19

For the Leader. A Psalm of David.

The heavens declare the glory of God, the sky proclaims His handiwork. Day after day reveals His splendor, night after night shows forth His wisdom. No speech is uttered, not a word is spoken, not a sound is heard. But their eloquence resounds throughout the whole world, their testimony reaches the ends of the earth.

In the heavens has He set a tent for the sun. It emerges like a bridegroom leaving his chamber, like an athlete set to run his course. It rises at one end of the heavens and makes its circuit to the other end. None can hide from its radiance.

The teaching of the Lord is perfect, reviving the soul; the testimony of the Lord is trustworthy, making wise the simple. The commandments of the Lord are right; they bring joy to the heart. The precepts of the Lord are pure, enlightening the eyes.

The fear of the Lord is pure, it will endure forever. The ordinances of the Lord are true, they are altogether righteous. They are more precious than the finest gold, they are sweeter than honey, than the drops that fall from the honeycomb.

I am careful to observe them, great is the reward for those who keep them. Yet what person can see his own errors?

O Lord, cleanse me of my hidden faults, guard me against willful sins, that they may not have dominion over me. Then shall I be innocent, then shall I be free of grave transgressions.

May the words of my mouth and the meditations of my heart be acceptable to You, my Rock and my Redeemer.

Psalm 92
A Psalm, A Song for the Sabbath Day

It is good to thank You, Lord,
To praise Your name in song,
Each morning to tell of Your kindness,
To recount each night Your unfailing love.

On harp and lute and lyre
Will I play in Your honor,
Your works have filled me with joy,
Your deeds have filled my heart with song.

How great are Your works, O Lord,
How deep the wisdom of Your creation,
The ignorant do not know this,
The fools cannot understand it.

When the wicked sprout as the grass,
When evil men blossom and prosper,
I know they will soon be destroyed,
But You, O Lord, will be exalted forever.

The righteous will bloom like the palm tree,
Like a cedar they will grow tall and upright,
Rooted in the House of the Lord,
They will blossom in the courts of our God.

Green and vibrant even in old age,
They will testify
That God is upright,
There is no inequity in Him.

Psalm 93

God is enthroned in the majesty of creation,
The Lord robed Himself in might
And established the world securely
That it cannot be moved.
Your kingship is from the beginning of time,
You are eternal.

The rivers, O Lord,
The rivers raise up their voice,
The rivers send up a mighty shout,
The mighty waters,
The raging waves of the sea,
They all proclaim,
Mighty is the Lord in His universe.

The testimonies to Your presence are firmly established,
Your creation is graced with holiness,
Lord, You are eternal.

ISAIAH'S CALL

In the year that king Uzziah died I saw the Lord sitting upon a throne high and lifted up, and His trailing robes filled the temple. Above Him stood the seraphim. Each one had six wings; with two he covered his face, with two he covered his feet, and with two he flew. And one called to another and said: Holy, holy, holy, is the Lord of hosts; the whole earth is full of His glory. And the doorposts shook at the voices calling and the temple was filled with smoke. Then I said: Woe is me! for I am undone, because I am a man of unclean lips, and I dwell among a people of unclean lips, and mine eyes have seen the King, the Lord of hosts. Then one of the seraphim flew to me, with a glowing stone in his hand, which he had taken with the tongs from off the altar. He touched my mouth with it, and said: Now, this has touched your lips, and your iniquity is taken away, your sin expiated. And I heard the voice of the Lord saying: Whom shall I send, and who will go for us? Then I said: Here am I; send me.

Then He said: Go and tell this people: You listen but you do not understand, you see but you do not know. The heart of this people is hardened [*hashmen,* literally "fattened"], its ears dulled, its eyes closed, lest it sees with its eyes, and hears with its ears, and understands with its heart, and changes, and finds healing. And I said: How long, O Lord? He answered: Until cities lie wasted, without inhabitants, houses without people, and the land left desolate, until the Lord has banished the people, and there be widespread abandonment throughout the land. If a tenth of them survive, they too will be consumed. But a holy seed will endure, as the stump of an oak or a terebinth which remains after they have been felled. (Isaiah 6)

ISAIAH'S VISION OF THE MESSIANIC AGE

There shall come forth a shoot out of the stock of Jesse, and a branch out of his roots shall blossom. And the spirit of the Lord shall rest upon him, the spirit of wisdom and understanding, the spirit of counsel and might, the spirit of the knowledge and of the fear of the Lord. And his delight shall be in the fear of the Lord; and he shall not judge after the sight of his eyes, neither reprove after the hearing of his ears. But with righteousness shall he judge the poor, and reprove with equity the meek of the earth; and he shall smite the earth with the rod of his mouth, and with the breath of his lips shall he slay the wicked. And righteousness shall be the girdle of his loins, and faithfulness the girdle of his reins.

And the wolf shall dwell with the lamb, and the leopard shall lie down with the kid, and the calf and the young lion and the fatling shall graze together, and a little child shall lead them. And the cow and the bear shall feed in the same pasture; their young ones shall lie down together; and the lion shall eat straw like the ox. And the sucking child shall play over the hole of the asp; and the weaned child shall put his hand on the adder's den. They shall not hurt nor destroy in all My holy mountain, for the earth shall be full of the knowledge of the Lord, as the waters cover the sea.

And it shall come to pass in that day, that the root of Jesse shall be for an ensign of the peoples, and the nations shall seek after him; and his dwelling place shall be glorious. (Isaiah 11:1–11)

EZEKIEL'S VISION OF THE CHARIOT

In the thirtieth year, in the fourth month, in the fifth day of the month, while I was among the exiles by the river of Kevar, the heavens opened and I saw divine visions. . .

As I looked, a stormwind from the north, a huge cloud with flashing fire, and a radiance round about it, while out of the midst of it gleamed something with a lustre like that of shining metal. Within it were figures resembling four living creatures that looked like this: their form was human, but each had four faces and four wings and their legs went straight down; the soles of their feet were round. They sparkled with a gleam like burnished bronze. . .

As I looked at the living creatures, I saw wheels on the ground, one beside each of the living creatures . . . Wherever the spirit wanted to go, there the wheels went, and they were raised together with the living creatures; for the spirit of the living creatures was in the wheels.

Over the heads of the living creatures, something like a firmament could be seen, seeming like glittering crystal, stretched out straight above their heads . . . Above the firmament over their heads, something like a throne could be seen, looking like sapphire. Upon it was seated, up above, one who had the appearance of a man. Upward from what resembled his waist I saw what looked like shining metal; downward from what resembled his waist I saw what looked like fire; he was surrounded with splendor, resembling the rainbow that appears in a cloud on a rainy day. Such was the vision of the glory of the Lord, as it appeared to me.

And when I saw it I fell upon my face. Then I heard the voice of someone speaking, and he said to me: O mortal man, stand upon your feet, that I may speak with you.

And spirit entered into me when He spoke to me, and set me upon my feet; and I heard Him that spoke to me.

And He said to me: Son of man, I send you to the children of Israel, to rebellious nations, that have rebelled against Me; they and their fathers have transgressed against Me, even to this very day; and the children are brazen-faced and stiff-hearted, I do send you to them; and you shall say to them: Thus says the Lord God. And they, whether they will hear, or whether they will forbear—for they are a rebellious house—yet shall know that there has been a prophet among them. (Ezekiel 1:1–2:5)

EZEKIEL'S VISION OF THE VALLEY OF DRY BONES

The hand of the Lord was upon me, and He carried me out by His spirit, and set me down in the midst of the valley, and it was full of bones; and He caused me to pass by them round about; and behold, there were very many in the open valley; and lo, they were very dry. And He said to me: Son of man, can these bones live? And I answered, O Lord God, You know. He said to me: Prophesy upon these bones, and say to them, O you dry bones, hear the word of the Lord. Thus said the Lord God to these bones: Behold I will cause breath to enter into you, and you shall live. And I will lay sinews upon you, and will put flesh upon you, and will cover you with skin, and put breath in you, and you shall live; and you shall know that I am the Lord. So I prophesied as I was commanded; and as I prophesied, there was a voice, and behold a trembling, and the bones came together, bone to bone. And I looked, and lo, there were sinews upon them, and flesh came up, and skin covered them above, but there was no breath in them.

Then He said to me: Prophesy to the wind, prophesy, son of man, and say to the wind: Thus said the Lord God: Come from the four winds, O breath, and breathe upon these slain, that they may live. So I prophesied as He commanded me, and breath came into them, and they lived, and they stood up upon their feet, a very great army.

Then He said to me: Son of man, these bones are the whole house of Israel. Behold, they say: Our bones are dried up, and our hope is lost; we are as wholly destroyed. Therefore, prophesy and say to them: Thus said the Lord God: Behold, I will open your graves, and cause you to come up out of your graves, O my people, and I will bring you into the land of Israel. And you shall know that I am the Lord, when I have opened your graves, and caused you to come up out of your graves, O My people. And I will put My spirit into you, and you shall live, and I will place you in your own land; and you shall know that I the Lord have spoken it and performed it, said the Lord. (Ezekiel 37:1–14)

THE VISION OF DANIEL

1.

In the third year of the reign of Cyrus, King of Persia, a word was revealed to Daniel called Beltshazzar and the word was true; and it was meant for a long time later. He was given to understand the word; its meaning was revealed in the vision.

In those days I, Daniel, was in mourning [for the fate of my people] three weeks. I did not eat choice foods, meat and wine did not touch my lips, I did not anoint myself, until the end of those three weeks.

On the twenty-fourth day of the first month, as I stood at the great river, the Tigris, I raised my eyes and saw a man dressed in linen, his loins girded with fine gold of Ophir, his body sparkling like the precious stone of Tarshish, his face as bright as lightning, his eyes like torches of fire, his arms and legs like purified bronze, and the sound of his utterance like the sound of a multitude.

I, Daniel, alone saw the vision. The people who were with me did not see the vision, but they were seized with a great trembling, and they fled to hide themselves. I was left alone and saw this great vision, and I was enfeebled, my appearance was distorted, and my vigor was gone. Then I heard his voice, and when I heard him I fell down stunned, with my face touching the ground. Then a hand touched me, and raised me shaking on my knees and the palms of my hands. And he said to me: Daniel, greatly beloved, give heed to the words I will tell you; stand in your place, for I have now been sent to you. When he told me, I stood stunned.

He said to me: Fear not, Daniel, for ever since you set your heart to gain understanding and you fasted in contrition before your God, your prayers have been heard, and I have come in response to your prayers. For twenty one days the patron angel of Persia contended with me, but

Michael [the patron angel of the Jewish people], one of the chief angels, came to assist me; until then I had been left alone to deal with the kings of Persia. Now I have come to tell you what will happen to your people in the end of days, for this vision deals with the distant future. (Daniel 10:1–14)

2.

In that day shall arise Michael, the great prince, who is the patron angel of your people. It will be a time of trouble, the like of which has never been since there was a nation. At that time will your people be delivered, all of them whose names are inscribed in the book [of the righteous]. Many of those now sleeping in the dust will awake, some for eternal life and some for shame and everlasting contempt. The enlightened will shine as the brightness of the firmament, and those who lead many to righteousness will shine as the stars forever. And you, Daniel, keep these words secret, and close the book with seals until the time of the end; many will seek for answers, and knowledge will increase.

Then I, Daniel, looked and saw two others standing, one on this side of the river and one on the other side. And one of them said to the man robed in linen who hovered above the waters of the river: How long will it be before those wondrous events happen? And I heard the man robed in linen who hovered above the waters of the river, as he raised his right hand and left hand and swore by Him who is the life of the universe, that within a span of time, and another span of time and a half span of time, when the power of the holy people will be broken, all these things will be accomplished. I heard but did not understand, and I said: Lord, when will be the end hinted at in these words. But he said: Go, Daniel, for these things will remain hidden and closed until the time of the end.

Many will purify themselves and be cleansed and become refined, but the wicked will continue in their wrongdoing, and none of the wicked will understand, but the enlightened will understand. From the time the daily Temple offering was ended, and abomination of idolatry was put in its place, there will transpire a thousand and three hundred and thirty days. Fortunate the one who waits and will reach the thousand and three hundred and thirty days. Now go your way toward the end, remain at peace, and you will reach your appointed destiny at the end of days. (Daniel 12)

2. *The Talmud*

The Talmud is the second great milestone in the literary history of Judaism. It represents approximately a thousand years of Jewish thought. Its foundations were laid by the work of Ezra during the middle of the fourth century B.C.E., in the community of the returned exiles from Babylonia, who inaugurated the second Jewish commonwealth in Palestine. Its period of greatest productivity came in the centuries that followed the disastrous Judean uprising against Rome in 70 C.E. The Talmud exists in two versions, a Palestinian and a Babylonian. Both were edited in the fifth century. The Talmud is not an independent body of literature, however; it proceeds instead as a supplement to the Bible. The Bible remained the fundamental source of belief and practice in Judaism, but the Talmud became its authoritative exposition and implementation.

The Talmud is not a unitary work, reflecting the mind of one author or group of authors. It is an edited anthology of the deliberations of the academies where Judaism was expounded, recording views that reflect a consensus among the scholars on a given subject of discussion. It also reflects the views of individual teachers. Much of the material that is expounded in the pages of the Talmud is law, reflecting the biblical emphasis on law, but there is also a good deal of moralistic and pietistic material. The former is called *halakhah* and the latter is called *aggadah.* Biblical precedents, together with the claims of the existential situation in which the Jews found themselves, are reflected in the discussions of the talmudic sages.

The established religious community, with its concerns of meeting the challenges of the world, does not as a rule operate with the categories of mystical experience. Some teachers of the Talmud cultivated the mystical life, but others focused their attention on problems of law, on the ordered disciplines of faith, on guiding the people in a time of turbulence and uncertainty. The editors of the Talmud reflect a preference for the latter interests. Indeed they appeared to have looked with some suspicion on the excursions into mystical speculation. They seem to have regarded it as a destabilizing interest which might impede their people in the pressing demands of dealing with reality. While recording the views of those teachers who sought to cultivate mystical interests, the Talmud indicates that the religious authorities of the time tried to discourage this tendency. They did not think that the quest for closeness to God was dependent on experiencing a direct encounter with God, to which mystics were drawn. They looked upon this as a dubious and perilous adventure. Instead of seeking direct encounters, they channeled their mystical quest through the study of Torah, but this study was pursued not to gain knowledge. The Torah and the commandments were rather seen as a ladder by which a person might reach the higher goal of cleaving to God. Indeed, subsequent developments in Jewish mysticism were often to move in this direction.

We include here several selections from the Talmud which reflect the interest in mysticism, as well as the discouraging attitudes of some talmudic authorities. These selections also indicate that in some instances mystical pursuits became intertwined with magic, which was, no doubt, an additional factor that inspired the effort to discourage it.

THE WORK OF THE CHARIOT

The Mishnah cites certain subjects of great delicacy which are not to be expounded in public, because of the danger of misunderstanding. One is the discussion of forbidden incestuous marriages, the second is speculation on the mysteries of creation, and the third is the secrets surrounding the divine chariot on which duly qualified spirits may ascend to the heavenly realm. A passage from the Palestinian Talmud is cited which offers a legendary embroidery on the divine potencies released through the chariot speculations; another episode is cited which describes the perils to which those who venture into this awesome realm expose themselves.

1. The subject of forbidden incestuous marriages may not be expounded in the presence of three, nor the work of creation in the presence of two, nor the work of the chariot in the presence of one, unless he is a sage who has innate understanding. Whoever speculates on these four, it would have been better if he had not come into the world: what is above and what is below, what came before and what will come after . . . (Mishnah Ḥagigah 2:1)

2. Our Rabbis taught: Once Rabbi Johanan ben Zakkai rode on a donkey when going on a journey, and R. Eleazar b. Arakh followed him. He [R. Eleazar] said to him [R. Johanan]: Master, teach me a chapter of this work on the chariot. He answered: Did not the sages teach: . . . nor the work of the chariot in the presence of one unless he is a sage, who has innate understanding? R. Eleazar said to him: Master, will you permit me to say something on my own? Say it, he replied. When R. Eleazar b. Arakh began his discourse on the work of the chariot, R. Johanan ben Zakkai descended from the donkey, saying, It is improper that I listen to a discourse in honor of my Creator while I ride on a donkey. They seated themselves under a tree. A fire descended from heaven and encompassed them; the ministering angels danced before them as the attendants of a wedding canopy do to bring rejoicing to a groom. One angel called out of the fire: The work of the chariot is indeed in accord with your exposition, Eleazar b. Arakh. At once all the trees opened in song: "Then shall all the trees sing before the Lord" (Ps. 96:13). When R. Eleazar completed his discourse on the work of the chariot, R. Johanan ben Zakkai stood up and kissed him on the head and said: Praised be the Lord God of Abraham, Isaac and Jacob who has given Abraham our father a wise son who knows to expound the work of the chariot. (TJ Ḥagigah 2:1)

3. Four entered into the orchard of mystical knowledge: Ben Azzai, Ben Zoma, Aḥer and Rabbi Akiba . . . Ben Azzai looked and died . . . Ben Zoma looked and was affected mentally . . . Aḥer cut down the plants . . . Rabbi Akiba departed in peace. (Ḥagigah 14b)

THE NAME OF GOD

We have previously alluded to the mystical speculations which surrounded the pronunciation of God's proper name. The identification of the name with the essence it represents tended to suggest that the pronunciation of God's name, Y H W H, would release the awesome potency of God Himself. We are told of the miraculous consequences released by this practice, of the perilous results which followed its unauthorized use, and of the efforts of the rabbis to discourage it.

1. The following will have no share in the world-to-come . . . Abba Saul says: Also one who pronounces the name of God as written. (Mishnah Sanhedrin 11:1)

2. Abba Saul says: . . . R. Mani said: This is illustrated by the Cuthites who pronounce God's name in an oath. R. Jacob b. Abba says: God's name is written YH, but it is pronounced as though written AD. [YH stands for YHWH and AD for Adonai, but the sage was reticent even to spell out the name or the substitute.] (TJ Sanhedrin 11:1)

3. They [the Romans] brought in Rabbi Ḥanina b. Teradyon. They asked him: Why did you study Torah? He replied: I did as the Lord my God commanded me. They immediately decreed that he be executed by burning, his wife slain, and his daughter placed in a brothel. This fate befell him because he used to pronounce the name of God as written. But how did he allow himself to do this? Did we not learn: These will have no share in the world-to-come . . . Abba Saul says: Also one who pronounces the name of God as written? He did so in order to learn the pronunciation, as we have learnt: You shall not learn to follow after the abominations of those nations (Deut. 18:9), but you may study about them in order to understand and to teach. Why then was he punished? Because he pronounced the name in public. His wife was sentenced to be slain, because she did not rebuke him for it. (Avodah Zarah 17b–18a)

4. Samuel passed and he heard a Persian cursing his son with the name of God, and he died. The Persian said: My son is gone, and someone has heard me pronounce the name. (TJ Yoma 3:7)

5. Rabbah said: Seafarers told me that the wave which sinks a ship appears with a white fringe of fire at its crest, and when one strikes it with a staff on which is inscribed *eheyeh asher eheyeh, YH, H ẓeva'ot,* it subsides. [*Eheyeh asher eheyeh,* usually translated, "I am what I am," is the name by which God first revealed Himself to Moses, as described in Ex. 3:14; *YH* is an abbreviation of the four letter name of God, YHWH;

Ḥ zeva'ot is an abbreviation of *YHWH* ẓeva'ot, usually translated, "Lord of hosts."] (Bava Batra 73a)

THE THREAD OF BLUE

We have previously called attention to the mystical associations which attached themselves to the color blue. Resembling the sky, the abode of the deity, and of the ocean, from which all life commenced, the color blue was seen as a special locus of the divine. The mysterious attributes of the mollusc *murex* from which the color was extracted, and the fact that the Bible prescribed a blue colored thread to be added to the fringe on the corner of a garment (Numbers 15:27–41), added to the mystical idealization of this color.

1. And the Lord spoke unto Moses saying: Speak to the children of Israel and bid them make themselves throughout their generations fringes in the corners of their garments, and that they put with the fringe of each corner a thread of blue. And it shall be to you for a fringe, [*ure'item oto*] *that you may look upon it* and remember all the commandments of the Lord and do them and that you go not about after your own heart and your own eyes. (Numbers 15:27–41)

2. Rabbi Meir said: The text does not say, "that you may look upon *them*" [plural: the fringes], but "that you may look upon *him*" [singular: the Hebrew *oto* usually translated "it" may also mean "him"]. The text suggests here that whoever fulfills the commandment of the fringe, the Scripture regards it as though he had received the divine Presence, for the blue resembles the sea, and the sea resembles the sky and the sky resembles the throne of glory, as it is written (Ezekiel 1:26): "And above the firmament over their heads was the likeness of a throne, as the appearance of a sapphire stone." (*Sifrei* on Numbers, *ad loc.*)

3. It was taught in the name of Rabbi Hezekiah: When the children of Israel robe themselves in a fringed garment, let them not think that they are robed merely in blue, let the children of Israel look at the fringe as the glory of the *Shekhinah* upon them, for it is written (Num. 15:39): "And they shall be to you for a fringe that you may look upon Him." Our text does not say upon *them* [*otam*, the fringes], but upon Him [*oto*], referring therefore to the Holy One, praised be He. (*Midrash Tehillim* on Psalm 90:18)

4. Said Rabbi Judah bar Ilai: Why did the Torah prescribe the blue thread in the fringe? It is because the blue thread resembles sapphire and the staff of the Lord was of sapphire, which teaches us that whenever the children of Israel look upon this thread of blue, they will be reminded of all the signs and wonders which the Lord performed by means of this staff. (*Mekhilta* and *Mekhilta deRabbi Simeon ben Yoḥai* on Ex. 17:6)

THE PARABLE OF THE SONG OF SONGS

For the mystic, the visible is only a vessel which houses an invisible, inner reality. Love on a mortal plane is an intimation of a higher love, the love between God and man. The Song of Songs is a poem portraying the love between a young man and a maiden. In the mystic reinterpretation, this poem became a parable of the love between God and Israel. It was no doubt because of this reinterpretation that the Song of Songs became the much appreciated book of the Bible, and came to be read in the synagogue on Passover, the occasion that served as the most vivid reminder of God's love for Israel, their liberation from Egyptian bondage. The passages cited describe how the rabbis translated the various exclamations of the mortal lovers into equivalent statements of the higher love between God and Israel.

1. Said Rabbi Akiba: God forbid, no one in Israel ever challenged the Song of Songs . . . for all of *ketuvim* is holy, but the Song of Songs is holiest of the holy. (Mishnah, Yadayim 3:5)

2. Let him kiss me with the kisses of his mouth,
Your love is more delightful than wine.
Your ointments have a goodly fragrance,
Your name is an oil poured forth,
Therefore do the maidens love you.
Draw me after you, let us make haste
The king has brought me to his chambers,
We will rejoice and exult in you.
We shall extol your love above wine.

I am black and beautiful, O daughters of Jerusalem,
As the tents of Kedar, as the curtains of Solomon.
Do not stare at me because I am swarthy,
The sun has burnt me,

My mother's sons were angry with me,
They made me a keeper of vineyards,
My own vineyard I did not tend.

(Song of Songs 1:1–6)

3. The sages said: Let not the parable be deemed as something trivial, for through the parable a person can grasp the teaching of the Torah. It is like the case of a person who lost a gold coin or a jewel in his house. Does he not look for it with a candle worth a meager sum? Similarly be not disdainful of the parable—through it a person grasps the teaching of the Torah. As proof of this, we cite the case of King Solomon, who, by means of the parable, was able to master the nuances of the Torah.

Let him kiss me with the kisses of his mouth. To what event does this allude? It was taught in the name of Rabbi Nathan: The Holy One, praised be He, in the glory of His own greatness chanted it, for it is written: The Song of Songs by Shelomoh [Solomon], that is by the king who is the source of *shalom* or peace . . . Rabbi Johanan said: It alludes to the event at Sinai, as it is written: "Let him kiss me with the kisses of His mouth," that is, let Him bring forth kisses [words of teaching] from His mouth . . . Another interpretation: The rabbis said: Each commandment went to each Israelite in turn and said to him: Will you accept me? So many laws are implied in me, so many rules, so many penalties, so many decrees, so many alleviations and so many restrictions, and so much reward; and every Israelite answered: Yes, yes. At once the commandment kissed him on his mouth. . .

I am black and beautiful, O daughters of Jerusalem. I am black with my own deeds and beautiful with the deeds of my ancestors . . . I am black with my deeds at the sea, as it is written: "And they were rebellious at the sea, at the Sea of Reeds" (Psalms 106:7), and I am beautiful with my deeds at the sea, as it is written: "This is my God and I will glorify Him" (Ex. 15:2) . . . I am black with my deeds at Horeb, as it is written: "They made a calf in Horeb" (Psalms 106:19), and I am beautiful with my deeds at Sinai, as it is written: "All that the Lord had spoken we will do and we will hear" (Ex. 27:7) . . . I am black with my deeds all year and I am beautiful with my deeds on Yom Kippur. . .

Look not upon me that I am swarthy, the sun tanned me . . . So did the community of Israel speak to the prophets: Do not judge me by my swarthiness. No one loved me more than Moses, but because he had said: "Listen to me you rebels," it was decreed that he was not to enter Eretz Israel. No one loved me more than Isaiah, but because he had said: "And I live among a people of unclean lips," God said to him: Isaiah, it is well and good for you to say about yourself, "For I am a man of unclean lips," but how did you dare say, "And I dwell among a people of unclean lips?" Come and see what follows: And one of the seraphim flew to me and in his hand a glowing coal [*riẓpah*] (Isaiah 6:6). Said Rabbi Samuel: *riẓpah* suggests *ruz peh,* crush the mouth, crush the mouth of one who slanders My children. . .

We have a similar illustration in the case of Elijah. It is written: "And he said, I have been very jealous for the Lord of hosts, for the children of Israel have forsaken Your covenant" (I Kings 19:10). God said to him: Is it My covenant, or is it your covenant? Elijah continued: "They have thrown down Your altars." God said to him: Are they My altars or your altars? Elijah continued: "And they have slain Your prophets with the sword." God said to him: They were My prophets, why should that have provoked you? Elijah then said to Him: "I alone am left and they seek to take my life." Consider now the additional statement in the text: "And he looked and under his head there was a cake baked on hot stones [*reẓufim*]" (I Kings 19:6). What is the significance of describing the cake as *reẓufim,* baked on hot stones? Said Rabbi Simeon ben Gamaliel: It alludes to *ruz peh,* crush the mouths of one who has slandered My children. (Shir haShirim Rabbah 1:1, 5, 6)

EARLY MYSTICS

3.

Mystical Midrashim

The Talmud did not channel all the literary activity during that period. We have various midrashic works expounding various religious themes, some of a halakhic and some of an aggadic nature, which were composed in the talmudic period or shortly thereafter. In almost all cases the date of a particular work's composition only brings to a close a trend of thought which had much earlier beginnings. In many cases these midrashim proceed through expounding biblical texts, but in some cases there is what appears an independent exposition, although here, too, texts are introduced to illustrate or confirm a homily. Some of these Midrashim are well-known and are highly prized segments of a special category of rabbinic literature, but a number of them suffered neglect in the course of the centuries. Especially midrashim which expounded mystical themes were neglected and in some cases were recovered only thanks to modern scholarship.

Two volumes of such Midrashim, each consisting of twenty-five texts, were published in 1950 and 1953 by the Mosad Harav Kook in Jerusalem under the title *Batei Midrashot*. They were prepared from manuscript by S. Aaron Wertheimer, and revised by his grandson Avraham Joseph Wertheimer.

We include here selections from two mystical Midrashim, the *Hekhalot Rabbati* and the *Alphabet of Rabbi Akiva*.

We have discussed references to *merkabah* mysticism in the Talmud, but it is clear that those scattered references do not portray fully the interest in this type of mysticism during that period. We have discussions of this subject in certain apocryphal works, such as the Book of Enoch, which were frowned on by the religious authorities. But some of these works which have been preserved appear to have had a wider following in Jewish religious circles. This is particularly true of such texts as *Hekhalot Rabbati,* the "Greater *Hekhalot,*" which had a marked influence on the Jewish liturgy. This work appears to have taken form in the latter part of the sixth century, though some of the material included in it is much earlier, going back in some cases to the second century.

The term *Hekhalot* means palatial halls or chambers, the heavenly domain to which the mystic riding on the divine chariot ascended. The overall theme of this work is a description of the grandeur of the heavenly domain, the beatitude experienced by the mystic venturing to enter its courts, and the prerequisites the chariot rider must possess to negotiate the journey successfully. Some of the secrets revealed to the visitor in the celestial realm attempt to lift the enigma of continued Jewish suffering at the hands of persecutors by picturing the eventual Day of Judgment and the coming of the messiah.

An elaborate hierarchy of angels is encountered, some of them identified by a specific name and function. Among them is *Metatron,* who appears frequently in the Talmud, and who was regarded as the original Enoch, transferred to the heavenly realm and transfigured into a kind of prime minister in the celestial court; *Hadarniel,* who acts as guide to the heavenly visitor and serves as a protagonist of the Jewish people; and *Zagzagael,* who is privy to the divine secrets and who is said (in the Midrash, Deuteronomy Rabbah, 11) to have taught Moses the secrets of the ineffable name of God.

Several selections in the liturgy which extol the glory and perfection of God were clearly inspired by texts in the *Hekhalot Rabbati.* These include the *Kedushah, En keElohenu,* and *HaAderet vehaEmunah,* which has been included in the *Yom Kippur* liturgy.

The *Alphabet of Rabbi Akiva (Ottiyot deRabbi Akiva)* is a study of the mystical meaning of the Hebrew alphabet. Since Hebrew was regarded as the holy language it was assumed that the very names and structures of the letters conveyed hidden meanings. The *Alphabet of Rabbi Akiva* belongs to the early period of Jewish mysticism, and it has been placed within the same time category as the *Merkabah* literature, i.e. sixth century, though an exact date cannot be assigned to it. The poet Eleazar haKallir clearly borrowed from it, and historians have placed his activity in the seventh century. Two versions of this text have been published. The selections in this study are taken from the first version and are identified by page references to the Wertheimer edition (*Batei Midrashot,* vol. II, Mosad Harav Kook, Jerusalem 1923).

The formal character of this Midrash is an exposition of the mystical meaning of the Hebrew alphabet, but this is only a technique. The substantive character of this work is to be seen in the ideas which are emphasized. We have here great stress on the world-to-come, on the vindication of Israel, when retribution will be visited on its persecutors. A prominent role is assigned to the angel *Metatron,* who is described by various titles. There are various allusions to hell, but we are told that sinners will be rescued by God's own intervention from its fierce tortures. There is stress on the virtues of humility and of God's special love for the poor. One teaching presented here was destined to play a significant role in the later stages of Jewish mysticism, in the Kabbalah as well as in Ḥasidism, that "the holy one, praised be He was destined to give. . .a new Torah through the messiah" (p. 368). The implication is that the Torah, as we now have it, reflects the existential state in which man now finds himself, but in the more refined and spiritual state he will attain in the messianic age he will need a new level of Torahitic instruction (see the chapter "The Meaning of the Toraḥ in Jewish Mysticism," in Sholem's *On the Kabbalah and its Symbolism*).

THE REWARDS OF CONTEMPLATING THE CHARIOT

1. Said R. Ishmael: What song should be sung by one who desires to contemplate the mysteries of the chariot, to enter upon it in peace and return in peace?

2. The greatest of his rewards is that it brings him into the celestial chambers and places him before the divine throne and he becomes knowledgeable of all future events in the world: who will be thrust down and who will be raised up, who will be weakened and who will be strengthened, who will be impoverished and who will be made affluent, on whom will be decreed death and on whom life, from whom will be taken away an inheritance and to whom will be given an inheritance, who will be endowed with Torah and who with wisdom.

3. Greater than this is that he becomes knowledgeable of human behavior. If a person commits adultery he knows it; if a person commits murder he knows it; if he is suspected of having relations with a woman during her menstrual period, he knows it. Greater than these is the fact that he becomes a savant in the arts of magic.

Greater than this is that whoever should raise his fist at him and hit him would be covered with leprosy. Greater than this is the fact that whoever should slander him would be smitten with wounds and growths which produce festering boils on the skin.

Greater than this is that he becomes distinguished among all other people in his behavior and is honored among higher and lower beings. Whoever should inadvertently injure him will suffer injury, and misfortunes will descend on him by heavenly decree, and whoever should raise his hand against him will suffer retribution from the heavenly tribunal (*Pirkei Hekhalot Rabbati* 1:2-5).

THE AFFLICTIONS AND CONSOLATION OF ISRAEL

1. Said R. Ishmael: The angel Zagzagael, the prince of the inner court, told me: My friend, sit in my lap, and I will tell you what will happen to the Jewish people. I sat in his lap, and he looked at me and wept, and the tears dropped from his eyes and fell on my face. I said to him: Noble, heavenly majesty, why do you cry? He answered me: My friend, come and I will bring you inside and I will disclose to you what awaits Israel, the holy people. He seized me and brought me into the innermost, secret chamber where the documents are kept, and he opened up and showed me a listing of troubles, one worse than the other. I asked Him: Whom will these befall? He said to Me: The Jewish people. I asked him: Will they be able to endure them? He said to me: Come tomorrow, and I will show you worse troubles than these. The next day he took me into the inner chambers and he showed me troubles worse than the first; some were consigned to the sword, some to famine and some to captivity. I said to him, Noble majesty, are the Jews the only ones who committed sin? He said to me, Each day many new troubles are decreed against them, but when they come into the synagogues, and they chant the response: Amen, may the great name of God be magnified, we do not permit them to be carried out.

When I left him I heard a voice speaking Aramaic, saying thus: The Temple is to be destroyed, the maidens and the young men are to be for spoil, the children of the king are to be killed, the wife of the king will be defiled, the table on which the offerings were prepared will be taken as booty by the enemy, Jerusalem will be exiled, and Eretz Yisrael will be devastated.

When I heard this mighty voice, I became faint and fell backward until the angelic prince Hadarniel strengthened me and revived me and set me on my feet and said to me: Friend, what happened to you? I said to him: Noble, heavenly majesty, Perhaps there is no longer hope for the Jews? He answered me: My friend, come and I will take you to the hidden chambers of consolation and deliverance. He took me into the hidden chambers of consolation and deliverance and I saw groups of angels weaving robes of deliverance and making crowns and setting in them precious stones, and pounding all kinds of spices and preparing wines for the righteous in the hereafter.

I saw one crown especially distinguished; the sun and the moon and twelve constellations were set in it. I said to him: Noble, heavenly majesty, for whom is this special crown? He said to me: It is for David, king of Israel. I said to him: Noble, heavenly majesty, show me the honor due to David. He said to me: Wait, my friend, three hours, until David, king of Israel, enters, and you will see him in his glory. (*Hekhalot Rabbati* 6:3-5)

2. He seized me and put me in his lap and said to me: What do you see? I said to him: I see seven streaks of light flashing like one. He said to me: Close your eyes that you may not become shaken up, for they have gone forth in honor of David. At once all the *ofahim* and the *seraphim* and the holy *ḥayot*, and the treasure houses where the snow is stored, and the clouds of glory, and the constellations, and the stars, and the ministering angels, and the flaming fire of the Temple became astir, and proclaimed: "To the chief musician. A Psalm of David. The heavens declare the glory of God" [Psalm 19]. Then I heard a stormy sound emanating from the Garden of Eden, declaring: "The Lord will be King forever." David, king of Israel, marched at the head, and the other kings of the house of David followed him; each one bore a crown on his head, but the crown of David was the most glorious of all the crowns, and its lustre sparkled from one end of the world to the other.

After David entered the heavenly Temple he found a fiery throne set for him, forty miles long in height and twice the length and twice the width. David seated himself on the throne facing the divine throne, all the kings of the house of David sat before him, and all the kings of the kingdom of Israel sat behind him. Then David stood up and chanted songs in praise of God, the like of which no one in the world ever heard before. When David began and said: "The Lord will reign forever," the chief angel Metatron and his angelic host responded: "Holy, holy, holy is the Lord of hosts." The *ḥayot* offered praise saying: "Praised be the Lord from His place." The heavens recited: "The Lord will reign forever." The earth chanted: "The Lord is King, the Lord was King." All the kings of the house of David joined in the chant: "The Lord will be King throughout the earth."

Said R. Ishmael: When I came and disclosed all this from the proceedings before the throne of glory all my colleagues rejoiced and arranged a day of celebration. Moreover, the chiefs in their rejoicing declared: Bring before us all kinds of musical instruments and let us drink to their playing, for Hadriel, the Lord God of Israel will do all kinds of wonders in executing judgment against wicked Rome, let us celebrate with harp and lute. (*ibid.*, 7:1–3)

THE SONG OF THE ANGELS

(*HaAderet vehaEmunah*)

Majesty and faithfulness belong to the eternal God,
Understanding and blessing belong to the eternal God,
Splendor and greatness belong to the eternal God,
Knowledge and communication belong to the eternal God,
Nobility and glory belong to the eternal God,
Decision and firmness belong to the eternal God,
Uprightness and lustre belong to the eternal God,
Might and softness belong to the eternal God,
Adornment and purity belong to the eternal God,
Unity and awe belong to the eternal God,
Crown and glory belong to the eternal God,
Teaching and insight belong to the eternal God,
Dominion and sovereignty belong to the eternal God,
Beauty and victory belong to the eternal God,
Magnificence and strength belong to the eternal God,
Power and gentleness belong to the eternal God,
Redemption and glory belong to the eternal God,
Beauty and righteousness belong to the eternal God,
Summons and sanctity belong to the eternal God,
Jubilation and exaltation belong to the eternal God,
Song and praise belong to the eternal God,
Adulation and eminence belong to the eternal God.

(*Hekhalot Rabbati* 28:1)

THE ALPHABET

1. Said Rabbi Akiva: What does the *aleph* signify? Through its phonetic structure (*alph*) the Torah meant to teach us: To truth (*a*met) train (*l*emad) your mouth (*p*ikha), so that you may make yourself fit for this world. Your mouth (*p*ikha) you must train (*l*emad) to truth (*a*met), so that you may make yourself fit for the world to come. Why is this? Because God Himself is known as truth, and the throne on which He sits is truth, and mercy and truth find welcome before Him, and all His teachings are teachings of truth and all His decrees are decrees of truth, and all His ways are mercy and truth. . .

Another interpretation of what the *aleph* signifies: I will open (*a*phtaḥ) to speech (*l*ashon) the mouth (*p*eh), and the mouth (*p*eh) to speech (*l*ashon) I will open (*a*phtaḥ). Said the Holy One, praised be He: I will open to speech the mouths of all the children of flesh and blood that they may constantly praise Me, and declare My sovereignty over the world, for were it not for the songs they sing to Me each day I would not have created the world . . .

Another interpretation for "I will open to speech the mouth and to speech I will open the mouth." Said the Holy One, praised be He: I will give speech to the children of Israel in the discourses of the Torah so that they may praise Me constantly, for if Israel did not exist no one would acknowledge My greatness or declare My praise. Were it not for the songs that Israel sings to Me each day I would not have created the world. Even Israel, for whose sake the whole world was created, was brought into the world only for the sake of song, as it is written (Isaiah 43:21): "This people that I created for My sake, that they might declare My praise." (pp. 343,345)

2. Another interpretation of what the *aleph* signifies: Said the Holy One, praised be He: I spoke (*a*marti) to My people (*l*eami) of My glory (*p*earti), and of My glory (*p*earti) I spoke (*a*marti) to My people (*l*eami). The term *amarti* applies to speaking of Torah, as it is written (Deut. 32:2): "My doctrine (*likḥi*) shall come down as the rain, My speech (*imrati*) shall distill as the dew," and doctrine (*lekaḥ*) is specifically defined as meaning Torah (in Prov. 4:2): "I have given you a good doctrine (*lekaḥ*), forsake not my Torah."

How were they admonished not to forsake the Torah? At the giving of the Torah, the Holy One, praised be He, called together the children of Israel and said to them: I have something precious and I am prepared to give it to you forever if you will accept My Torah and keep My commandments. They replied to Him: Master of the universe, what is the something you are prepared to give us if we keep Your Torah? The Holy One, praised be He, answered them saying: It is the world-to-come. To this the children of Israel replied: Give us a sample of the world-to-come. The Holy One, praised be He, answered them: The sample is the Sabbath, which is one sixtieth of the beatitude of the world-to-come. . . And how do we know that the world-to-come is one unbroken Sabbath? For it is written (Ps. 92:1): "A Psalm, a song for the Sabbath day. It is good to praise the Lord, to sing to Your name, O Most High."[1] At that point groups of angels descended from heaven. Some held in their hands harps, some flutes, some lyres and other instruments of music, and they played before Him songs, as it is written: ". . . and to sing to Your name, O Most High."

The psalm continues: "To declare Your lovingkindness in the morning." This refers to the world-to-come, which has been compared to the dawn, as is alluded to in the verse (Lam. 3:23): "(The Lord's mercies) are new each morning, great is Your faithfulness." The psalm goes on: ". . . and Your faithfulness in the night." This refers to the present world, which has been compared to night, as it is written (Ps. 104:20): "You make the darkness and it is night, when all the beasts of the forest creep forth." But do the beasts of the forest creep around only at night, not in the daytime? This alludes to this world which is like the night, and the kings of the nations are like wild beasts which roam in the forest at night. When dawn breaks, as the wild beasts return to their lairs, so will the kings and princes of the nations, when the world-to-come dawns and the messiah's kingdom is established, return to the forest and their places, and come down from their high station, and return to the dust. They will have no share in the world-to-come. Thus it is written (Zech. 14:9): "Then will the Lord be King over all the earth." (pp. 346–347)

3. Another interpretation (for the letter *bet*): Why does the Torah begin with the letter *bet* (*b*ereshit), and end with the letter lamed (yisrae*l*)? Because when you join the first and the last letters they form the word *bal* (nothing) and when you read them in the reverse order they form the word *lev* (heart). Said the Holy One, praised be He, to Israel: My children, if you pursue these two attributes, humility (*bal*), and heart (*lev*), I will consider it as though you have kept the entire Torah, from *bet* to *lamed*. (p. 355)

4. Another interpretation (for the meaning of the letter *dalet*): Said the Holy One, praised be He: I said (*d*ibarti) to raise (*l*ehakim) the poor

---

1. The perfections of the world as described in this psalm were regarded as a reflection of the world-to-come, not of this world (*Midrash Tehillim* on. Psalms 92:1).

(*d*al), the poor (*d*al) to raise (*l*ehakim) I said (*d*ibarti). People dislike the poor; no one loves the poor but I alone. People disparage the poor and the wisdom of the poor is not heeded, as it is written (Eccl. 9:16): "The poor man's wisdom is despised, and his words are not heeded." But I am a stronghold for the poor, as it is written (Ps. 9:10): "The Lord is a stronghold for the oppressed." And when a poor man comes before Me in prayer, I do not turn him away empty-handed, as it is written (Ps. 74:21): "The oppressed will not be turned away disappointed" [the usual interpretation takes this as a prayer: May the oppressed not be turned away disappointed]. My *shekhinah* is close to him each day, as it is written (Ps. 34:20): "The Lord is near to those who are broken-hearted." The broken-hearted refers to the poor. Whoever shuts his ears from listening to the cry of the poor will himself not be heeded when he cries in bitter complaint, as it is written (Prov. 21:13): "Whoever shuts his ears not to listen to the poor will himself call, and not be answered." Moreover, the Holy One, praised be He, watches over the poor constantly, as it is written (Isa. 66:2): "On this man will I look often: the poor and the one who is humble of spirit." And their words are sweeter to me than those of any other people, as it is written (Ps. 69:34): "The Lord listens to the needy, and does not despise His imprisoned ones." What is meant by "His imprisoned ones?" This refers to the sick and the wounded who, during their illness are like prisoners in this world, until God sends them healing and releases them. (p. 361)

5. Another interpretation for "the Lord is near to the broken-hearted" (Ps. 34:20). Is He only near to those who are broken-hearted and not to those who are anxious of heart? Is it not stated (Isa. 35:4): "Say to the anxious of heart, Be strong, fear not." But this is meant to suggest to us that God withdraws His presence from all who are proud-hearted. All such people are deemed by Him as an abomination, as it is written (Prov. 16:15): "All the proud-hearted are an abomination to the Lord, My hand on it—he will not be cleared." "Abomination" is but another name for idolatry, as it is written (Deut. 7:26): "You shall not bring an abomination into your house." This suggests that one who is proud in spirit is as though he had worshipped idols. Moreover, it is as though he had erected an altar in his heart and brought idolatrous offerings on it. . . And what is meant by "my hand on it—he will not be cleared"? It is an allusion to father Abraham who by his charitable deeds made himself worthy of heaven and earth, of this world and of the world-to-come, as it is written (Gen. 22:22): "And Abraham said to God, I raise my hand to the God the Most High, the possessor of heaven and earth." Even if a person should be as charitable and perform acts of loving-

kindness like Abraham, but if he be guilty of haughtiness, he will not be spared from *gehinnom*. (p. 370)

4. *Sefer Yeẓirah*

Sefer Yeẓirah is the earliest tract of cosmological mysticism to have come down to us. It is a short but enigmatic work, consisting altogether of some 2,000 words but abounding in pronouncements that have baffled scholars through the centuries. It has been ascribed to the patriarch Abraham and to Rabbi Akiva, but its true author remains unknown and it has been conjectured that he lived sometime between the third and sixth centuries. The book has been translated into Latin, French and German, and several translations into English are also extant, the best known of which, by K. Sterning, appeared in 1923.

The central problem in the book is to account for the mystery of creation. The author's solution reflects an affinity with the Pythagorean doctrine reducing ultimate reality to mathematical concepts or numbers. It also reflects the biblical teaching that God performed the act of creation through the utterance of words, which are in turn constituted of letters of the alphabet.

The book opens with its central thesis that God created the world by means of thirty-two paths of wisdom, which are further defined as ten *sefirot* or primordial numbers and the twenty-two letters of the Hebrew alphabet. The ten *sefirot* generated these basic elements: the spirit of God, ether, water, fire, and the six dimensions of space: height, depth, east, west, north and south. The twenty-two letters of the alphabet are divided into three categories. The first is what were called "mother" letters. These are *aleph* (a), *mem* (m) and shin (sh). It has been suggested that they are so characterized because they stand for the three primary divisions of the alphabet, the mutes (*mem*), the sibilants (*shin*) and aspirates (*aleph*). These three are also so designated because they are the key letters in the Hebrew words for the basic elements in all existence, air (*avir*), fire (*esh*), and water (*mayim*). The next group of letters are seven "doubles", so called, it has been explained by some scholars, because of a variation in sound, through a sign in the letter, such as a dot or a *dagesh*. These letters are given as *bet* (b), *gimmel* (g), *dalet* (d), *kaf* (k), *pe* (p), *resh* (r) and *tav* (t). The *resh* (r) is not so affected in modern Hebrew usage, but it is in other languages with which the author may have been familiar, such as Greek or Arabic. The remaining twelve are called simple letters. The significance of this theory about *sefirot* and letters is to suggest that the mystery of creation lends itself to ordered discourse, which proceeds through number and language. The translations below are based on the critical edition of the text by Ithamar Greenwald in *Israel Oriental Studies* I (1971), 132–177.

1. The Lord, the Lord of hosts, the God of Israel, the living God and the King of the universe, the Almighty, Merciful and Gracious, the Exalted, who abides in eternity, whose name is august and holy, shaped (*hokak*, literally, "engraved") and created the universe with thirty-two wondrous paths of wisdom, comprising three categories: numbers, letters and words.

2. Ten non-corporeal *sefirot* and twenty-two basic letters, three "mother" letters, seven double letters, and twelve simple letters.

3. Ten non-corporeal *sefirot*, corresponding to the ten fingers, five paralleling five, with the covenant of unity in the center, as indicated by the term for "word" (*milah*) which is formed by tongue and mouth, and which also defines the organ that bears the covenant of circumcision.

4. Ten non-corporeal *sefirot*, ten and not nine, ten and not eleven; understand with wisdom, and discern with understanding; analyze them

and probe them, clarify the matter and establish the Creator on His throne.

5. Ten non-corporeal *sefirot.* They comprise ten dimensions; the dimension of beginning, the dimension of the end, the dimension of good, the dimension of evil, the dimension of height, the dimension of depth, the dimension of east, the dimension of west, the dimension of north, the dimension of south. One Lord alone, God, the faithful King, rules over all from His holy abode for ever and ever.

6. Ten non-corporeal *sefirot.* Their appearance is like a flash of lightning and they have no end. His word is in them, surging forth and receding. They hasten like a whirlwind to do His bidding and they bow down before His throne.

7. Ten non-corporeal *sefirot.* Their end is merged with their beginning and their beginning is merged with their end, as a flame is joined to the burning coal. For the Lord is one and there is none like Him, and what can you count before One?

8. Ten non-corporeal *sefirot.* Curb your mouth from speaking of them and your heart from speculating about them. And if your mouth ventures to speak and your heart to speculate, turn back. For this reason it is written (Ezekiel 1:14): "And the living creatures [Ezekiel's characterization of certain angels which carry the divine chariot] surged forward and returned." This reticence was pledged in a covenant. (ch. 1, Mishnayot 1-8)

5.
Baḥya Ibn Paquda

Baḥya ben Joseph ibn Paquda was a pietistic mystic who was active in eleventh-century Spain. He was a *dayan,* a member of a court of rabbinic law, but he decried the overemphasis on behavioristic disciplines, as opposed to inner spirituality. He stressed feeling, inner devotion, as the way of cultivating a sensibility for the divine. His own sensitivity is reflected in several hymns which he wrote, the best known of them being *Tokheḥah,* an exhortation to pietistic devotion. It was included in the High Holy Day liturgy in some Sephardic communities. The hymns were written in Hebrew, but his major work, *Ḥovot haLevavot,* was originally written in Arabic, and it was translated into Hebrew by Judah ibn Tibbon in 1160. Scholem finds a distinct influence of Islamic, specifically, Sufi, mysticism in this work (*Kabbalah,* pp. 35f), but its primary exposition proceeds by invoking biblical and Talmudic references, which invest it with the authority of classical Jewish teaching. The book has been translated into many modern languages and a translation into English from the original Arabic was recently published by Menahem Mansoor (*The Book of Direction to the Duties of the Heart,* Routledge & Kegan Paul, London 1974). The selections included here are translations from the Hebrew version of ibn Tibbon.

The values stressed by Baḥya are the familiar subject matter in all forms of pietistic mysticism, but two of his conceptual positions are especially noteworthy. The first is his positive attitude toward reason as a vital channel for acquiring sound knowledge about God. Secondly, he held that in every generation and in all countries prophet-like figures arise to admonish their fellow-men and lead them back from their waywardness to their home in God (Penitence, ch. 6). Here is the foreshadowing of the concept of the rebbe that we encounter in later Ḥasidism. *The Duties of the Heart* became one of the most popular works in Jewish spirituality and it was highly esteemed as a basic text in the disciplines of Jewish piety even in circles not inclined to mysticism.

THE DUTIES OF THE HEART

God graced man with the capacity of speech and with fullness of perception and comprehension, but the greatest gift He bestowed on him is wisdom. This represents the life of his spirit and the light of his intelligence, through which he can learn to do God's will, and save himself from His displeasure in this world and in the next. Thus the verse declared: "The Lord bestows wisdom, from Him comes knowledge and discernment" (Prov. 2:6); Job's friend Elijah is quoted as declaring: "God inspires a man, it is the Almighty who breathes knowledge to him" (Job 32:8); and Daniel said: "He imparts wisdom to the wise" (Daniel 2:21); and the verse also states: "I the Lord your God instruct you for your benefit, I show you the way to go" (Isa. 48:17).

Wisdom embraces three divisions: the first is physics, which is the knowledge of the nature of bodies and their accidents; the second is practical wisdom, and some include in this category the wisdom of morals; it embraces the knowledge of mathematics, astronomy, and music; and the third division is the divine science, which is the knowledge of divine matters, including the knowledge of God, praised be He, the knowledge of His Torah and other concepts like the soul, the mind, and angelic beings.

All the divisions of wisdom, according to their respective subject matter, are gates the Creator, praised be He, opened to rational beings through which to understand the Torah and the world. Some branches of this wisdom are needed more to clarify the Torah, and others are needed more for their usefulness in the world. The branch which is needed for the affairs of the world is the lower wisdom which is concerned with the nature of bodies and their accidents and the middle branch of wisdom which is the science of mathematics. These two branches of wisdom deal with the hidden realities of this world, and how we can adapt them to our benefit and enjoyment. They also teach us about all the arts, and the various pursuits needed for our bodily life and for the affairs of the world. But the branch of wisdom which is most needed for the understanding of the Torah is the supreme wisdom, which is the divine science, and we are under obligation to study it in order to comprehend and to be drawn to the Torah.

But it is forbidden to study it [the Torah] in order to gain worldly benefits. Thus did our sages teach: "I have commanded you this day to love the Lord your God, to heed His voice and cleave to Him" (Deut. 30:16); this means that a person should not say, "I will study Bible so that people call me scholar, I will study Mishnah so that they call me Master, I will study Talmud so that I be deemed a sage and sit in the academy," but let him study out of love, and the honors will follow in the end. The sages also said: Perform good deeds for their own sake, and speak of them as an end in itself. Do not turn them into a crown with which to adorn yourself, nor a spade to dig with (Nedarim 62a). We also have the comment by Rabbi Eleazar on the verse, "Happy is the man who reveres the Lord, who takes great delight in His commandments" (Ps. 112:1): *"in His commandments,"* not in a reward for his commandments, as we studied in the Mishnah (Avot 1:3): Be not like servants who serve a master so as to receive a reward, but be like servants who serve the master without expecting a reward; and let the fear of God be on you (Avodah Zarah 19a).

The Creator opened for us three gates for the knowledge of His Torah and His law: the first is the sound mind; the second is the text of Torah revealed to His prophet Moses, and the third is the traditions we have received from early masters which were transmitted to them by the prophets, peace be upon them. These gates have been explained satisfactorily by the great sage, Rabbi Saadia.

The science of the Torah, however, is divided into two parts: one involves the knowledge of the duties which are performed by bodily organs, and this is externally visible; the second involves the knowledge of the duties of the heart, which embrace the realm of the conscience, and this represents the science of the inner life.

The duties of external conduct are two-fold: one consists of rational commandments, which we would be under obligation to carry out even if they were not ordained in the Torah, and the other consists of duties based on traditional prescription, which reason neither demands but neither does it reject. The latter includes the prohibition of eating milk with meat, the prohibition of wearing a garment made of mixed materials, wool and cotton [*sha'atnez*], the prohibition of seeding a field with diverse seeds [*kilayim*] and the like. The rationale for all these eludes us, and we do not know why they were proscribed to us. But the duties of the heart are all rooted in reason, as I shall explain, with the help of God.

All the commandments are subdivided into positive and negative. There is no need to clarify this in relation to the duties of external conduct, as they are well-known to all. But I will mention some of the duties of the heart, as circumstances will suggest, so that they serve as an illustration of others I will not mention. Among the positive commandments in the category of duties of the heart are: the belief that the world had a Creator; that He created it *ex nihilo;* that there is none like Him; that we are under obligation to acknowledge His unity, to worship Him with our hearts; to contemplate the wonders manifested by His creatures, so that these serve as tokens of His nature; that we trust in Him, humble ourselves before Him, and feel awed by Him; that we feel embarrassed when we realize that He observes our open acts and secret thoughts; that we yearn to please Him; that our conduct be devoted solely to glorifying His name; that we love Him, and love those that love Him in order to be close to Him; that we spurn those who spurn Him; and similar duties not embraced in external behavior.

The negative duties of the heart are the opposite of all these. Included among them are: that we shall not covet; that we shall not exact vengeance or bear a grudge; that our minds shall not focus on forbidden things, that we lust not after them, that we do not give consent to carry them out; and similar rules which apply to the inner life that none can see except the Creator. Thus it is written: "I the Lord search the heart, I probe the emotions" (Jer. 17:10). Similarly it is written: "The soul of man is a lamp of the Lord, searching out all his inward parts" (Prov. 20:27).

I also said to myself that perhaps these duties are so well-known to everybody and all people adhere to them so that there is no need for a special work to be devoted to them. But as I reflected on the behavior of people in most of the generations described in our literature I found them remote from this category of duties, except for special zealots who are meticulous about them. As to others it has always been necessary to exhort them and to instruct them. How much more so is this necessary with most of the people in our time who have neglected the knowledge of behavioral duties and more so the duties of the heart. Those of them who do feel stirred to study the Torah do so that the ignorant may regard them as scholars, and that they gain fame among the great. They turn away from the way of the Torah to concentrate on subjects which cannot gain for them special excellence or save them from spiritual stumbling, which one would not be held accountable for if he did not know them. But they ignore the core study of religion and the basic concepts of the Torah which they should not neglect and without which it is impossible to keep any commandments.

I then resolved to write a book on this subject, structuring it according to the basic principles of the duties of the heart and the commandments applying to the inner life, to make it a miscellany adapted for common use, and to include in it enough of the subject to serve as a guide to the upright path. It will seek to lead people back to the noble practices of our ancient teachers, and the moralistic values of the pious [*ḥasidim*]; it will seek to waken people from the sleep of folly, to deepen them in the fine points of this science, and to bring to their minds the knowledge of God and His teachings; it will seek to save souls and to make each person more sensitive in performing his duties; it will seek to bestir the negligent, set straight the overzealous and encourage the tardy; it will seek to give direction to beginners and point a way to the perplexed.

And when you, brother, read my book and grasp its subject matter, make it a point to remember it, and judge yourself honestly in the light of its teaching. Go into it deeply, let it bear fruit in your life, and take it to your heart and conscience. If you find any error in it, correct it, or if you note anything missing in it, add to it. Focus on the thrust of its practical objective in what it seeks to communicate, but do not try to gain renown or take pride in the knowledge it conveys. Judge me charitably when you encounter mistakes or when you note my limitation in dealing with any phase of the subject. I wrote in haste for I was afraid death might overtake me and I will be unable to accomplish my objective. For you must realize that a creature of flesh and blood is limited in understanding and human nature does not allow him to attain perfection, as it is written: "Mortal men are a mere illusion, and people of rank are not dependable. If put on the scales they are lighter than a mere breath" (Ps. 62:9). I have already acknowledged to you my limited powers in order to atone for my errors. (*Ḥovot haLevavot*, introduction)

6.

Moses Maimonides

Moses ben Maimon (1135-1205) was born in Cordoba, Spain. At the age of thirteen, when his native city was invaded by a fanatical Moslem sect, the Almohades, who inaugurated a policy of persecution against non-Moslems, he joined his family in their flight from Spain. He lived for a time in Fez, North Africa, in Safed, Palestine, and finally in Cairo, Egypt.

Maimonides made monumental contributions to every phase of Jewish knowledge and thought. His philosophic classic, *The Guide for the Perplexed,* defends the legitimacy of reason as an aid to religious knowledge, and he has therefore been regarded by some as a rationalist. But the strong mystical trend in his writing represents a significant chapter in the history of Jewish mysticism. Indeed, the great masters of Kabbalah and Ḥasidism often quoted Maimonides, not only from his legal writings, but also from his philosophic treatise, *The Guide.*

The most noteworthy contribution of Maimonides to mysticism is his doctrine of prophecy. In the thought of Maimonides, prophecy ceased to be a singular phenomenon of God's revelation vouchsafed to chosen individuals, and became instead an episode in a larger category of man's encounter of the divine; it became a phase of mystical experience. As R. J. Z. Werblowsky put it: "Medieval Jewish philosophy, dominated by Maimonides, tended to efface the distinction between prophecy and the contemplative life of mystical *devekut*. On the one hand prophecy became the ideal and legitimate aim of all spiritual life, on the other hand it lost its original characteristics of specific contents and message, and became a mystical or semi-mystical 'state' " (*Joseph Karo*, Oxford University Press, London 1962, p. 49).

Maimonides listed eleven degrees of prophecy. The first two are only what he calls "stepping stones" to prophecy, but they correspond to the experience of creative spirits in thought and action who have testified to an infusion of energy from a transcendent source that inspired them to act and to speak. Many students of creativity have indeed interpreted the experience which energizes the creative act as a mystical experience. (See Rufus Jones, *The Testimony of the Soul*, Macmillan, New York 1937, pp. 208f)

The medium through which the divine influence enters the mind of the prophet is the "Active Intellect." This goes back to the teaching of Aristotle, that the universe is directed by a series of "Intelligences" which emanated from God; the last of these "Intelligences," called "the Active Intellect," directs the terrestrial sphere. The notion that the "Intelligences" *emanated* from God made them coterminous with God, and this fitted in with the Aristotelian belief that the universe was eternal. Maimonides accepted the Aristotelian's doctrine of "Intelligences" but he held them to have been created by God, *in time*, which harmonized with his belief that the universe was created rather than eternal. Maimonides identified the Intelligences with angels; the Active Intellect, he held, directed the earthly sphere, and it was this Intelligence which channeled the divine influence to the prophet. There were three conditions a person had to meet if he was to be a recipient of the divine influx: the perfection of his intellectual faculties; an active imagination to robe the concepts perceived in the imagery necessary to aid communication; and a sound moral life. Such a person can be chosen by God to be the recipient of a prophetic communication.

Like all students and practitioners of the mystical life, Maimonides called for meditation as the vital energizing condition that established the channel linking man with God. The focus of meditation was to be on the perfection of God as revealed in the wondrous panorama of His creation. In the moment of illumination which occurs in this process, truths not reached by reason will dawn on the prophet. Such truths can never contradict reason, but reason cannot establish them. This is the area of revelation which is an indispensable complement to reason in bringing man the knowledge by which to order his life.

Maimonides was careful to caution that not everyone who is qualified by intellectual, imaginative and moral perfection will necessarily become a prophet. There remains an element of divine grace which is involved in the fulfillment of the seeker's quest. But to whatever extent a person achieves these attributes his meditative discipline will bear for him a precious fruit. It brings God out of His remoteness and He enters into an intimate relationship with him as lover and beloved.

REASON AND REVELATION

1. I maintain that human knowledge is limited, and as long as the soul is in the body it cannot know what is beyond nature. It cannot see beyond, because it is confined within nature. Thus when our intelligence should seek to probe the beyond it will be unable to do so, for this subject is outside its reach. It is only what is within nature that it can know and contemplate . . . But know that there is a level of knowledge beyond that of the knowledge of philosophers, and this is prophecy. Prophecy is another world, and proof and argumentation do not apply here. Once it has been authenticated that we have before us a prophetic vision, there is no need for supporting evidence. (Letter to Rabbi Ḥisdai haLevi)

2. I say somewhat in the figurative language of the psalm (Ps. 115:1): The heavens are the heavens of the Lord, but the earth has He assigned to the children of man, that is to say, God alone has an authentic knowledge concerning the heavens, their nature, their substance, their form, their motion, and their causes. However, what is below the heavens He has endowed man with the capacity to know, because this is his world, his home which is under his control, and he is part of it; and this is the truth. The causes which would illuminate the mystery of the heavens are denied us. They are too far from us, they are beyond us in space and rank. The one principle one may infer from them is that they point to the existence of their Mover. But other problems concerning them are beyond the reach of the human intellect. It is, in fact, a defect in one's intelligence or a kind of madness to weary the mind with that which is outside his faculties of comprehension. It is for us to halt where

our competence reaches and to leave subjects which cannot be reached by logical reasoning to him [Moses] who was granted a mighty influx of divine illumination so that it was said of him (Nu. 12:8): "Mouth to mouth I speak to him." (*Guide* II 24)

NATURE OF PROPHECY

1. Know that the true essence of prophecy is an emanation sent forth by God, praised be He, through the medium of the Active Intellect, in the first instance to man's rational faculty, and then it will extend to his imaginative faculty. This is the highest degree and the greatest perfection man can obtain. This is made possible through the highest perfection of the imaginative faculty. This state cannot be found in a person or acquired by him merely by cultivating his intellectual and moral faculties, even if these were of the highest excellence, unless he were also endowed at birth with highest perfection of the imaginative faculty . . . You already know the function of the imaginative faculty: it is to retain sense impressions, to combine them and to imitate them. You know, too, that its most powerful and most significant action takes place when the senses are at rest and are not active. Then will the divine inflow reach it, to the extent of its receptive capacity.

This is the basis of dreams with a positive meaning, and this itself is the basis of prophecy. The difference is only in degree, not in kind. You are familiar with the statement of the sages (Berakhot 57b), that a dream is one sixtieth of a prophecy . . . They reiterated this subject in the Midrash Bereshit Rabbah (15:15), stating: A dream is an unripe form of prophecy. This is a wonderful comparison. An unripe fruit is the fruit itself but it fell off before its completion, before it ripened. Similarly, the action of the imaginative faculty during sleep is the same as in prophecy, except that it was cut short and did not reach its proper end. But why should I tell you this by citing rabbinic texts and overlook a text in the Torah (Nu. 12:6): "If there be a prophet among you, I, the Lord, will make myself known to Him in a vision, in a dream will I speak to him." Thus He, may He be exalted, has informed us of the true nature of prophecy. He has taught us that it is a state of perfection that is activated in a dream or a vision.

The term for vision, *mareh,* derives from the verb *ra'oh,* to see. This indicates that the imaginative faculty reaches a state of perfection to a point where the object of its vision appears to it as though it had an external existence, and that it reached him through resultant sensations Through these two channels, that is, through vision and dream, do all degrees of prophecy occur, as will be explained later. It is also known that the subject which preoccupies a person and engages his faculties and on which his heart is focused while he is awake will be the subject on which the imaginative faculty will act during sleep, when the intellect will extend its influence on it, in accordance with its preparedness . . .

We have made clear the three prerequisites: intellectual perfection through study, the perfection of the imaginative faculty by endowment at birth, and the perfection of one's morals by withdrawing the mind from a concern with bodily pleasures and overcoming one's desire for foolish and evil self-aggrandizement. Those who have attained perfection vary in the extent to which they possess these three, and the extent to which they differ with regard to these three qualities will they differ in the degree of prophecy attained by them. (*Guide* II 36)

2. After our previous explanation of the nature of prophecy, as mandated by reason and as clarified by our Torah, it becomes necessary for me to mention the different degrees of prophecy, according to these two sources of authority. Not all of those that I shall include as degrees of prophecy is a prophet. The first and second degrees are preliminaries to prophecy. Whoever has achieved one of them is not to be included in the category of prophets discussed previously. If such a person is sometimes designated as a prophet it is only in a general way, because he is indeed very close to the prophets . . .

The first of the degrees of prophecy consists in divine assistance which attaches itself to a person, activating and stirring him to perform a mighty good deed such as rescuing an important community from evil men, delivering one noble individual, or bestowing some benefit on a multitude of people. Such an individual comes by himself upon this influence which stirs him and moves him to act, and this is called the *spirit of the Lord.* It is said of a person who has this experience that the spirit of the Lord came upon him, or that the spirit of the Lord clothed him, or that the spirit of the Lord rested upon him, or that the Lord was with him, or other such characterizations. This was the category of all the Judges of Israel, who are all included in this general characterization (Judges 2:18): "The Lord raised up for them judges, and the Lord was with the judges, and He saved them . . ."

The second degree consists in a person's discovery that he is as though possessed by one special interest and a singular power has been born in him and has moved him to speak, and he delivers discourses of wisdom, or he composes hymns, or he pronounces words of caution and admonition, or he expounds subjects of a behavioral or a religious nature. He does all this while awake, and while his faculties function in their usual manner. Of such a person it is said that he speaks with the holy spirit. It is under this type of influence of the holy spirit that David composed the book of Psalms and Solomon the book of Proverbs, Ecclesiastes, and the Song of Songs. Similarly, Daniel, Job, and the books of Chronicles and the other books included in the Writings [*Ketuvim*] were also written with the aid of this category of action of the holy spirit. (*ibid.*, II 45)

3. From one individual you can draw an inference concerning all members of the species, and it can be established that this characteristic pertains to all constituent individuals in the species. I mean to say that from one instance of the pronouncements of the prophets it is possible to infer evidence concerning all pronouncements in this category. After this preliminary remark you will understand that just as a person may see in his sleep that he has gone to a certain country, married, remained there for a long time, and became the father of a son whom he called by a certain name, and certain things happened to him, so are the parables of the prophets seen or enacted in the vision of a prophecy. When the parable calls for any action, the prophet will perform it. He will set intervals of time between actions, according to the prompting of the parable, and he will journey from place to place—all this will be part of the prophetic vision; they are not real actions communicated to the senses. Some are reported in the books of the prophets in unqualified terms. Since it is made clear that the subject is a prophetic vision, it was not necessary to remind us concerning each detail of the parable that it occurred in the prophetic vision. Thus the prophet states: "And the Lord said to him," and he does not need to explain that it occurred in a dream. The multitude thinks that these actions, these journeys, these questions and answers occurred in a form perceived by the senses, not in a prophetic vision . . .

From what I mentioned you can draw inferences to clarify what I did not mention. All these accounts are of the same nature, they exemplify the same principle; they are all cases of a prophetic vision. Whatever is stated in that vision—that he did thus, or heard, or went, or came, or spoke, or was spoken to, or stood, or sat, or climbed, or descended, or set out on a journey, or asked, or was asked—all of it occurred in a prophetic vision. Even when these events extended over a long period of time, and involved particular dates and persons and places, once it has been made clear that the incident is a parable, know with certainty that all of it occurred in a prophetic vision. (*ibid.*, II 46)

ON CLEAVING TO GOD

1. We shall now return to the subject of this chapter, which is to summon a person to concentrate all his thoughts on God alone, after he has attained to a knowledge of Him as we mentioned earlier. This is the type of service characteristic of those who have been enlightened with the truth, and the more they will focus their thoughts on God and be with Him, the more will their service be enhanced. But whoever will think of God and continue to remember Him, without enlightenment, following after his imaginings or some belief conveyed to him by someone else, is in my opinion outside the palace and is indeed remote from it. He is as one who neither mentions God in truth, nor does he think of Him, for that which is in his imagination and what he utters with his lips does not correspond to any existing reality. It is a deceptive notion contrived by his imagination, as we explained in the chapter on the divine attributes.

The proper type of worship is to be undertaken after intellectual clarity has been achieved. Having attained a knowledge of God and His works, as the intellect establishes it, then you can begin to devote yourself to Him and seek to draw close to Him, and the bond between you and Him, that is the intellect, will grow stronger. Scripture states (Deut. 4:35): "It has been shown you so that you may know that the Lord is God"; and it is also written (Deut. 4:39): "Know this day and reflect in your heart that the Lord, He is God"; and it is similarly written (Ps. 100:3): "Know that the Lord, He is God." The Torah has thus made it clear that the highest type of worship which we have commented on in this chapter can only take place after sound knowledge has been achieved . . .

I have made it clear to you that the intellect which has been bestowed on us as an emanation from God is the bond which links us to Him. You have the choice: you can, if you wish, deepen this bond, or you can, if you wish, weaken it gradually until you will put an end to its functioning. The only way this bond can be strengthened is by activating it in the love of God, and by making this love your conscious goal, as we explained. You will weaken it by turning your thoughts to other things. You must realize that even if you were the most enlightened of persons with regard to the true knowledge concerning God, when you turn your thought to the necessities of eating or of business, you have at once interrupted the link between yourself and God, praised be He, and you are no longer with Him and He is not with you, for the relationship between you and Him has at that time been terminated . . .

d you must know that all those forms of worship such as reading the Torah, prayer, and the performance of other *mitzvot* have as their only objective to condition ourselves to concentrate on the commandments of God and to withdraw from worldly pursuits, in effect to be wholly involved with Him, and liberated from whatever is not concerned with Him. But if you pray by moving your lips and turning your face to the wall while thinking of your business affairs, if you read the Torah with your tongue while your heart is focused on the construction of your house, without discerning what you read, and, similarly, if you perform the *mitzvot* only with your limbs—like one who digs a ditch or cuts wood in the forest, without reflecting on the meaning of that action, neither of the one who authorized it or the reason for it—then do not imagine that you have achieved the goal. You will then be rather close to those of whom it is said (Jer. 12:2): "You are near to their lips but far from their hearts." (*Guide* III 57)

2. A person must not say: I shall perform the commandments of the Torah and pursue the study of its wisdom that I might be the beneficiary of all the blessings promised therein, or that I might merit the life of the world-to-come, and I shall avoid the transgressions which the Torah warns us against, in order to be spared the curses mentioned in the Torah or so that I may not be cut off from the life of the world-to-come. This is not the proper way to serve God, for one who serves Him in this manner serves out of fear and it is not the level of service exemplified by prophets or wise men. This type of service is pursued only by the ignorant, women and children, who are taught to serve out of fear till they grow in understanding and serve out of love.

One who serves God out of love studies the Torah and practices the commandments and pursues the paths of wisdom for no ulterior consideration, not out of fear of evil that might befall him nor in anticipation of the benefits. But he pursues the truth because it is the truth, and the good, and its general aspects, will prevail in the end. This is a very high attainment, and not every wise man attains it. This was the attainment of Moses, whom the Holy One, praised be He, characterized as His friend, because he served only out of love, and this is the level of service which Moses commanded us, as it is written (Deut. 6:15): "You shall love the Lord your God," and when a person will love God with the proper love, he will at once perform all the commandments out of love.

And what is the proper love? It is that a person shall love the Lord with a very mighty and overflowing love so that his soul shall be attached to the love of God, constantly dwelling on it, as one who is lovesick and cannot take his mind away from his love for a particular woman, but dwells on it at all times, on lying down and on rising up, when eating and drinking. Even more than this must be the love for God in the hearts of His lovers, dwelling on it constantly, as we have been commanded (Deut. 6:5): "with all your heart and all your soul," and this was conveyed in a parable by King Solomon, when he said (Song of Songs 2:5), "I am lovesick." The entire Song of Songs is a parable dealing with this theme . . .

It is well-known that the love of the Holy One, praised be He, cannot become fixed in a person's heart unless he meditates on it constantly, in a proper manner, and he must withdraw from everything else in the world, as is commanded us (Deut. 6:5): "You shall love the Lord your God *with all your heart and all your soul.*" One can only love God through the knowledge that one has of Him, and the love will be commensurate with the knowledge; when it is little it will be little, and when much it will be much. Therefore, must a person dedicate himself to pursue the disciplines of knowledge which reveal to him his Creator, to the extent that human intellect is capable of comprehending it. (*Mishneh Torah, Hilkhot Teshuvah* 10:1–6)

3. It is incumbent on us to love the honored and awesome God and to fear Him, as it is written: "You shall love the Lord your God" (Deut. 6:4), and it is also written: "You shall fear the Lord your God" (Deut. 6:13). And which is the path that leads us to love and to fear Him? When a person contemplates His great and wondrous works and His creatures and recognizes therefrom His wisdom which is beyond assessing and endless, he at once loves, praises, and extols, and is filled with a great longing to know the great Name, as David said (Psalms 42:3): "My soul is thirsty for God, for the living God." And when he contemplates these very matters he at once recoils and becomes afraid realizing that he is but a lowly and dull creature, of little knowledge, standing before the Perfect One, as David said (Psalms 8:4–5): When I see the heavens, the work of Your fingers, what is man that You are mindful of him? (*ibid., Hilkhot Yesodei haTorah* 2:1–2)

7. Sefer haBahir

The *Sefer haBahir,* sometimes also called *Midrash R. Neḥunya ben haKanah* because the opening is a homily quoted in his name, is the earliest work in Kabbalah. The book is of unknown authorship. It originated in Germany or in the east, but it first made its appearance in Provence during the 13th century. It is a short book, consisting of no more than some 12,000 words. Its theme is the mystical rhythm of divine activity which engendered and continues to direct the world. A host of parables are cited to illustrate its esoteric teachings, but the parables themselves are sometimes enigmatic and difficult to follow.

In elucidating the mystery of creation the *Sefer haBahir* draws on the concept of the ten *sefirot,* which are regarded as divine attributes, and they are called by various names, such as "words," "beautiful vessels," "kings," "voices," "crowns," "lights," and "powers." The *sefirot* in their togetherness are pictured as a cosmic tree from which souls blossom forth. Some have seen in the *Bahir's* portrayal the inclusion of God Himself among the ten *sefirot*, His role being that of the supreme crown. The *sefirah hokhmah*, "wisdom," is invested with a certain priority among the *sefirot*: it is pictured as the spring which waters the cosmic tree in which the other *sefirot* are arranged. The *Sefer haBahir* is the earliest source for teaching the concept of *gilgul*, the transmigration of souls.

The teachings in the *Sefer haBahir* clearly reflect an affinity with teachings in earlier mystical literature. The references to the mystical significance of the blue thread in the *ẓiẓit*, the fringe on each corner of a garment, is in essence a talmudic quotation on the subject. But whereas the Talmud cautions against mystical studies, the *Sefer haBahir* urges it even when one is prone to err in it. The interpretation of the ten fingers as an allusion to the ten *sefirot* is reminiscent of the *Sefer Yeẓirah*, but the association of this with the high priests raising his hands when blessing the people does not occur in the *Sefer Yeẓirah*. Gershom Scholem has called attention to gnostic elements in many of the concepts in this volume. The author was undoubtedly at home in the mystical tradition but he had the freedom to shape his ideas in accordance with his own disposition.

A German translation of the *Sefer haBahir* by Gershom Scholem appeared in 1933 and a new Hebrew edition by Reuven Margaliot, with notes and references, appeared in 1951. The selections below are translated from the Margaliot edition.

THE PURSUIT OF MYSTICAL STUDIES

1. His disciples asked R. Reḥumei: Why is it written (Habakkuk 3:1): "A prayer of Habakkuk the prophet. Upon *Shigyonot*." Instead of "a prayer," it should have said "a psalm" [the contents resemble a psalm of praise]. But whoever turns his heart away from the affairs of the world and concerns himself with the work of the Chariot, it is regarded by the Holy One, praised be He, as though he had prayed all day, for it is written "a prayer." What is meant by *Shigyonot*? This alludes to the verse (Prov. 5:19): "Because of your love for her err [*tishgeh*, usually translated "be enraptured," but the root *shagah* also means to err] always." What does this refer to? To the work of the Chariot, as is suggested by the verse (Habakkuk 3:2): "O Lord I have heard the account about You and am afraid" [one is prone to err in mystical studies and one is rightly afraid, yet one should pursue them]. (*Sefer haBahir* 68)

2. Said R. Reḥumei: What is the meaning of the verse (Prov. 6:23): "The way of life is the reproof of instruction"? This teaches us that one who studies the work of creation and the work of the Chariot cannot but

stumble, as it is written (Isa. 3:6): "And this stumbling is under your hand." These are matters that one cannot grasp unless one stumbles over them, and the Torah calls it, "the reproof of instruction," but in truth one thereby attains the path of life. Therefore whoever seeks the path of life should bear the reproof of instruction. (*ibid.* 150)

THE SEFIROT

1. All agree that they [the angels] were not created the first day, so that they might not say, Michael stretched out [the world] in the south side of the sky, Gabriel in the northern side, and the Holy One, praised be He, in the middle. But "I the Lord made everything, I stretched out the heavens Myself, I spread out the earth—it was *from Me*" (Isa. 44:24). As written, the Hebrew word for "from Me," *me'iti,* means literally, Who was with Me? I am the one who planted this tree for the whole world to play with, and I spread out everything in it, and I called it "all," because everything is attached to it, and everything emerges from it, and all are in need of it; they look to it, and wait for it. From it the souls blossom joyously. I was alone when I made it, and no angel can exalt himself over it to say, I preceded you, for even when I stretched out My land in which I planted and rooted this tree and I caused them to rejoice together and I rejoiced with them, who was with me to whom I disclosed this secret?

Said R. Reḥumei: From what you say, may one infer that what was needed for this world, the Holy One, praised be He, created before the heavens? He said to him: Yes. To what may this be likened? To a king who wanted to plant a tree in his garden. He examined the entire garden to know if there was in it a spring with flowing water to sustain it, and he could not find one. He said: I will dig for water, and bring forth a spring so that the tree might be sustained. He dug and brought forth a spring flowing with living water, and then he planted the tree which bore fruit. It succeeded because the roots always watered it from the spring.

And what is this tree that you speak of? He said to him: It refers to the potencies of God [the *sefirot*] in graded order, and they are like a tree. As a tree, by being watered, bears fruit, so the Holy One, by means of water, increases the powers of the tree. And what is the water of the Holy One, praised be He? It is wisdom. And this also refers to the souls of the righteous that are carried from the spring to the great channel and ascend and are attached to the tree. And through what are they carried? Through the people of Israel: when they are righteous and good, the *shekinah* abides among them and in their works in the lap of the Holy

One, praised be He, and He prospers them and increases them. (*Sefer haBahir* 22, 23, 119)

2. Why was [Aaron's blessing] pronounced with the raising of the hands? He could have blessed them by pronouncing the blessing. The reason is that there are ten fingers in the hands, an allusion to the ten *sefirot* with which heaven and earth were finished. And those ten correspond to the Ten Commandments, and those ten embrace all the 613 commandments. And if you will count the letters in the Ten Commandments you will find that there are 613, and that they include all the letters of the alphabet, except the *tet*. Why is this? It is to teach us that the letter *tet* represents the "stomach," and the "stomach" is not included among the *sefirot* [stomach seems to be used here as a euphemism for the serpent, which is associated with physical lusts and gluttony and which is shaped like the alimentary canal of which the stomach is part; the letter *tet* is shaped like a curled up serpent; in Phoenician, *tet* also designates the ninth letter of the alphabet, as in Hebrew, and it is also the name of the snake-god].

And why are they called *sefirot*? The term is explained by the verse (Ps. 19:2): "The heavens, in their sapphire-like radiance, declare (*me-sape-rim*, that is, through their sapphire-like radiance) the glory of God." (*ibid.* 124, 125) — See Dan on this {1. Early Kabb 2. Midrash

THE THREAD OF BLUE

1. And what is meant by *earth*? It is the source from which the heavens were formed,[1] and it is the sea of wisdom. Corresponding to it is the thread of blue which is included in the fringe in the corner of a garment (Deut. 22:12). For R. Meir stated (Menaḥot 43b); Why was blue singled out from all colors? Because the blue resembles the sea and the sea resembles the sky, and the sky resembles the throne of divine glory as it is written (Ex. 24:10): "And they saw the God of Israel and under His

1. Gershom Scholem (*Das Buch Bahir*, Schocken, Berlin 1933, section 65) emends the text to read *min hashamayim* instead of *mimenu shamayim*, rendering this to mean "that which was hewn from the heavens." But the point here is to express the paradox that the earth is that from which the heavens were hewn. The term *ereẓ*, earth, as here used is of course not the physical earth but wisdom which is the ground of all being, as the text continues to expound. The *Zohar* (II 271a) confronts the difficulty that according to the Bible the heavens were created before the earth, and suggests that the reference here is to a divine potency, the *sefirah*, in other words, whose emanation proceded the creation of everything. As noted earlier in the section on the *sefirot*, "what was needed for this world the Holy One, praised be He, created before the heavens."

feet there was like a sapphire pavement and as the heavens for purity," and it is also written (Ezekiel 1:26): "As the appearance of the sapphire stone so was the appearance of the throne." (*Sefer haBahir* 96)

2. Why do we add a thread of blue in the *ẓiẓit* and why do we have thirty-two threads [of the white, eight threads in each of the four corners of the garment]? This is comparable to the case of a king who had a beautiful garden in which there were thirty-two paths. He appointed a watchman, and disclosed to him alone that there were thirty-two paths, saying to him: Guard them and walk in them daily, and whenever you will tread in them, it will be well with you. What did this watchman do? He appointed guardians over them, saying: If I should remain alone in these paths—it is impossible for one watchman to guard all these paths. Moreover, people will say, this king is a miser. Therefore did this watchman appoint other watchmen for each of the paths. These are the thirty-two paths [watched over by the thirty-two threads].

And why was the thread of blue added? Said the watchman: Perhaps these watchmen might say, This garden is ours. He gave them a sign and said: See this is a sign of the king that the garden is his, and that he established these paths, and they are not mine; and here is his seal. To what may this be compared? To the case of a king and his daughter who possessed slaves who wanted to go on a distant journey, but they feared the king's anger. The king then gave them his seal, but they were afraid of the daughter and she gave them a token. They said: Now with these two seals [the white and the blue] the promise in the verse (Ps. 121:7) will apply: "The Lord will keep you from all evil, He will guard your soul." (*ibid.* 92, 93)

REINCARNATION

1. Why is it that there is a righteous person who enjoys good, and there is a righteous person who suffers affliction? It is because in the latter case that righteous person was formerly wicked, and he is now suffering punishment. But is one punished for offenses committed during one's youth? Did not R. Simon say that the heavenly tribunal inflicts punishment only for misdeeds committed after the twentieth year of a person's life? He replied to him: I do not refer to misdeeds in the course of the person's life. I refer to the fact that that person pre-existed prior to his present life. His colleagues said to him: How long will you mystify your statement? He said to them: Consider the analogy of the person who planted vine in his garden and he hoped that they would grow good

grapes, but they grew bad grapes. He realized that he had not succeeded. He did a new planting, fenced it in, after he had cleared out the bad vine. He planted a second time but saw he had not succeeded. He fenced it in, did a new planting after he cleaned out the bad vine. He saw that he had not succeeded and he plucked out the bad vine and did a new planting. How long does this go on? He said to them: For a thousand generations, as it is written (Ps. 105:8): "The matter which He ordained for a thousand generations." (*Sefer haBahir* 195)

2. What is the significance of the phrase "from generation to generation" (Ps. 106:10)? Said R. Pappias: It alludes to the verse (Ecclesiastes 1:4): "One generation goes and one generation comes." [*ba*, which also means "came"], on which Rabbi Akiva commented: It is the same generation which came before. To what may this be compared? To a king who had servants whom he robed, in accordance with his means, in finely embroidered silk garments. But they misbehaved. He rejected them and took off their garments, and they departed. He took the garments and washed them well until they were without stain, and he kept them in readiness. He acquired new servants and robed them in those garments, without knowing whether those servants would be good or bad. Thus they acquired garments which had been used previously and others had worn before them. But the earth abides forever, and this is the meaning of the verse (Ecclesiastes 12:7): "The dust returns to the earth as it was, but the spirit returns to God who gave it." (*ibid.* 121, 122)

8. Sefer Ḥasidim

Jewish mysticism entered the mainstream of Jewish life with the Ḥasidei Ashkenaz, a pietistic movement of the 13th century Jewish community in Germany. It was not a formal, organized movement, as 18th century Ḥasidism eventually became under the inspiration of Israel Baal Shem Tov, but many of the ideas characteristic of later Ḥasidism were clearly foreshadowed by the earlier movement. We have a testament of their faith in a volume called *Sefer Ḥasidim,* or the Book of the Pious, to which many teachers contributed. Its principal creator, however, is generally said to have been a certain Judah, commonly called Yehudah heḤasid, or Judah the Pious.

There is no subtle philosophizing in the *Sefer Ḥasidim.* There is no reference to the role of a living master, such as the "rebbe" who played so crucial a role in the organized ḥasidic community of the later period. One detects here traces of influence of medieval German culture, including some of the current superstitions for which there is little precedent in classic Jewish teaching. But its central ideas—which show a ready parallelism to the ideas which dominated later Ḥasidism—include the stress on religious inwardness, the quest for nearness to God, devotion in prayer, and the primacy of simple piety over mere learning. The book is permeated with yearning for God and it sets forth the path by which the soul, stirred by this yearning, can find its peace in God's presence.

There is a strong ascetic tendency in this volume, a call to selflessness, and an admonition to discipline one's appetites and minimize worldly pleasures. It calls for an equanimity of spirit and indifference to insult. While this mood was prevalent in contemporary German culture, the *Sefer Ḥasidim* bases itself primarily on classic talmudic texts. It demands that acts of service to God be performed as ends in themselves, rather than out of ulterior motivations, such as expected rewards in this world or in the hereafter. It warns against routinized or habituated piety, calling instead for deep feeling and inner devotion. Extended statements on theological and pietistic practices are quoted from the *Mishneh Torah* of Maimonides.

The book is prefaced by Yehudah heḤasid's will. This is a catalogue of various taboos which he enjoined upon posterity. One of them, which was widely adopted, was a warning against marrying a woman who bears the same name as one's mother, or marrying a man who bears the same name as one's father. If one did so in violation of his warning, he recommended that the name of one of them be changed, for thus "there might be hope."

The *Sefer Ḥasidim* exists in two different editions. The one from which our selections are quoted appeared originally in 1538, on the basis of a manuscript written by Abraham ben Moshe haKohen of Bologna; it was re-edited by Reuven Margaliot and issued by Mosad Harav Kook in 1957. Another edition, based on a Parma manuscript and edited by Yehudah Wistinetzki, appeared in Frankfurt a.M. in 1924.

Yehudah heḤasid and his circle are also credited with having written a number of pietistic hymns, the best known of which is the hymn in adoration of God known as *Shir haKavod*. It is recited by many congregations in the Sabbath morning service.

THE TRUE SERVICE

1. The basis of ḥasidic piety is the fear of God, which is shown when a person lusts for some pleasure and he ignores his temptation out of the fear of God. This fear is not of punishment in the hereafter; it is not motivated by a desire for benefits in this world or the next, but it is a fear

lest one not be wholly devoted to the love of the Creator, praised be He, as it is written (Deut. 18:13): "You shall be wholehearted with the Lord your God." Such a person is called a fearer of God. The great and wonderous force for attaining this is the discipline of rejecting food, for satiety in food produces bad thoughts. How is this to be understood? If dishes of fish and meat or other delicacies be placed before him he need not avoid them altogether but, out of fear of God, he should avoid filling his stomach with them to the point of satisfying his lust fully. Similarly, if the opportunity for performing a commandment came to him, and it is difficult for him to perform it, but he is not inhibited. This characteristic was present in Abraham of whom it was written (Gen. 22:12): "Now I know that you fear God." (*Sefer Ḥasidim* 12)

2. When you pray, recite your prayers to the tune of a melody that is pleasant and agreeable to you . . . and then you will pray with devotion and your heart will be drawn after the utterance of your lips . . . Thus will you be filled with love and joy toward the One who knows your heart, and you will praise Him with great endearment and exultation. This is the method by which the heart is properly conditioned. (*ibid.* 158)

3. If a poor person and an affluent person be sick, and many go to visit the affluent person, one should go to visit the poor one, even if the affluent person is also learned in the Torah. But if the learned and the poor one are both in need, the honor due to the Torah takes precedence. However, if the scholar is not devout, while the poor and ignorant person is, the latter must be given precedence, for it is written (Psalms 11:10): "The beginning of wisdom is the fear of the Lord." (*ibid.* 361)

4. Said Rabbi Judah: An individual must not afflict himself with fasting lest he become dependent on others. But a person whose evil passion gains ascendency over him may fast to humble his passion. However, a teacher, a scribe and a workman may not fast, for it will curtail their work. When a person fasts he must be careful not to show anger that day, for fasting makes a person irritable and it is preferable for a person to be satisfied and at peace with people and not quarrelsome, than to indulge in fasts. (*ibid.* 617)

5. It is preferable for a person to pray and read the *Shema* and the benediction in any language he understands than in Hebrew if he does not understand it . . . Thus they wrote the Babylonian and Palestinian Talmuds in Aramaic so that even unlearned people might understand the commandments, and for this reason, too, the practice was to have translation into Aramaic accompany the Torah reading. A person should also judge whether he can pray with concentration and then he is to

pray, otherwise he is not to pray at that time, because prayer requires concentration. (*ibid.* 785)

6. Every mitzvah a person can perform he should perform, and whatever he cannot perform, let him *think* of performing it.

This is illustrated by the story of a man who was a shepherd and he did not know how to pray. Each day he used to say: Sovereign of the universe, You surely know that if You had cattle to entrust to my safekeeping, others I charge for this, but for You I would do it for nothing, because I love You. He [this shepherd] was a Jew.

Once a learned man passed and he found that this shepherd prayed thus. He said to him: You fool, don't pray thus. The shepherd asked him: Then how shall I pray? At once the learned man taught him the order of the prayers, the *Shema* and the *Amidah*, so that he should not continue to say what he had been accustomed to say. After this learned man passed, he [the shepherd] forgot all that he had taught him, and he did not pray, and what he had been accustomed to say he was afraid to say, because that *ẓaddik* kept him from it.

That learned man was told in a dream at night: If you do not tell him [the shepherd] to continue saying what he had been accustomed to say before you met him, and if you do not return to him, know the evils which will befall you, because you robbed Me of one destined for the world-to-come. He at once returned to him and asked him: What is the text of your prayer? He said to him: Nothing, because I have forgotten what you taught me and you ordered me not to say that if He had cattle . . . The sage said to him: Thus did I dream; say what you had been accustomed to say.

So we see that it is not Torah and good deeds, but his intention of doing good which is accounted to a person as something great, for God seeks the heart. Therefore shall a person think noble thoughts toward the Holy One, praised be He. (*Sefer Ḥasidim*, Parma, ed. Wistinetzki, 4–6)

THE MORAL DIMENSION

1. It is written in the Torah (Lev. 19:17): "You shall surely rebuke your neighbor and not bear sin because of him." This obligates us to rebuke a fellow-Jew who in resignation or laziness fails to perform any of the two hundred and forty-eight positive commandments or who violates any of the prescribed negative commandments. Our sages have taught (Arakhin 16b) that whoever had the opportunity to chastise any

fellow-Jew for violation of a positive or negative commandment and watched resignedly without doing so is deemed culpable for all those offenses. This is how another text puts it: Whoever had the opportunity to protest and rebuke misdeeds in his own household and failed to do so is culpable for the offenses in his household; whoever had the opportunity to protest offense in his city and failed to do so is culpable for the offenses in his city; and whoever had the opportunity to protest offenses anywhere in the world and failed to do so is culpable for the offenses anywhere in the world (Shabbat 54b).

And how do we know that one must persist and rebuke a second time if one is not heeded the first time? This is taught to us by the following (Baba Metzia 31a): Whence may we infer that if one has rebuked once, he is to rebuke a second time? We may infer it from the verse (Lev. 19:17): "You shall surely rebuke your neighbor." [*Hokheaḥ tokhiaḥ*, the term for rebuke is repeated.] The one who rebukes must adapt his words to the nature of the one being rebuked. If he is a gentle person he must rebuke him gently; if he is strong he is to rebuke him according to the gravity of his offenses. He is to invoke analogies and cite proofs to bring him around to his views.

He must not show partiality to an elder or a person of distinction if he is not to be deemed under censure for failing to rebuke him. Nor is he to show partiality to a teacher, for it was taught by a sage (Berakhot 19b) that when there is danger of profaning God's name, we must not be concerned with showing deference to a teacher . . .

The person who is to rebuke others is under obligation to rebuke himself for his own offenses and to mend his ways before criticizing others; otherwise they will not listen to him. Thus the sages commented on the verse (Zephaniah 2:1): "Gather yourselves together, gather together, O sinful nation." Adorn yourself, then adorn others (Sanhedrin 18a).

One must not desist from rebuking his neighbor till he turns him to the right course and desists from offenses in worldly matters and in his relationship to God. Whoever fails to rebuke a neighbor shares in his guilt. Thus the conclusion of the verse ordaining the duty to rebuke is: "And you shall not bear sin because of him." (*Sefer Ḥasidim* 5)

2. Do not assume that the need to probe one's ways and turn back from evil applies only to offenses involving action, such as robbery or fornication or theft and the like, but as a person must turn back from these so must he turn back from character traits such as anger, hatred, envy, mocking and lusting after food and the like. He must turn back from all of them. The latter offenses are in fact more serious than those

involving action, for when a person becomes accustomed to them, it is difficult to detach himself from them, as they become ingrained in his character. It is this which is referred to in the verse: "Let the wicked man forsake his way" (Isaiah 55:7). (*ibid.* 27)

3. It is forbidden to accustom oneself to flattering speech. One must beware of saying what he does not mean, but must speak what is in his heart; one must match his speech with what he believes in his heart. One must not deceive anybody, including a non-Jew . . . Similarly one must not pressure another to eat when he knows that he will not eat, nor may one push presents to another when he knows he will not accept them. One may not open a barrel of wine suggesting that he is doing it in the other person's honor, when the barrel had to be opened in any case, but he should tell him that he is not doing it because of him. The same applies to all similar situations, even a single word of guile or deception is forbidden, but one must be truthful in speech, upright in spirit, and his heart free of all perversity and vanity. One must be a person of integrity in all aspects of his being; one should not be quarrelsome, scornful or mocking, for mockery and levity bring a person to lewdness. One is not to indulge in excessive joking, nor be overly sad and grieving, but meet everyone in a gracious manner. One should not be ambitious and greedy for wealth, nor lazy and shrinking from work, but of a generous eye, modestly pursuing his occupation, engage in the study of Torah, take pleasure in the little that is his portion. One must not be a contentious person, envious and lusting, nor avid for honor, for envy, lust and avidity for honor undermine a person's life in the world. (*ibid.* 51)

4. If you have heard a person commit an error in teaching, do not tell him that he is in error, if this should cause him embarrassment, but mention it to one of his relatives or to his friend and do not disgrace him. A person should not tell his neighbor that so and so sought the hand of his daughter for his son in marriage, because the other person is embarrassed and he takes pleasure and becomes proud. (*ibid.* 139)

5. It happened that a person was riding alone in the desert at night and saw a great host of large wagons; on the wagons people were riding, and people were also pulling the wagons. He wondered what they were doing. When he approached them he recognized some of them as people who had died. He asked them what the reason was that some were pulling the wagons all night and some were sitting on the wagons. They told him that it was in expiation of their sin, that when they were alive they played with women and with girls. Now they pulled the wagons to a point of exhaustion when they could not pull any longer and then those who rode descended and pulled while they rested, and when they were

exhausted the others went up to rest . . . Whoever acted in this world like an animal must work in the next world like an animal. And whoever oppresses people or terrorizes people will be treated in the next world like an animal, and this includes one who is unduly harsh with his animal. (*ibid.* 169)

A HYMN IN HONOR OF GOD

Shir haKavod

Sweet melodies will I sing to You
And hymns compose,
For my soul yearns for You
My soul yearns for Your presence,
To know the mystery of Your Being.
When I but bring Your praises to my lips
My love for You wells up within my heart;
Therefore will I extoll You
And honor Your name with songs of adoration.
I will tell of Your glory
Though I have not seen You;
I will speak of You in similies
Though I cannot know Your essence.
You revealed a semblance of Your splendor
In the mystic visions of Your faithful servants, the prophets.
They envisioned Your grandeur and Your might
From the stupendous work of Your creation.
They speak of You not as You are,
But by inference drawn from Your handiwork.
They portrayed You in countless forms
That are all but imperfect aspects of Your oneness.
They envisioned You as a sage and as a youth,
As a sage sitting in judgment
And as a youth in the day of battle,
As a warrior staking his strength in combat,
Wearing the helmet of victory on His head,
Defeating His foes by His right arm, by His holy might.
I will proclaim His renown,
For He has conferred His love on me,
And He will be to me a crown of splendor.

I see His head luminous as pure gold,
His holy name inscribed upon His forehead.
Adorned by His people with a crown
Of grace and glory, magnificence and beauty.
O may the Temple of righteousness,
His noble ornament,
Be remembered in His favor,
May He keep His beloved people in glory,
Crowned with the sovereign diadem of beauty.
His splendor is my renown, and mine is His,
And He is near to me when I call on Him.
He revealed the ways of His providence,
To His humble servant Moses
Who glimpsed the fullness of His eternal mystery.
He loves His people,
His humble seed He glorifies,
He who is surrounded by man's praise
Takes delight in them.
The essence of Your word is truth;
O You who have called into being the generations,
Extend Your care to a people that yearns for You.
Receive the multitude of my hymns,
And may the song of my prayer come before You.
Let my prayer be like incense,
Let a poor man's song be to You
As the song once chanted at the altar of sacrifice.
May my prayer come before You.
The sustainer of the universe and its Creator,
The Just, the Mighty One.
Accept the silent promptings of my heart,
For all my being is astir with longing for Your Presence.

THE WORLD OF THE KABBALAH

9.

Abraham Abulafia

One of the most influential figures in the early Kabbalah was Abraham Abulafia (1240–1292). He came to the Kabbalah after he had become disillusioned with the more conventional interpretations of Judaism. He had studied Bible, Talmud, philosophy and medicine, but his primary quest was to unravel the mystery surrounding God and His universe. However, what he sought was not a theosophy, not a way of understanding reality, but a way of going beyond it, of finding the channel leading to an intimate experience of the divine. He was an adherent of Maimonides, but felt the need to go beyond rationalism, and he found it in a unique system of meditation which focused on the letters of the Hebrew alphabet, released from their particularization in the finitude of words into their original essence, where they functioned as notes in a melody. The one reality toward which the music of the letters in their endless permutations and combinations were directed was the names of God. The ultimate reward which this discipline offered was union with God, which invested a person with the prerogatives of prophecy.

Abulafia pursued this goal by adopting an ascetic regimen of living. Withdrawn from the world, clad in white, immersed in prayer and meditation, uttering the divine name with special modulations of the voice and with special gestures, he induced in himself a state of ecstasy. In this state he believed that the soul had been liberated from the "seals" and "knots" that kept it in bondage to the material world, and was able to be reunited with God. In such moments of ecstasy he felt himself possessed with prophetic endowments.

Abulafia believed himself charged with the mission of prophet and messiah and in 1280 he reported a call to confer with the Pope in the name of Jewry. He reported that the Pope gave orders to arrest him, and to have him burnt if he should appear in Rome, but this did not daunt him. When he entered Rome he discovered that the Pope had died during the night. But Abulafia was arrested and held in the College of the Franciscans for twenty-eight days before he was freed.

Abulafia was a prolific writer. He produced more than twenty treatises, but none of these works were published. Perhaps it was his unusual doctrine that may have inspired apprehension in some circles that would otherwise have wanted to spread his writings. His prescription of specific directions for venturing into the highest strata of mystical experience and assuming the role of prophecy and messiahship (at least for self-liberation) was certainly a daring departure even for a kabbalist. But his position was widely known through his oral discourses which made a deep impression on his listeners.

Modern scholarship, especially the work of Adolph Yellinek and Gershom Scholem, has brought some of his work, still in manuscript, to the attention of the larger scholarly world. It reveals him to have been a truly original spirit who thought and wrote in an unprecedented idiom and who contributed a highly significant chapter to the history of Jewish mysticism.

THE TWO LEVELS OF KABBALAH

The Kabbalah, which eludes most rabbis who concentrate on the study of Talmud, is generally divided into two parts. One part deals with knowing God through the method of the ten *sefirot,* which are called "plants", so that whoever effects disunity among the *sefirot* is guilty of cutting down the "plants", and it is the *sefirot* that manifest the secret of divine unity.

The other part involves knowing God through the method of the twenty-two letters of the alphabet . . . These two methods are not perceived by the senses, nor known as axioms, nor are they part of commonly accepted knowledge, and therefore are most scholars unaware of them. As for the knowledge of God through His works, this is not within the concern of the Kabbalah. This involves the science of research. My work here does not follow the method of those scholars who are called philosophers, the scholars in research . . . Undoubtedly, the first category of kabbalistic study must precede the second, but the second is of greater importance than the first. The latter was the goal in the creation of the human species, and the one who attains it is the only one whose mental faculties have reached complete self-realization. It is to him that the Lord of all existence has revealed Himself and disclosed to him His secret.

The first group are called prophets to themselves, and those who know God through His work share this designation with them, to some extent. Those who are called prophets in this sense meditate in their hearts on the changing substance of their thoughts, and their deliberations are purely subjective. The light of God illumines some of their thoughts sometimes with a tiny light. They themselves recognize that this emanates from outside themselves, but they receive no verbalized message that they should recognize as speech; it is only light.

But both these groups are prophets who begin by being illumined with the light of life, and from this stage they rise from light to light, through meditation on the ramification of their thoughts which are rendered sweet by their fusion with the divine realm. Through the enhancement of their merit they approach the highest distinction to a point where the speech they hear within themselves is linked with the fountain from which all speech derives. They ascend from speech to speech until their inner human speech is potent in itself and becomes ready to receive the divine speech, whether it be the form of the speech, or the contents of the speech itself. These are the true prophets, in justice and in righteousness. Thus the mastery of the knowledge of the ten *sefirot* precedes the additional knowledge of the names of God, and not vice-versa. (A. Yellinek, *Philosophie und Kabbala*, Leipzig 1854, pp. 15f.)

THE ENCOUNTER WITH GOD

Make yourself ready to meet your God, O Israel. Get ready to turn your heart to God alone, cleanse your body, and choose a special place where none will hear you, and remain altogether by yourself in isolation. Sit in one place in a room, or in the attic, but do not disclose your secret to anybody. If you can do this in the day time in your own home, do even if only a little. But it is best to do it at night. Be careful to withdraw your thoughts from all the vanities of the world when you are preparing yourself to speak to your Creator, and you want Him to reveal to you His mighty deeds.

Robe yourself in your *tallit* and put the *tefillin* on your head and hand so that you may feel awed before the *shekhinah* that is with you at that time, cleanse your garments. If you can, let your garments all be white, for this is a very great aid to experiencing the fear and love for God. If you are doing this at night kindle many lights so that your eyes will see brightly.

Then take in hand pen and ink and a writing board, and this will be your witness that you have come to serve your God in joy and with gladness of heart. Begin to combine letters, a few or many, reverse them and roll them around rapidly until your heart feels warm. Take note of the permutations, and of what emerges in the process. When your heart feels very warm at this process of combinations and you have understood many new subjects that you had not known through tradition or through your own reason, when you are receptive to the divine influence, and the divine influence has touched you and stirred you to perceptions one after another, get your purified thoughts ready to envision God, praised be He, and His supreme angels. Envision them in your heart as though they were people standing or sitting[1] about you, and you are among them like a messenger whom the king and his ministers wish to send on a mission and he is ready to hear about his mission from the king or his ministers.

After envisioning all this, prepare your mind and heart to understand mentally the many subjects that the letters conjured up in you, concentrate on all of them, in all their aspects, like a person who is told a parable or a riddle or a dream or as one who ponders a book of wisdom in a subject so profound as to elude his comprehension which will make you receptive to seek any plausible interpretation possible.

All this will happen to you after you will have dropped the writing tablet from your hand and the quill from your finger or they will have fallen away by themselves, because of the intensity of your thoughts. And be aware that the stronger the intellectual influx will become in you,

---

1. The Hebrew has *ḥoshvim,* which means "thinking," but this is obviously a misprint for *yoshvim,* "sitting."

your outer and inner organs will weaken and your whole body will be agitated with a mighty agitation to a point where you will think you are going to die at that time, for your soul will separate from your body out of great joy in having comprehended what you have comprehended. You will choose death over life, knowing that this death is for the body alone, and that as a result of it your soul will enjoy eternal life.

Then you will know that you have attained the distinction of being a recipient of the divine influx, and if you will then wish to honor the glorious Name, to serve Him with the life of body and soul, cover your face and be afraid to look at God, as Moses was told at the burning bush (Ex. 3:5): "Do not draw near, remove the shoes from your feet, for the ground on which you stand is holy."

Then return to your bodily needs, leave that place, eat and drink a little, breathe in fragrant odors, and restore your spirit until another time and be happy with your lot. And know that your God who imparts knowledge to man has bestowed His love on you. When you will become adept in choosing this kind of life, and you will repeat it several times until you will be successful in it, strengthen yourself, and you will choose another path even higher than this. (Gershom Scholem, *HaKabbalah shel Sefer haTemunah veshel Avraham Abulafia*, ed. J. Ben-Shlomo, Jerusalem 1965, p. 210f.)

DISCLOSING THE MYSTERIES

God knows and the people of Israel know that, with my limited knowledge of the Torah, I am not moved by sinister motives. I have not come to make disclosures of the concealed teachings in the Torah, as is assumed by some people who have not attained any of the qualities that constitute true perfection, nor is it because I regard myself as having attained a level of wisdom or in status as a kabbalist more perfect than any of those who preceded me, and who did not disclose what I disclose in the mysteries of the Torah. Nor is it because I think that if I do not make the disclosure, it will not be disclosed by another more perfect than I. But I am inspired to take this step for two factors. One is divine, and the other human. The divine factor is the fact that we are approaching the end, that is, the time is drawing close for the redemption of the people of God and their emergence from darkness to light. The human factor is the lack of people knowledgeable in the wisdom of the Kabbalah in our time. (Scholem, *HaKabbalah*, p. 200)

THE SEVEN PATHS IN THE KNOWLEDGE OF THE TORAH

There are seven paths in the knowledge of the Torah.

The first path consists in understanding the simple meaning of the Torah text, for a biblical text may not be detached from its simple meaning. This is the way best suited for the multitude of people, men, women and children. It is well known that each person in the beginning, in his childhood and early youth, belongs to this category. Since some people are learned and some altogether unfamiliar with anything except the letters, and it is said concerning everyone (Job 11:12): "Man at birth is like the colt of a wild ass," it is appropriate that the uneducated, except for the knowledge of the letters, be taught some traditions so that they may possess religion in its conventional form . . .

The second path includes those who study various commentaries, but what they have in common is that they revolve around the simple meaning and pursue it from all angles as in the expositions of the Mishnah and the Talmud which expound the surface meaning of the Torah. This is illustrated by the interpretation of the phrase "circumcision of the heart." The Torah ordains that it be circumcised, as it is written (Deut. 10:16): "And you shall circumcise the foreskin of your hearts." This commandment cannot be observed literally. It must, therefore, have an explanation. This is to be understood in the light of the verse (Deut. 30:6): "And the Lord your God will circumcise your heart," with the accompanying verse (Deut. 30:2): "And you shall return to the Lord your God." The term "heart" must, therefore, be taken here as alluding to a return to God. But the circumcision of the child on the eighth day cannot be understood in the same way, for it cannot be applied to penitence . . .

The third path embraces the study of the biblical text from the perspective of *midrash* and *aggadah*, and the derivatives from these types of study. This is illustrated by the inquiry as to why there is no mention that "God saw that it was good" after the second day of creation, and the answer that it was because the organization of the waters was not completed on the second day. There are other such expositions. This path is called *derash* to indicate that here there is room to search and probe [*derash* means to search] and also that this subject may be expounded in public [*derash* is also used in the sense of expounding]. . .

The fourth path embraces parables and riddles. In this path begins the divergence between the select few and the multitude. The multitude will understand things according to the three paths mentioned earlier. Some will follow the simple text and some will seek explanations for them and some will understand them according to *derash*. But the select few will realize that these are parables and they will search after their meaning, and here they will encounter *homonyms* [the double usage of terms], as the subject has been explained in the *Moreh* [Maimonides' *Guide for the Perplexed*].

The fifth path includes only the secrets of the Torah. The four paths mentioned earlier are shared by people of all nations, their masses in the first three and their wise men in the fourth. The fifth path begins the levels of secret wisdom possessed by Jews alone. In this we are differentiated from the world's general populace as well as its wise men, but also from the Jewish sages, the rabbis, whose views revolve around the circle of the latter three paths mentioned above. I cite as an illustration of this path: the secret meanings disclosed to us by the fact that the letter *bet* with which the Torah begins is large, and large letters of the alphabet appear in all the twenty-four books of the Bible . . . or the inverted form of the base in the two letters *nun* enclosing the chapter describing the movement of the holy ark (Nu. 10.35). There are many similar mysteries which are handed down by tradition . . . and nothing of the truths revealed by these mysteries has been disclosed to any people except ours. One who follows the way of the nations may mock, thinking that these were written that way without any reason and they thus misrepresent the tradition, and they are guilty of grave error. But those who have mastered the truths of these paths recognized their distinction and these mysteries have been made clear to them, for they are holy. This path is the beginning of the general wisdom of combining letters. This path is appropriate only for those who fear God and meditate on His name.

The sixth path is very deep, and who can attain it? It is concerning it that the verse says (Job 11:9): "The measure thereof is longer than the sea." It is fitting for those mentioned before who withdraw from the world in their desire to draw close to God to a point that they themselves shall experience His active presence in themselves. These are the people who seek to resemble in their activity the actions of the Active Intellect. This path embraces the secret of the "seventy languages" [in Hebrew, *shivim leshonot*] which, by the rules of *gematria* [the system of numerical equivalents for letters of the alphabet], is equivalent to the "combination of letters" (in Hebrew *ẓeruf ottiyot;* both have the numerical equivalence of 1214). This involves the return of the letters to their original essence in memory and in thought, analogous to the ten non-corporeal *sefirot* which involve a holy mystery and all things holy have at least ten constituents. Thus Moses ascended no higher than the ten heavenly realms, and the *shekhinah*, the divine presence, descended no more than the ten heavens, and the world was created by ten divine commands, and the Torah was given with the Ten Commandments, and there are many cases involving ten which illustrate this. Under the rubric of this path is also included *gematria, notarikon* [the reading of letters in a word as abbreviations for other words] and the interchange of letters, and then new interchanges to be repeated up to ten times. This halts only because of the weakness of the human intelligence, for there is no limit to this process of permutation.

The seventh path is a special path and it includes all others and it is the holy of holies and it is fitting for prophets only. This is the circle that revolves around all things. In attaining it one comprehends the message that descends from the Active Intellect to the power of speech. It is a divine influence that emanates from God, praised be He, through the mediation of the Active Intellect reaching the power of speech, as our master said in the *Moreh* [*Guide for the Perplexed*] in section two, chapter thirty-six, and this is the path by which true prophecy, in its essence, is attained. This is the knowledge that grasps the essence of God's proper name, to the extent that the choicest in the human species, the prophet, may comprehend it. It is through this channel that He fashioned for him [the prophet] the divine communication. It is improper to describe the manner in which this path, the holy of holies, proceeds, by writing about it in a book. It is impossible to disclose this to anyone, not even the main points, unless in his yearning he has learnt as a preliminary, in a direct communication from a teacher, the forty-two and the seventy-two letter names of God. I have therefore included here in my description, which is the essence of brevity, all that is needed to be said on the subject. (Yellinek, *Philosophie*, pp. 2–5)

THE MUSIC OF THE ALPHABET

I will now explain to you how the method of *zeruf* [letter combination] proceeds. You must realize that letter combination acts in a manner similar to listening with the ears. The ear hears sounds and the sounds merge, according to the form of the melody or the pronunciation. I will offer you an illustration. A violin and a harp join in playing and the ear hears, with sensations of love, variations in their harmonious playing. The strings touched with the right hand or the left hand vibrate, and the experience is sweet to the ears, and from the ears the sound travels to the heart and from the heart to the spleen [the seat of emotion]. The joy is renewed through the pleasure of the changing melodies, and it is impossible to renew it except through the process of combinations of sounds. The combination of letters proceeds similarly. One touches the first string, that is, analogically, the first letter, and the right hand passes to the others, to second, third, fourth, or fifth strings, and from the fifth it proceeds to the others. In this process of permutations new melodies emerge and vibrate to the ears, and then touch the heart. This is how the technique of letter combination operates . . . And the secrets which are disclosed in the vibrations rejoice the heart, for the heart then knows its God and experiences additional delight. This is alluded to in the verse (Ps. 19:8): "The Torah of the Lord is perfect, reviving the soul." When it is perfect, it restores the soul. (Scholem, *HaKabbalah,* p. 208)

THE PEAK OF MYSTICAL EXPERIENCE

This science [of letter combination] is closer to the attainment of prophecy than any other types of study. A person who knows the essence of reality through studying it in books is called *ḥakham* [scholar]. When he knows it because someone who acquired it by contemplating the divine names or who learnt it from a teacher transmitted it to him, he is called *mevin* [one who understands]. One who knows it from his own heart, through contemplating the mysteries of existence, is called *da'atan* [a gnostic, a knower]. But one who knows the truth about the reality of existence through a fusion of the three methods mentioned above—knowledge through study in books, understanding received from true kabbalists, and wisdom attained by one's own contemplation—may not necessarily be called a prophet, especially if he has not been touched by the Active Intellect or he has been touched by it but is not aware that he has been touched by it. But if he has been touched by it and he comprehends that he has been touched by it, it is clear to me and to every perfect person that he is to be called "master," for his name is like "the name of his Master" [the angel *Metatron,* often mentioned in esoteric teaching, is also so designated], whether it be in one or more, or in all of His names. For he is not separate from his Master, he is his Master and his Master is he, since he is attached to Him in an attachment so strong that he cannot be separated from Him by any means, so that he is He. And just as his Master who is dissociated from all corporeality is always called *sekhel* [knowledge], *maskil* [the knower], and *muskal* [the known], since these are all actively one in

Him, at the same time, so this special person, who bears the special title, when knowledge is activated in him, will be, in his own being, *muskal, maskil,* and *sekhel,* just like his Master. Then there will be no difference between them, except that his Master has His supreme perfection from within Himself, and not through the action of any of His creations, while this one reached his status through the mediation of creatures. (Scholem, *HaKabbalah,* p. 209)

10.
Joseph Gikatilla

Joseph ben Abraham Gikatilla (1248–1325), one of the most influential of the early Spanish kabbalists, was born in Medinaceli, Castile and lived for many years in Segovia. He studied under Abraham Abulafia, but he soon developed his own style in Kabbalah. His earliest work, *Ginat Egoz,* centers kabbalistic theosophy on the hidden meanings in the names of God. It shows the influence of Abulafia in stressing the mystic symbolism of the alphabet, the vowel points and system of punctuation. The title *Ginat* is a composite of the three words whose initial letters are *gematria, notarikon* and *temurah,* concepts which, as we noted earlier, played an important part in the Abulafian system of Kabbalah.

Gikatilla's most influential work was the *Sha'arei Orah* in which he delineates his thinking about the names of God into categories based on the ten *sefirot,* a dramatic departure from his approach in the *Ginat Egoz.* He identified the first *sefirah, keter,* with the *En Sof,* the Infinite.

As the Kabbalah finally developed under the influence of the *Zohar,* the *sefirah keter* is only one of the *sefirot,* while the transcendent infinite God is beyond it.

Gikatilla gives a synopsis of the *Sha'arei Orah* in his introduction to the book, extracts from which are translated below. The names of God and their proliferating derivatives, all of them stemming from the primary name, YHWH, spell out God's ways in creation, and they are explicated and verbalized in the Torah and the commandments. The entire Torah is thus, in the words of Gikatilla, "woven out of the name YHWH." Sometimes the Torah employs anthropomorphic terms in speaking of God; it speaks of Him as though possessed of eyes, ears, hands and the like, and as though employing those organs to perform human functions. But these anthropomorphisms, when ascribed to God, are only a euphemism. They refer to spiritual forces, the *sefirot,* and to actions effected on a spiritual plane. It is only on the human plane that those references relate to the physical. Gikatilla objected to the uses of the divine names in magic rites, not because he denied the potency in the names, but because he thought it a desecration to use what is of such transcendent holiness for profane purposes.

Gikatilla also wrote various other works, including *Sefer Sha'arei Ẓedek,* which attempts to explain the mysteries of the *sefirot*; commentaries on the Song of Songs and other parts of the Bible; a commentary on the Passover Haggadah; a commentary on the *mitzvot*; a manual of disciplines in practical Kabbalah; and a collection of prayers.

A summary of Gikatilla's *Sha'arei Orah* was translated into Latin in 1516 by the apostate Paul Riccius, who was active in the Christian Kabbalah.

THE NAMES OF GOD

You asked me, beloved friend, to illumine for you a way to the knowledge of the names of the Holy One, praised be He, to enable you through them to effect your desire and to reach your goal. And because I noted that your intention is even nobler than your request itself, I have been forced to advise you on the particular way which will bring you light, and which God, praised be He, approves, and the one which He does not approve. When you attain this knowledge, and you call, the Lord will answer you, and you will be one of His intimates, and you will love Him with all your being, and you will take delight in the Lord and He will fulfill the desires of your heart.

Surely you know, surely you heard, that the Lord is the everlasting God, heavenly and earthly beings are in dread of Him. The earth quakes in dread of Him, and who can withstand His anger, who can prevail in the face of His indignation? (Nahum 1:6) He puts no trust in His angels, and even the heavens are not pure in His sight, how much less is man, a loathsome, tainted creature, who gulps down iniquity like water (Job 15:15–16). How can man born of woman dare make use of God's holy names and turn them into a tool for personal ends? What kind of a person is it who is presumptuous enough to touch the royal crown and turn it to personal use? Our sages said (Mishnah, Sanhedrin 10:1): Whoever pronounces God's name as written will have no share in the world-to-come. The saintly R. Ḥanina ben Teradyon, who pronounced the name not for profane purposes or for personal ends, but rather in a spirit of reverence, and in order to study and to understand the ways of God, praised be He, was nevertheless punished (Avodah Zarah 17b–18a). Certainly we, poor in knowledge and deficient in virtue, must desist from this. You have certainly noted the admonition (Ex. 20:7): "You shall not mention the name of the Lord your God in vain." Though this is primarily an admonition against a false oath, it is phrased in a way which implies a warning against bringing God's name to one's lips in vain. For the verse could have stated: Do not take an oath in God's name falsely. The phrase used, "You shall not mention," includes both connotations.

Our master Moses, when he ascended to heaven, learnt from the ministering angels the secret about mentioning the name of God, praised be He, and he cautioned the Israelites concerning this, saying (Deut. 32:3): "When I mention the name of the Lord, acclaim the greatness of our God." And if the angels are cautioned against pronouncing God's name, certainly lowly man is similarly cautioned. Surely this applies to a person foolish enough to try and make practical use of the crown of his Creator. Above all, we need to desist from this because in our time no one has the knowledge to pronounce God's name and turn this to practical use. This being so, the one who pronounces it will only succeed in forfeiting his share in the world-to-come, and he will accomplish nothing. Concerning such persons did our sages say (Ḥagigah 16a): Whoever is not solicitous about the respect due his Creator, it would have been better if he had not come into the world.

Now, my son, listen to me, and be attentive to my advice. "My son, if sinners tempt you, do not give in to them" (Prov. 1:10). If they say to you, come with us and we will give you the secret about the names of

God and their pronunciation which you will be able to make use of, my son, do not follow them, avoid the path they travel, for all those names and the techniques for using them are only a trap to catch souls that will go down to destruction. If the early sages possessed secrets about the holy names, as a tradition handed down by the prophets, like the seventy-two letter name, the forty-two letter name and the twelve letter name and many other holy names, and they were able to effect through them signs and wonders in the world, they would not have used these names for personal ends. They would have used them temporarily in a time of crisis or for the sanctification of God. This is illustrated by the case of Rabbi Meir, who rescued his wife from the tent of prostitutes, and he said to the Cuthite who guarded her: Whenever you should see yourself in trouble say this, God of Meir, answer me, and you will be delivered; and though he said this to that Cuthite, when Rabbi Meir's help was needed, and he found himself imperiled, he did not use the potency of the divine name, but he ran away, as is recorded in the first chapter of the tractate Avodah Zarah (Avodah Zarah 18a-b). . .

Truth and the tradition of the covenant dictate that whoever wishes to gain his ends by means of the names of the Holy One, praised be He, must study with all his strength the teachings of the Torah concerning each of the holy names mentioned in the Torah like *eheyeh, yah, YHWH, adonai, el, eloah, elohim, shadai,* and *ẓevaot.* And a person is to know that each of these names is like a key to whatever it be that a person needs in this world. In contemplating these names he will find that the entire Torah and the commandments hinge on them. In comprehending the hidden meaning of each one of these names, he will come to know the greatness of Him who spoke and the world came into being, and he will feel fear and awe of Him, and he will yearn to cleave to Him through knowing His names, praised be He. Then he will be close to the Lord and his prayer will be accepted. This is alluded to in the verse (Ps. 91:15): "I shall strengthen him, for he knew My name, he will call me, and I will respond to him." The verse does not say, "I will strengthen him because he invoked My name," but "for he knew My name." Knowledge is the main thing, and then "he will call me and I will respond to him." This means that if he should be in some need and he will focus his prayer toward that name on which whatever he seeks is dependent, then "I will respond to him.". . .

Know that all His holy names mentioned in the Torah are all dependent on the four letter name, YHWH. You might ask, Is not the name *eheyeh* the basis and the source of all? Then know that the four letter name is like the body of the tree, while the name *eheyeh* is the root of the tree, from which more roots spread and branches reach out on all sides. All other holy names are all like branches and leaves that spread from the body of the tree, and each of the branches bears its own fruit. Apart from the holy names which are well known and which may not be erased, there are many appelatives derived from each name. Thus you may ask: What are the appelatives for YHWH? They are: Awesome One; He forgives iniquity; He overlooks transgression. What are the appelatives for *el*? They are: Great One, Merciful and Gracious One. What are the appelatives for *elohim*? They are such terms as: Mighty One, Ruler, Judge. All of these appelatives have appelatives of their own, and they make up all the words of the Torah. You end up by realizing that the entire Torah is woven together out of appelatives, and the appelatives out of the names, and the holy names all are dependent on the name of YHWH and are all united in it. It thus turns out that the entire Torah is woven out of the name of YHWH, and it is for this reason that it is characterized thus (Ps. 19:8): "The Torah of YHWH [usually rendered "of the Lord"] is perfect."

You are thus taught that by comprehending the holy names in their respective categories and the appelatives deriving from each, you will realize that everything hinges on His great name, praised be He, and you will yearn to cleave to Him, and you will be in fear and awe of him. "Then you will understand the fear of the Lord (YHWH), and will attain to the knowledge of God" (Prov. 2:5). Then you will be included among those of whom it is written (Ps. 91:5): "I shall strengthen him, for he knew My name." And then you will realize how great is the punishment due to be meted out to the person who mentions the name of God in vain, certainly to one who pronounces it as written, and above all to one who puts it to practical use. But before I begin to expound my intention in writing this work, I must place before you one introduction, and it is this.

As a general principle, know that the essence of the Creator cannot be grasped by another, and none of the myriad of heavenly beings know His abode, certainly not His true being. Thus you have noted what the angels testify: "Praised be the Lord from His place" (Ezek. 3:12), that is, wherever His abode may be. And if this is true of heavenly beings, it is certainly true of earthly creatures. This being so, what can all those organs ascribed to God in the Torah, like hand, foot, ear, eye and the like, mean? Know and believe concerning all those ascriptions, that though they point to His greatness and His truth, no creature can know and comprehend what is meant by this which is called (in Him) hand, foot, ear, and the like. And if we are made in His image and likeness, do not assume that it means an eye in the form of an eye, or a hand in the precise form of a hand, but in God's existence, praised be He, these designate spiritual forces deep in the reality of His being whence emanate the influences to all creatures, according to the decree of God. But there is no correspondence between hand and hand, and their forms are not alike, as the verse declares (Isa. 40:25): "To whom will you compare Me that I will be like?"

Know and understand that there is no resemblance between Him and us in essence or form. Only this—the form of the organs in us are fashioned with a symbolic similarity to hidden spiritual forces which are beyond comprehension except as a mnemonic for remembrance. This is comparable to the written phrase "Reuben the son of Jacob." These letters and their configuration are not the form or the essence of Reuben the son of Jacob. They are only a technique for remembering that the phrase, Reuben the son of Jacob in script is a symbolic correspondence to that well-known substance and form called Reuben the son of Jacob. God, praised be He, wanting to confer merit on us, created in us many hidden organs which become known by analogy to the structure of the divine chariot [apparently an allusion to the hierarchy of the *sefirot*]. If a person should prove himself worthy by cleansing any one of his organs, that organ will serve like a throne for that spiritual reality designated by the same name, eye for eye, hand for hand, and similarly with the others. How are we to understand this? If a person should be vigilant and not allow his eyes to gaze at anything obscene or anything else that is unworthy, but only at things associated with the holiness of God and His service, then that eye is like a throne for that heavenly reality called eye; and similarly with the and and the foot and the other organs. This is the significance of the statement by the sages (Genesis Rabbah 47:8): The patriarchs are the chariot . . .

Now I must enlighten you concerning a matter related to this. Know that attributes are related to organs. How is this? The attribute of the eye is sight; the attribute of the ear is hearing; the attribute of the hand is touch; the attribute of the foot is walking. Thus the attributes are a function of the organs. And since the sages associated attributes with God, we must interpret the attributes as we told you to interpret ear, hand, foot mentioned earlier. As there is no similarity between us in regard to organs, so is there no similarity between us with regard to attributes. Since in this work we shall make reference to attributes, beware and be very careful lest you stumble and think that God praised be He, has any limited or defined attribute, for this is not so. But as the terms eye and ear are without particularization of measure or limitation or image, the same is the case with the attributes. Our sages referred to the holy names as attributes, as we are taught in the first chapter of the tractate Rosh Hashanah (17b): Said Rav Judah, There is a covenantal commitment that the thirteen attributes [of God] will not be without efficacy, and the thirteen attributes are spelled out in the verse (Ex. 34:6–7): "The Lord, the Lord is a merciful and gracious God . . ." The principle you must believe is that there is no comparison between the attributes of God, praised be He, and our attributes, except as a symbolic remembrance in name alone. Concerning this did our sages say in many passages: Come and see that the attributes of the Holy One, praised be He, are not like the attributes of a creature of flesh and blood.

After we have given you a key by means of this introduction, we must now enter upon the explanation of each of the holy names mentioned in the Torah and enlighten you concerning every instance where one of these names is mentioned, so that you realize what a fountain of life-giving waters flows from all His names, praised be He. When you will understand this then will you succeed in your way, and then will you be enlightened. (*Sha'arei Orah*, introduction)

THE SECRET OF THE NAMES

Know that all His names, praised be He, are borne by and included in the proper name, the name of YHWH, may He be praised. Some are related to it by analogy to the roots, some to the branches, some to the top of the tree, while the proper name, may He be praised, stands at the center, and is called the middle column. The other names are included in it from both sides, like the top of the tree, its roots and its branches. How are we to understand this?

The first letter of the name of YHWH stands for two names. The tip of the letter *yod* pointing upward symbolizes the great primordial existence in its full essence, and this is designated by the name *eheyeh* [literally, "I shall be," usually translated "I am"], which is called the Infinite. It is called *ayin, Nothing,* because it stands for His concealment to heavenly and earthly beings, as no one can understand anything about Him. And if someone should ask: What is He? The answer is Nothing, that is, no one can understand anything concerning Him.

This is alluded to in the statement: You may probe the heavens from one end to the other, but you may not probe what is above and what is below (Pesikta Rabbati 21, 109a). This is the mystery conveyed by the tip of the letter *yod,* the upper tip, which stands for the supreme crown (the first *sefirah*), called Nothing, that transcends all conception. No one can know anything concerning Him, except for the belief in His existence, but His existence is not comprehended by anyone other than Himself. It is for this reason that He is called *eheyeh*, which designates *existence* as such, but He alone knows the nature of this existence. It is designated *eheyeh*, with the initial letter *aleph*, as in the terms *akum* (I will arise), *ada* (I will know), *avin* (I will understand), *aseh* (I will do), *avo* (I will come)—a designation for an unspecified state of being. The name *eheyeh* is used to suggest, *I alone know My being*; and this is the significance of the tip of the letter *yod* in the name. It is symbolized by the tip of the letter *yod*, rather than through a full letter of its own, because no one can assess it, imagine it or even portray it through the form of a particular letter.

The name *eheyeh*, which is related to the depth of primordial existence, and embraces the attribute of unmitigated compassion that overcomes all expressions of sternness, is also called *el*. This is alluded to in the verse (Isa. 40:19): To whom [*mi*] will you compare God [*el*]? It suggests that even as far as the letters which signify the essence of existence, there is no particular form of a letter to symbolize it, except for the letter which stands for the *sefirah binah*, discernment, which does point to it,[1] but no other. In this sense we may also explain the above verse: To *mi*, whom, may you compare *el*? By means of the *sefirah binah*, called *mi*, we may picture His existence, but through nothing else. And know that this is the secret of the tip of the letter *yod* in God's proper name, which symbolizes the supernal existence unbounded and undefined.

The secret conveyed by the tip of the letter *yod* brought into being the full letter *yod*, which stands for the *sefirah ḥokhmah*, wisdom, yearning without end; and this is the secret meaning of the verse (Job 28:12): "Wisdom—whence will it derive?" Whence, *meayin*, also means "from nothing," or wisdom derives from Nothing or *keter* (the supernal crown, the first *sefirah*). The secret reference of the term *ḥokhmah* is the second *sefirah*, while the secret reference of the term "nothing" is to the first *sefirah*. Both these *sefirot* are alluded to in the mystery of the letter *yod*, its tip and its full form. Thus we learn that the letter *yod* of God's proper name embraces two of the holy names, which correspond to two upper

---

1. The allusion here is to the letter *heh*, which stands for the *sefirah binah*, sometimes called *mi*, who, because it points to an aspect of God, that permits the inquiry *who?* but to which no answer can be given. Gikatilla explains this partly in the next section. See also Scholem, *Major Trends*, p. 221.

sefirot, called *eheyeh yah; eheyeh* is the secret meaning of the tip of the letter *yod,* while *yah* is the form of the letter [*yah* is the sound of the letter yod]. (*Sha'arei Orah,* sha'ar 5, *sefirah* 6; ed. Joseph Ben-Shlomo, Mosad Bialik, Jerusalem 1970, vol. I, pp. 190f.)

11. *The Zohar*

The *Zohar* is the most influential book in the history of Jewish mysticism. It is the classic text of the Kabbalah. The *Zohar* is presented as the work of an early sage of the Talmud, Rabbi Simeon bar Yoḥai, but internal evidence has led scholars to regard it, in its present literary form, as the work of a medieval teacher, Moses de Leon of the 13th century (d. 1305). The title means "The Luminous," an allusion to a favorite concept of the mystics that a divine light shines in all things, in the material world as well as in the teachings of the Torah. The quest of the mystic is to penetrate the shell of existence and to establish contact with the inner light, which is truly the dimension of divinity, the hidden grandeur of all existence. Structurally, the *Zohar* presents its themes in the form of a commentary on the Bible, following the order of the weekly portions, but many lengthy and independent comments are introduced as well. Often difficult to comprehend, it must be studied by anyone who wishes to grasp the spirit of this important section in the literature of Judaism.

The *Zohar* is not a unitary book; it is a composite of several parts, written by different hands at different times, but these are all treated as though a unit, and are usually referred to by the one general name of *Zohar*.

Part of zoharitic literature is the *Tikkunei Zohar*, sometimes called in short *Tikkunim*. This was completed shortly after the *Zohar* itself and is an interpretation of the first section of Genesis (chapters 1–5). In style and spirit it is similar to the *Zohar* and it is sometimes cited to illustrate zoharitic teachings.

The most basic teaching of the Kabbalah which is expounded at length in the *Zohar* is the doctrine of the *sefirot*, the ten divine potencies which emanate from God and which effectuate His will in creation. Kabbalists visualized the grouping of these potencies in a structure resembling the shape of a person. It was the *sefirot*, so arranged, that Scripture alluded to in saying that God made man in His own image; in other words, He made him in the man-like image assumed by the *sefirot*. Indeed, according to the Kabbalah, all biblical references to God's actions really allude to the role of the *sefirot* while God as He is in Himself is beyond our knowledge and beyond our discourse. The man-like image of the *sefirot* is sometimes called the "supernal man."

According to the *Zohar*, there is no reference to the *sefirot* in the Torah because we study the Torah on the level of literalism. The Torah has an inner meaning, and the doctrine of the *sefirot*, as well as other esoteric teachings popular with the kabbalists, were to be found by one who has mastered the secret wisdom hidden in the Torah.

The *Zohar* stresses the importance of a mystical approach to Torah study, which is the essential attribute of man's true perfection. The tales are only outer garments which clothe a body; the body is the precepts of the Torah. But even the precepts are not the ultimate essence. They incarnate an inner meaning, and this is the soul of the Torah. The wise man, one who has attained mystical illumination, can attempt to penetrate to that soul. But the *Zohar* suggests that there is a limit to what even the mystically illuminated man can know, as long as he is confined to this world of finitude. In the hereafter, in the messianic epoch, our capacities will be enhanced and "the truly wise, the servants of the supreme King," are then destined to reach even further, to "the very soul of the soul of the Torah."

The *Zohar* stresses God's love as the operative principle governing the universe. The problem of evil was explained as an incident in the complex of forces directing the world, which, when seen from the perspective of the whole, no longer appear as evil. It does not project a central role for the figure of the master as found in other schools of mysticism, such as Ḥasidism, but it does show a tendency to idealize Moses. This idealization goes so far as to downgrade the virtues of Abraham in favor of the real hero, Moses, who is called "the faithful shepherd." It should be noted that this is in marked contrast to the general tendency in Jewish tradition to guard against the over-idealization of Moses. The Passover *Haggadah,* which celebrates the exodus from Egypt, does not even mention his name. He is usually portrayed as a human figure who struggled with inner doubts, who occasionally lost patience with his people, who sometimes yielded to human weaknesses.

The *Zohar* was regarded as among the most hallowed texts in Jewish tradition and some selections from it were included in the liturgy.

THE SEFIROT

1. Elijah began the discourse: Sovereign of the universe, You are one but not according to a numerical order, You are above the highest, You are the mystery above all mysteries; thought is altogether powerless to comprehend You. You brought forth ten spheres of perfection which we call the ten *sefirot,* and through them You direct hidden worlds which have not been revealed, and worlds which have been revealed; and through them You remain hidden from mortal men. You bind them together and invest them with unity, and because You are in their inner being, whoever effects disunity among these ten, it is as though he had effected disunity in You.

These ten *sefirot* act according to this order: one long [because embodying love, it emanates in greater profusion from God], one short [because embodying sternness, it is released by God in less profusion], and one intermediate [a harmonizing principle to merge the other two in the right proportion]. You direct them, but no one directs You, none above, none below, none on any side. Some of them [the lower order of *sefirot* which have to be animated by the higher] You assigned the role of garments, and it is from the "garment" *sefirot* that human souls are derived. You have prepared a number of bodies for them, so-called in comparison with those *sefirot* called garments, in which they are robed.

The *sefirot* are pictured in an arrangement corresponding to the structure of the human body: *Ḥesed* [lovingkindness] is the right arm; *Gevurah* [sternness] the left arm; *Tiferet* [beauty, the harmonizing principle, sometimes also called *raḥamim* or compassion] the torso; *Hod* [majesty] the two thighs; *Yesod* [the foundation] the extremity of the body, which bears the sign of the covenant of circumcision; *Malḥut* [sovereignty, which applies the general wisdom of the Torah to the existential world] the mouth, which is associated with the Oral Torah. The brain corresponds to the *sefirah Ḥokhmah* [wisdom], the inner essence of thought; *Binah* [analytical knowledge, generally translated as discernment] corresponds to the heart, as it is stated: The heart discerns [Berakhot 41b]. We have an allusion to the latter two [wisdom and discernment] in the verse: "The hidden things belong to the Lord" (Deut. 29:28). The crown on top is the crown of sovereignty, and its link with the last *sefirah* is alluded to in the verse: "He declares the end from the beginning" (Isaiah 46:10). This corresponds to the area on which the *tefillin* are placed. Within the crown are the ten letters that spell God's name: *Yod, he, vav, he.* These correspond to the path of the emanations [of the ten *sefirot* on their downward path toward the material world]. It waters the tree of the *sefirot,* in its arms and its branches, with divine influences, as any water nourishes a tree and enables it to grow.

Sovereign of the universe, You are the cause of all causes, who waters the tree by means of a fountain and this fountain is as the soul to the body, which gives life to the body. But in You there is no likeness, no comparison to anything within or without. You created heaven and earth and set in the heavens sun and moon, stars and planets; and on earth You created trees and plants, and the Garden of Eden, and grasses, and animals, and birds, and fish, and people, so that by contemplating them we may come to know the higher realm, how the upper and lower worlds may be recognized.

None can know anything about You. Apart from You none is real unity, and there could be no unity in the upper and lower worlds; and You are known as the Lord of all. Among the *sefirot* each has a specific name, by which the angels are also designated, but You have no specific name. You sustain all the names, and You are the perfection of them all, but if You withdrew from them, all the names would become as a body without a soul.

You are wise but not with a particular attribute of wisdom, You are discerning but not with a particular attribute of discernment. You are beyond characterization except to accommodate people, to convey to them Your power and to show them how the world is governed by judgment and compassion, which are also called righteousness and justice, on the basis of human conduct . . . But You have no attribute of justice which represents sternness or an attribute of righteousness which represents compassion. You are beyond all these characterizations. (*Tikkunei Zohar*, introduction II)

2. Rabbi Judah began the discourse: "Her husband is known in the gates, where he sits with the elders of the city" (Prov. 31:23). Come and consider. The Holy One, praised be He, is exalted in His glory, He is hidden and inaccessible in His great remoteness. There is no one in the world and there never was anyone since the world was created able to grasp His wisdom, and thus to comprehend Him.

Because he is so hidden and inaccessible, and withdrawn in the supernal heights, neither those above nor those below can cleave to Him, so that all say: "Praised be the glory of the Lord from His place" (Ezek. 3:12). Earthly creatures say that He is above, as it is written: "His glory is above the heavens" (Ps. 113:4); heavenly beings say that He is below, as it is written: "Your glory is upon all the earth" (Ps. 56:6). This goes on until all, those below and those above, say: "Praised be the glory of the Lord from His place," since He is unknown and none can comprehend Him. Yet you say: "Her husband is known in the gates!" ["husband" is here taken as a euphemism for God, who is sometimes spoken of in the esoteric language of Kabbalah as the spouse of Israel].

But "her husband is known in the gates" does indeed refer to the Holy One, praised be He, who is known, and one may cleave to Him, according to the way one conceives Him in his heart. Each one, to the extent that he can grasp the spirit of His wisdom and as he conceives Him in his heart, will he know Him in his heart. Thus He is known in the gates, that is, through these conceptions. But to have authentic knowledge of Him—none can comprehend Him [*sha'ar* means a "gate" and *sho'ar* means "to approximate"; our conceptions of God, which are only approximations, are gates or openings to the divine mystery].

Rabbi Simeon said: "Her husband is known in the gates." What is meant by "gates"? It has the same meaning as the term in the verse: "Raise up your heads, O gates, and be lifted up, your everlasting doors and let the King of glory enter" (Ps. 24:7). Through these gates which are the supernal attributes [the *sefirot*] is the Holy One, praised be He, known. Without them no one could cleave to Him [the King of glory becomes accessible to us through the manifestation of His providence which is structured in the *sefirot*].

Come and consider that no one can know the human soul. It is only because of the organs of the body, and their actions which carry out the instructions of the soul, that it is known and yet unknown. The Holy One, praised be He, is similarly known and unknown, for He is the soul of the soul, spirit of spirit, hidden and inaccessible to all. But through these supernal attributes, which are openings for the soul, is the Holy One, praised be He, known. (*Zohar* I 103 a-b)

THE *SEFIROT* AND THE MYSTERY OF GOD

In the Beginning (Gen. 1:1): Rabbi Eleazar began the discourse: It is written (Isa. 40:26): "Lift up your eyes on high and see, Who created these?" To what place does this refer? It refers to the place where all eyes are turned. Where is this? It is the mystery which enlightens the eyes. There you will know that the mysterious Ancient One, about whom one can only ask questions, created these. And who is this? It is He whom we can only call "Who?", for beyond this we cannot inquire. The being at the extremity of the heavens is designated as "Who?". There is a level below this designated as "what?". How do we differentiate between them? The first unknown designated as "Who?" is subject to inquiry. Once a person has inquired and sought to probe and find out from stage to stage to the very end, then he reaches the level designated as "what?". What have you discovered? Everything is as hidden as before. (*Zohar* I 1b)

THE TORAH

1. How confused the people of this world are in their understanding, failing to see the path of truth in the knowledge of the Torah! The Torah calls them each day with love, but they refuse to turn their head to her. Though I have said that the Torah discloses elements from her concealment, she discloses a little and soon hides herself again; and this is certainly the case. And when she shows herself from her concealment, she does so only to those who know her and are well familiar with her.

To what may the matter be compared? To a beautiful woman who is loved by someone, but she remains closed up in her palace; and people do not know her one lover, he remains hidden to them. This lover, out of his love for her, passes the entrance to her house constantly and looks on all sides. She knows that it is her lover who passes her door constantly. What does she do? She opens a hidden opening in that palace and shows herself to her lover, but she soon withdraws and disappears again. All those close to her lover do not observe this, except her lover, and all his being responds to her, for he knows that it was out of her love for him that she has shown herself for a fleeting moment, to arouse more love in him.

This is the way of the Torah, she only reveals herself to those who love her; she knows that a particular wise man paces in front of her door daily. What does she do? She shows her face to him out of her palace and nods to him, but soon returns to her place of hiding. All those present do not know and do not take note of it but he, and all his being responds to her. It is for this reason that the Torah reveals and hides herself and follows the ways of love with her lover, to arouse in him more love.

Come and see, this is the way of the Torah: at first, when she begins to reveal herself to a person, she gives him a hint (*remez*). If he understands, well and good, but if not she sends after him and calls him a fool. The Torah tells the one she sends after him: Tell that fool to come here that I may speak to him. Thus it is written (Prov. 9:4,5): "Whoever is foolish let him come here . . . come eat of my bread." When he approaches her she begins to speak to him from the other side of the cover. She places before him subjects commensurate with his understanding so that he may progress gradually. This is *derash,* the inferential interpretation of Scripture. Then she speaks to him from the other side of a delicate veil, in allegories, and this is *haggadah.* When he becomes more familiar with her she shows herself to him in her inwardness and speaks to him concerning her hidden secrets and all the secret paths of knowledge she had kept enclosed in her heart from ancient days, and then he is a perfect man, a true master of the Torah, lord of the house, for she has revealed to him all her secrets, and did not keep anything back from him. (*Zohar* II 99a–99b)

2. Come and see: A person wears clothes which all can see. When fools see a person dressed in beautiful garments, they look no further. But the worth of the clothes is in the body that is robed in them, and the worth of the body is in the soul that abides in it.

So it is with the Torah. It has a body, the commandments of the Torah, and they are robed in garments, which are the narratives concerning matters of this world. Fools concern themselves only with the garments, which is the narrative portion of the Torah; they know no more, and they do not seek what is beneath that garment. Those who know more do not fix their attention on the garment but on the body inside the garment. The truly wise, the servants of the supreme King, those whose souls were at the revelation at Mount Sinai, concern themselves only with the soul, the essence of all, the real Torah. In the hereafter it will be granted to them to see the very soul of the soul of the Torah. . .

Woe to the wicked who say that the Torah consists of ordinary tales, and they see only this garment and no more. Fortunate are the righteous whose gaze penetrates to the inner meaning of the Torah, as is proper. Wine is kept in a jar, and so must the Torah be contained in an outer garment. It is for this reason that we must penetrate to what is beyond the garment. Thus we say that all these matters and all these tales are only garments. (*Zohar* III 152a)

THE MORAL DIMENSION

1. "And Abraham approached and said: Will you sweep away the righteous together with the wicked?" (Gen. 18:23). Said Rabbi Judah: Whoever saw another father of mercy like Abraham? Consider that in the case of Noah it is written: "And God said to Noah: The end of all flesh has been decreed by Me . . . make yourself an ark of gopher wood" (Gen. 6:13, 14); and he remained silent and said nothing, not pleading for mercy. But Abraham, when God said to him: "The outrage of Sodom and Gemorrah is so great . . . I will go down and see" (Gen. 18:20), it is at once reported: "And Abraham approached and said: Will you sweep away the righteous together with the wicked?" Said Rabbi Elazar: Even Abraham's action was not perfect, as it should have been. Noah did nothing, Abraham pleaded for justice as he should have, that the innocent shall not die with the guilty, descending in his plea that the cities be spared for the sake of righteous men in it, mentioning at first fifty, then reducing the numbers down to ten, but he did not complete his action, for he did not plead for unqualified mercy. Abraham apparently said, I do not wish to stake the reward for my own deeds. But who performed the perfect act, as the circumstances call for it? It was Moses. When God said: "They have rapidly strayed from the path . . . they have made themselves a molten calf and bowed down to it" (Ex. 32:7, 8), what follows? Moses implored the Lord God until he exclaimed: "And now, if you only forgive their sin! But if not, erase me, I pray, from the Book You have written" (Ex. 32:32). Though they had all sinned, he [Moses] did not stir from there until He told him: "I have pardoned as you have asked" (Numbers 14:20). Abraham was not so concerned, asking forgiveness only if there should be righteous ones but not otherwise. Thus there was no one to defend his generation like Moses, who was truly a faithful shepherd. (*Zohar* I 106a)

2. "In the beginning God created heaven and earth" (Gen. 1:1). The initial letters for the Hebrew phrase, heaven and earth (*et hashamayim ve-et ha-aretz*) make *ah va*, which is the core of the word *ahavah*, meaning love, with which heaven and earth were created: the heavens

were created with *ah* and the earth with all that is in it was created with *vah*. It is this which endows every tree and every blade of grass with longing. This is what is meant by the teaching that there is not a blade of grass below that is not watched over from above, stirring it with the call to grow. It is this to which the verse (Job 38:33) alludes in the statement: "Do you know the laws of the heavens, have you grasped the manner of His reign on earth?" (Supplement to *Zohar* I 15a)

3. "Let us make man in our image after our likeness" (Gen. 1:26). The name for man, *adam*, embodies the secret of male and female, all designed in the supernal, holy wisdom. The term for image, *ẓelem*, is masculine, and the term for likeness, *demut*, is feminine; one was to perfect the other, enabling man to be unique in the world, to exercise sovereignty over all. (*Zohar* I 47a)

4. Rabbi Simeon began the discourse: Whoever rejoices on a festival without giving the portion due to the Holy One, praised be He, is selfish. Satan hates him, and brings accusations against him, schemes his downfall, and causes him all kinds of trouble. The portion due to the Holy One, praised be He, consists in bringing happiness to the poor, to the extent one can.

On those days the Holy One, praised be He, goes out to see those broken vessels of His, and when He sees that nothing has been done to make them happy, He cries over them. He reascends to the heavenly realm, intending to destroy the world.

The members of the heavenly academy then come before Him and say: Sovereign of the universe, You are called "merciful," and "gracious," extend mercy to Your children. But He tells them: Is not the world built on the foundation of mercy, as it is written (Ps. 89:3): "The world is built on mercy" [the Hebrew *olam*, here rendered "world," is sometimes translated as "forever"]? Only on this can the world endure. The angels on high then say to Him: Sovereign of the universe, that person ate and was sated and could have extended his beneficence to the poor, but gave them nothing. The Accuser then comes and asks permission to pursue that man.

Was there a person greater than Abraham, who bestowed good to all creatures? One day he made a feast, as we are told (Gen. 21:8): "The child grew, and was weaned, and Abraham made a great feast when Isaac was weaned." Abraham made a feast and invited the great men of his generation to that feast. At every festive celebration, as we have been taught, that Accuser appears. If he sees that the celebrant had first bestowed some beneficence to the poor and the poor were in his house, then he departs. If not, he enters and surveys the festivities without the participation of the poor and without a prior gift to the poor. He then ascends on high and launches accusations against that celebrant. When Abraham had invited the great of his generation to the feast, the Accuser came down and stood at his door in the disguise of a poor man, but no one paid attention to him. Abraham attended to the kings and important men, Sarah nursed all the children, for people had not believed that she had given birth, thinking that her baby was a foundling; they therefore brought all their babies with them and Sarah nursed them in their presence. This is alluded to in the verse (Gen. 21:7): "Who could have foretold Abraham that Sarah would yet nurse *children*" [in the plural]?

The Accuser was at the door when Sarah said (Gen. 21:6): "God has brought me laughter." The Accuser immediately presented himself before the Holy One, praised be He, and said to Him: Sovereign of the universe, You have called Abraham, "My friend!" He made a feast and contributed nothing for You, nor to the poor; he did not offer up to You even a single pigeon. Moreover, Sarah has said that You have made her an object of laughter.

The Holy One, praised be He, said to him: Who in this world is like Abraham? Nevertheless, the Accuser did not swerve from there until he had spoiled all that festivity. God thereupon ordained that Isaac be offered up as a sacrifice, and that Sarah die in anguish over the fate of her son. All this trouble came to him because he had not given anything to the poor. (*Zohar* I 10b–11A)

THE EVIL IMPULSE

1. Rabbi Isaac was present before Rabbi Elazar, and he said to him: Surely the love which a person feels for God is aroused by the heart, for it is the heart which inspires love for Him. Why then is it written, "with all your heart" and then "with all your soul?" [Deut. 6:5: "You shall love the Lord your God with all your heart, with all your soul, and with all your might"]. This suggests that there are two types of love, one with the heart and one with one's soul. If the heart is primary, why the reference to one's soul?

He said to him: Surely heart and soul are distinctive but they merge into one, for heart and soul and possessions [the rabbinic interpretation for "might" in Deut. 6:5] are all united, but the heart is primary and the basis of them all.

Why is the term for heart written *levavkha,* with the Hebrew letter *bet* double [instead of the simpler and more usual term *libkha*]? It alludes to two "hearts," that is, the two passions which stem from the heart: the passion for the good (*yeẓer hatov*) and the passion for evil (*yeẓer hara*). Each of these two is called "heart," one is called the heart for the good, the other, the heart for evil. This is suggested by the double *bet* in the Hebrew term *levavkha*, two "hearts," the good impulse and the evil impulse.

Why does it say "with all your soul" (*bekhol nafshekha*)? It should have said simply, "with your soul." What is the significance of the term "all"? This is meant to include the three levels of the soul, *nefesh* [the lowest level which represents the animating vitality], *ruaḥ* [spirit, a higher level], and *neshamah* [the soul proper, which is the divine spark, realized only by one who has mastered the hidden mysteries of the Torah]. This is alluded to by the term *bekhol nafeshekha*, with all your *nefesh*, that is, with all the dimensions of the soul which are rooted in the *nefesh*. The term "with all your might" ["might" is taken as referring to possessions] refers to different possessions; therefore the text uses the term "all". The love of God involves surrendering to Him all these, to love Him with each of them.

You might wonder: How can a person love Him with his evil passion? Does not the evil impulse challenge a person not to come close to God? How then can he love Him with this attribute? But this is an added love for the Holy One, praised be He, when the evil impulse is subdued because of the great love a person has for God. When the evil impulse has been overcome and the person has broken it—this is a love for the Holy One, praised be He, since a person has thereby associated the evil impulse in the service of God.

This secret is known to those who understand the mysterious workings of the *sefirot*. Whatever the Holy One, praised be He, has made in the realms above and in those below—all is intended to manifest His glory and all is intended to serve Him. Has it ever happened that a servant shall dispute his master and challenge everything the master desires? It is the will of the Holy One, praised be He, that people ever pursue His service and go in the true path, so as thereby to bestow on them many blessings. Since this is the will of the Holy One, praised be He, how did the evil servant come to dispute his Master's will, and influence people to pursue the evil path and cause them not to do the will of their Lord? Surely he must be acting in accordance with his Master's will.

The case is analogous to a king who had an only son whom he loved very much, and because of this love, he instructed him not to go near a woman of ill repute, because whoever goes near her becomes unworthy of entering the king's palace. This son agreed lovingly to follow his father's will. Outside the king's palace there was a harlot, of beautiful appearance. In time the king said: I would like to test my son's attachment to me. He called on that harlot and said to her: Go and tempt my son so that I can test my son's attachment to me. What did that harlot do? She went after the king's son, she began to embrace him, to kiss him, to tempt him with all kinds of temptations. If the son is honorable, and obedient to his father, he will rebuke her and pay no attention to her; he will push her away. Then will the father rejoice in his son, and bring him into the inner part of the palace and present him many gifts and bestow on him great honor. Who brought about all this honor for the son? You must agree that it was that harlot. Should that harlot be commended for this or not? Certainly praise is due her from all angles. Firstly, she carried out the instructions of the king; secondly, she was responsible for all the good that came to that son, and all the love the king lavished on him. Therefore, it is written (Gen. 1:31): "And behold, it was very good." "It was good" would refer to the angel who fosters life [the good impulse]; the additional word for "very," *meod,* [the Hebrew *meod* has a similar sound to the word *mot,* which means death] refers to the angel who fosters death [the evil impulse]. He is certainly very good for one who heeds the commandments of his master.

Come and see: If not for that challenger, the righteous would not inherit those hidden, higher blessings, which they are destined to inherit in the world-to-come. Fortunate are those who encountered this challenger, and fortunate are those who did not encounter him. Fortunate are those who encountered him and were rescued from him, for it is through him that they will inherit all those precious benefits of the world-to-come, concerning which it is written (Isa. 44:3): "No eye has seen a God like You doing such things for those who trust in Him." Fortunate are those who did not encounter him, because those wicked ones who do not heed their master and are induced to follow him inherit hell and are diverted from the realm of life.

What benefit does this challenger derive when the wicked heed him? Although he really does not derive any benefit, he fulfills the command of his master. Moreover, it is thus that he is strengthened. Because he is evil, he grows more potent by doing evil. One who is wicked does not become powerful until he slays someone. When he slays people, then his potency is enhanced, and he feels pleasure. That challenger who is called the angel of death does not become strengthened in his potency until he causes people to stray, and incites against them, and slays them—then he is pleased, and his potency is enhanced. Just as the life force is enhanced when people are good and walk in the righteous path, so does this challenger become more potent when the wicked heed him and he dominates them. May the Merciful One spare us from such a fate. Fortunate are those who were able to vanquish him and subdue him, meriting through him the life of the world-to-come, and to be confirmed in their attachment to the holy King. Such a one is surely alluded to in the verse (Ps. 84:6): "Fortunate is the man whose strength is in You, in whose heart are highways to you." (*Zohar* II 162b-163b)

THE FEAR OF GOD AND THE LOVE OF GOD

Rabbi Simeon began the discourse concerning the commandments of the Torah and stated: The commandments of the Torah which God gave to Israel are all stated in the Torah in comprehensive summation.

In the beginning [*Bereshit*, which may also mean "with" the beginning] God created. This alludes to the first commandment, and this commandment is the fear of the Lord, because this is referred to as "the beginning." Thus it is written (Ps. 111:10): "The beginning of wisdom is the fear of the Lord," and (Prov. 1:7): "The fear of the Lord is the beginning of knowledge." This precept is termed "the beginning," it is the gateway of faith and the whole world is sustained by it.

The fear of the Lord is expressed in three forms, two of them are without proper substance, but one is the essence of fear. There is one who fears the Holy One, praised be He, so that his children might live and not die, or because of his concern lest he suffer bodily punishment or monetary loss, and this induces in him constant fear. Thus we find a fear of God which is not a genuine fear. There is another type of person who fears the Holy One, praised be He, out of fear of punishment in the hereafter and the sufferings in hell. Both these types of fear are not genuine and do not constitute its essence.

Genuine fear is for a person to fear God because He is the mighty Sovereign, the Source of all worlds, before whom all existences are as nothing, as we have been told (Dan. 4:32): "And all the inhabitants of the earth are as nothing" [before Him]; and he is to set his heart on what is called fear. . .

Whoever fears God because he fears the stripe, as it has been said, is not infused with the fear of the Lord which the text says (Prov. 19:23): "The fear of the Lord brings life." The fear which rests on him is the evil fear of the lash, not the fear of the Lord.

The state which is described as the fear of the Lord is also called the beginning of knowledge. It is for this reason that this commandment is alluded to here, as it is the foundation of all other commandments of the Torah. Whoever keeps the commandment to fear God keeps them all. Whoever has not kept the commandment to fear has not kept the commandments of the Torah, because this is the gateway to all.

The second commandment is the one which is linked with the commandment of fear, and is inseparable from it; this is the commandment to love, that a person is to love his Master with a full love. What do we mean by a full love? It is what is called "great love." This is alluded to in the verse (Gen. 17:1): "Walk before Me and be wholehearted." It means wholehearted in love. This is what is referred to in the verse (Gen. 1:3): "And God said, Let there be light." This is a call for wholehearted love, which is called "great love." And here we have the commandment, that a person is to love God as is proper.

Said Rabbi Eleazar: Father, I heard an explanation of wholehearted love. He said to him: My son, say it before Rabbi Pinḥas who has attained that state. Said Rabbi Eleazar: Great love is a love which embraces two aspects, and if it does not embrace two aspects it is not genuine love, and concerning this have we learnt that the love for God is exemplified in two aspects. There is one who loves God because he has wealth, long life, children, mastery over his enemies, success in his undertakings, and for this reason he loves Him. And if the reverse should befall him, and the Holy One, praised be He, should deal sternly with him, he will change and will have no love for Him. This type of love is not a genuine love.

The love that is called perfect love is one which remains steadfast under both conditions, whether he is subject to suffering or to good fortune. The proper love with which one is to love his Master is as has been defined, even if He take your life from you.

Rabbi Simeon embraced him and kissed him. Rabbi Pinḥas came over and kissed him and blessed him, saying: Surely the Holy One, praised be He, sent me here, here is the tender light that I was told was hidden in my household which would eventually illumine the world.

Said Rabbi Eleazar: Surely fear must not be forgotten with any of the commandments, above all with this commandment of love is it necessary to associate fear. How is it to be associated with love? When love is expressed under favorable conditions, when one is given riches, length of days, children, sustenance, it is essential to cultivate fear lest he lapse into some offense. This apprehension is alluded to in the verse (Prov. 28:14): "Happy is the man who is always afraid"; for he adds fear to his love. Similarly it is necessary to cultivate fear when one is dealt with sternly. When a person sees that adversity comes upon him, he must arouse in himself the proper fear of God and not harden his heart. And it is against this that we are cautioned in the same verse: "And whoever hardens his heart shall fall into evil." Thus we have a fear which is expressed under the two conditions, and is included in the two aspects of love, and this is complete love, as it is mandated to be. (*Zohar* I 11b–12a)

12. Moses Cordovero

Moses ben Jacob Cordovero (1522–1570) was one of the most important kabbalistic thinkers of 16th century Safed. His teacher in classic rabbinic texts was Joseph Karo (1488–1575), the renowned author of the *Shulḥan Arukh*; his teacher in mystic lore was Solomon Alkabeẓ, his brother-in-law, who is best known as the author of *Lekhah Dodi,* sung at the Friday night service. Isaac Luria refers to him as his teacher, and though he came to differ with him in his thinking, he continued to hold Cordovero in high esteem.

Cordovero was part of a circle of mystics who tended to assume various ascetic disciplines. They would often leave their homes for days at a time and visit the graves of reputed kabbalists of ancient times that were situated near Safed. They would pray and meditate and discuss esoteric subjects. These excursions, known as *gerushin,* or "banishments," were meant to serve as acts of identification with the *shekhinah* in exile. Cordovero and his circle followed a rigid discipline of personal behavior, seeking moral purity and mutual help in their endeavor to transcend worldliness and reach a higher state of spiritual illumination. It was their hope that by their holiness they would effect the necessary impact in the heavenly sphere to hasten the coming of the messiah. Tradition has it that Cordovero was guided by celestial mentors that appeared to him in the spirit from among ancient prophets and sages and that he was also vouchsafed revelations from the prophet Elijah.

Cordovero left extensive writings which are an important contribution to kabbalistic literature. His *Pardes Rimonim* and *Elimah Rabbati* offer us a detailed exposition of his kabbalistic teachings. A more detailed discussion of the *sefirot* is found in *Shi'ur Komah.* The selections included in the present anthology are taken from his *Tomer Devorah* (Palmtree of Deborah, a title that bears allusion to the prophetess Deborah who is described as having expounded her teachings under a palmtree, see Judges 4:5), and from *Or Ne'erav* (Pleasant Light).

The primary problem to which *Tomer Devorah* addresses itself is to chart a moral code for a person to follow. In the rabbinic tradition, man's highest ideal in shaping his life is to imitate God's ways; as he is righteous, as He is merciful, so are we to be righteous and merciful within such measure as our finite existence allows. This goal came into some question in the Kabbalah which held that God as He is in Himself does not act in the world, but that the acting divine power is the realm of the *sefirot.* Cordovero reinterprets the ideal of imitating God into the imitation of each of the *sefirot.* The third chapter sets forth how man, in ordering his life, is called on to emulate the characteristics of divine wisdom. To the extent that he practices this, his life will exemplify one of primary qualities of the divine ordering of the world.

Or Ne'erav is a defense of kabbalistic study and an explanation of some basic concepts in kabbalistic thought.

THE CALL TO LOVE

I have found an additional therapeutic potion but it will not be as potent as when taken after the medicine mentioned earlier has been applied. This is the call for a person to cultivate two disciplines. Firstly, he must respect all creatures, recognizing in them the excellence of the Creator who fashioned man with wisdom. All other creatures, too, manifest the wisdom of the Creator. A person must realize their high worth since the

Source of all being, the Wise One, He who is exalted above all, concerned Himself with their creation. If, God forbid, he should mistreat them, he would be dishonoring their Creator. This would be analogous to the case of a wise craftsman who fashioned a vessel with great skill and then showed it to people, whereupon one of them began to disparage it and to belittle it. How angry this craftsman would be, because his skill would be disparaged through the disparagement of his handiwork. The Holy One, praised be He, will also be displeased by the disparagement of any of the creatures that He created. This is alluded to in the verse (Ps. 104:24): "How manifold (*mah rabu*) are Your works, O Lord." The term *rabu* also means *important*, as in the phrase *rab beto*. The text then adds: "in wisdom have You made them all." Since by Your wisdom were they brought into being, Your works have assumed great importance. It is therefore fitting that a person discern in them wisdom, not a cause for their disparagement.

Secondly, a person must condition himself to love people, even wrongdoers, as though they were his brothers. The love for all people must become fixed in his heart. He is to cultivate in his heart a love even for the wicked, saying: Would that these people become righteous, turning from their course in penitence, and then they would all become great and acceptable to God, as the faithful friend of the Jewish people [Moses] said (Nu. 11:29): "Would that all the people of the Lord were prophets." And how he would get himself to love them, if he learnt to focus his mind on their good points, overlooking their defects, concentrating not on the aberrations but on their good attributes. He is to say to himself: If this miserable pauper were very affluent, how pleased I would be in his company, as I am pleased to be in the company of so and so. But if they put beautiful garments on him, like those worn by so and so, there would be no difference between them. Why then should I disdain to give him honor? In God's eyes he is more important than I since he is troubled with privation and suffering by which a person is cleansed from sin.[1] Why should I dislike one whom God loves? Thus will his heart be drawn toward the good and he will condition himself to acquire all good qualities we have mentioned. (*Tomer Devorah*, ch. 2)

---

1. The term pauper is apparently a metaphor for the lack of good deeds; beautiful garments also seems to be used in metaphoric sense, referring to penitence, a usage suggested by Zechariah 3:4-5. The notion that suffering cleanses from sin is found in the Talmud (Yoma 86a).

WISDOM AND MORALITY

How shall a person train himself to possess the attribute of [the *sefirah*] wisdom? The divine wisdom, while concealed and immensely exalted, is embodied in all creatures. This is alluded to in the verse (Psalms 104:24): "How many are Your works, O Lord, in wisdom have You made them all." A person's wisdom should similarly be extended to all; he should teach, helping people in accordance with their capacities. He should influence them by his wisdom, not allowing any consideration to impede him.

The divine emanation of wisdom is two-faced. The higher aspect turns toward the *sefirah* Keter, the crown; it does not turn its gaze downward, but receives the influences from above. The second and lower aspect faces downward, to watch over the *sefirah* on which she bestows the influence of her wisdom. A person, too, should face in two directions. Firstly, he should withdraw from worldly involvements to be with his Creator so as to increase his wisdom and to perfect it. Secondly, he is to teach other people of that wisdom which the Holy One, praised be He, bestowed on him. Just as the divine wisdom extends its influence on the other *sefirot* in accordance with their intellectual capacities, and to the measure appropriate for their needs, so should he be careful not to extend in excess of what the intellectual capacities of the recipient would allow, so that no damage might result. Thus the higher *sefirah* does not bestow its influence in excess of the limits in the one receiving it.

It is in the nature of the divine wisdom, moreover, to exercise supervision over all existence; thought concerns itself with the welfare of each creature. Concerning the divine wisdom it is written (Isa. 4:8): "For My thoughts are not your thoughts." It is also written (II Sam. 14:14, as interpreted in *Meẓudat David*: "And He makes provision without rejecting anyone." It is further written (Jer. 29:11): "For I know the thoughts that I cherish, says the Lord, thoughts of good and not of evil, to give you a future and a hope." Similarly, it is important that a person have his eyes open to the condition of the people of God in order to help them; his thoughts are to be focused on the effort to bring back the straying and to devise plans for their benefit. As the divine mind seeks to help each being so must he concern himself with helping his companions. He should take counsel with God, and with His people, individually and collectively, and influence those who have deviated from the right course to return to proper behavior; he should serve as their guiding intelligence to direct them to the good path, even as the divine wisdom guides the realm of the *sefirot*.

Divine wisdom animates all beings with life, as it is written (Ecc. 7:12): "Wisdom gives life to all." Similarly, he is to serve as a life-giving influence to the whole world, and enable all to possess life in this world and in the next. In short he is to serve as a life-giving source for all beings.

The divine wisdom is the progenitor of all beings, as it is written (Psalms 104:24): "How many are Your works, O Lord, in wisdom have you made them all." They have life and continue to exist because of this. Similarly, he is to act as a father to all creatures of the Holy One, praised be He, and to Israel, especially, who are endowed with holy souls that emanate from this source. He is always to pray for mercy and blessing for his world as the divine Father extends mercy toward His creatures. He should constantly pray for the alleviation of suffering of those who are afflicted as though they were his own children, and as though he had created them; this is the will of the Holy One, praised be He. Thus the faithful shepherd [Moses] said (Nu. 11:12): "Did I conceive this people that You tell me to carry them to my bosom?" In this manner he should bear the entire people of God, as a nurse carries a suckling child; he should gather the lambs, lead gently the sucking one, look for the missing, concern himself with the lost, heal the broken ones, feed the needy, return the straying. He is to be compassionate toward all Israel, bear their burdens cheerfully, as the divine Father who is patient with all. He must not show embarrassment, nor hide himself, nor grow weary, but lead each one according to his needs. These are the attributes of wisdom in a father who is merciful toward his children.

Moreover a person's mercy should be extended to all creatures; he is not to show contempt or destroy any of them. Thus the divine wisdom extends to all created things, inanimate things, plants, animals, and persons. It is for this reason that we have been cautioned not to be disrespectful toward food. The divine wisdom is not disdainful of any being but has in fact endowed existence to all things, as the verse declares: "In wisdom have You made them all." It is similarly proper that a person show mercy toward all God's creatures. The Midrash tells us that our sainted teacher [Rabbi Judah haNasi] was punished because he showed insensitivity to a young calf, which, while on its way to slaughter, seemed to seek refuge near him. He said to the calf: Go, for this purpose were you created. He was afflicted with suffering, which is a consequence of judgment, while mercy is a shield against judgment. It was only when he showed mercy toward a weasel, citing the verse: "and His tender mercies are over all His works" (Psalms 145:9), that he was delivered from the judgment; he then drew the light of wisdom upon himself and his afflictions ceased. In the same manner a person must not be disdainful of any being in existence, since they all embody the divine wisdom. He must not uproot any plant unless it is because of some need, nor kill any living being unless it is because of need. In the latter case he is to perform the act of slaughter in a humane manner, with a knife carefully checked for sharpness and smoothness, acting in as merciful a manner as possible. To sum up, the divine wisdom releases an imperative to show compassion toward all beings, and not to injure them. We are only allowed to use them so that they may contribute to a higher level of life, the plant to animal life, the animal to human life. In that case it is permissible to uproot a plant and kill an animal, thus performing an objectionable act for the sake of a meritorious purpose. (*Tomer Devorah*, ch. 3)

THE IMPORTANCE OF MYSTICAL STUDY

1. We have noted that those who keep away from this Knowledge may be divided into three categories. Some shun it, saying that there is no need to believe in a secret dimension of the Torah, for various reasons. At times they look upon everything according to its literal meaning, and they have no interest in hidden teachings, for who can force them to believe in the ten *sefirot*, and other branches of this Knowledge? They only want to believe in the wondrous Unity. If they should be exposed to some elements of this Knowledge, especially if they should hear references concerning the *En Sof*, and different levels of meaning in the Torah, they will become unreservedly abusive of the error among the Enlightened, regarding them as heretics . . .

In refuting those who hold such opinions, one comes close to violating the talmudic injunction (Baba Kamma 69a): Let the wicked man wallow in his evil and perish. But it is in order to be concerned over the honor due to the Torah, to reprimand him for his presumption and to refute his position. There is no question that King Solomon alluded to such persons when he said (Prov. 18:2): "The fool does not take pleasure in understanding, but in expressing what is in his heart." One who is drawn after lusts, and is of limited understanding in the Torah and its secrets is called a fool, because he is drawn after the follies and intoxications of this lowly and fallen world. And he [King Solomon] states that this fool takes no pleasure in understanding, which refers to the secret teachings that are hidden in the revealed teachings, for this is the definition of understanding, as our sages said (Ḥagigah 14a): A person of understanding is one who understands one thing from another. The fool then does not wish hidden matters, which require understanding to draw them out, as the verse (Prov. 20:5) states: "A man of understanding will draw it out." He wishes only to express what is in his heart, which means the revealed matters that are a robe to the hidden. They appear as the simple meaning of what is stated and it is as though they are revealed to the heart. They do not appear so to the hearts of the Enlightened, only to the hearts of fools like him, and this is what is referred to by the phrase, "the expressions of his heart," that is, the expressions of his limited intelligence.

Concerning such persons did Rabbi Simeon bar Yoḥai state in the *Tikkunim*: The Hebrew term *brashyt* [*bereishit*, "in the beginning," with which the Torah begins] may be seen as a composite of two words, *atr ybsh*, "a dry place." This alludes to the foreboding in the verse (Isa. 19:5): "And the river will be parched and dry." When it is dry, the children below will proclaim the divine unity and recite *Shema Yisrael*, but there will be no response. This is expressed in the verse (Prov. 1:28): "Then will they call on Me and I will not answer." Therefore the person responsible for the disappearance of the Kabbalah and the wisdom from the oral and the written Torah, and who influences people not to cultivate them, claiming that there is only a literal meaning in the Torah and the Talmud—it is surely as though he had removed the flow from the river, and from that garden. Woe unto such a person! It would have been better if he had not been created in the world, and had not studied that written and oral Torah. It is ascribed to him as though he had returned the world to waste and desolation and caused poverty to abound in the world, and prolonged the time of the exile (*Tikkunei Zohar*, 43, p. 82a). . .

There is a second category of persons who spurn Knowledge, and their position is compounded of various arguments. They all agree in their esteem for this Knowledge, but some claim that it is so exalted that not all are worthy to be involved with it. They even feel warranted to strike out against those who do pursue it. They claim that they are avenging the honor of the Lord of hosts and the honor of His Torah against those who venture to step into an exalted realm, to speculate about divine matters, a subject remote from mortal minds, and one that is not becoming for lowly man to engage in. And if they should be pressed by the example of ancient sages who did concern themselves with this subject, they state that no one may be compared to them in saintliness to be entrusted with these lofty mysteries.

Some maintain that it is indeed proper for a person to pursue this Knowledge, but this requires a competent teacher, and it appears to them that no one has a thorough knowledge of it, and therefore they avoid studying even simple elements in it. If they should hear those who pursue it discuss any aspect of it, whether much or little, they raise their voices in a feigned piety, saying: May God forgive you, for your sin is great, and you are devoid of understanding, neither to the right of you, nor to the left of you; would it were given to me to understand what you are missing of this Knowledge.

The upshot of the matter is that [as they see it] no one understands this Knowledge and all are alike in this respect. It seems to these poor fellows that there is no difference between those who serve God and those who do not serve Him. It appears to some of them that it is necessary to precede this study with the science of astronomy and other sciences, which keep them from adopting the right course. Similarly, they will assume a pose of holiness and rationalize for themselves an excuse that they have not yet attained sufficient knowledge of the Talmud. Thus these poor fellows will manage not to study even a little of this Knowledge, certainly not to sate themselves with it, and thereby these poor fellows depart to the hereafter without Knowledge.

There is a third group that keeps away from this Knowledge by arguing that a person is prone to err in these subjects, and he commit a sin by falling into one of those errors affecting the divine. This group is nobly motivated but their action is not sound. It is true and they are right that a person is prone to err in these esoteric subjects, but this will not fault him. Our sages explained this in the *Sefer haBahir*: His disciples asked R. Reḥumei . . . What is meant by *shigyonot* [in Habakkuk 3:1]? This is to be understood in the light of the verse (Prov. 8:19): "Because of your love for her, err [*tishgeh,* usually rendered "be enraptured," but the root *ShGH* also means "to err"] always." What does this refer to? The work of the chariot [pursue it though you are prone to err].

The group whose approach is acceptable consists of those who pursue the right course. They have attained some mastery in Bible, and in the Gemara with its teachings, which have the same status to us as the Mishnah, and they have attained some mastery in this Knowledge. They study it for its own sake, in order to enter its secrets, to know their Creator, to attain the wonderful quality of reaching the true understanding of the teaching of the Torah, of praying before the Creator, to effect unification between God and His *shekhinah* through the performance of His commandments; and this is the service which is acceptable to the Creator of all existence.

This I know with certainty. Such a person will walk securely on his way, when he lies down he will be unafraid. And He who created him may be depended on to reveal to him what no one before him has known in the divine Torah, for every soul has a unique portion in the Torah. No one mastered it fully, without reservation, except Moses, peace be upon him. The Holy One, praised be He, revealed it to him in its generalizations and their constituent particulars, as the sages and their disciples of the future were due to expound it. (*Or Ne'erav* 1:1, 3, 4, 6)

2. Undoubtedly, one of the duties laid down by the Torah is for a person to know God, in accordance with his powers of comprehension. Thus the text states (Ex. 20:2): "I am the Lord your God," on which Maimonides offers the following comment in the beginning of his work (*Mishneh Torah, Hilkhot Yesodei haTorah* 1:1): The chief foundation and the basis of all wisdom is to know that there is a first Cause, who brought all beings into existence . . . And there is no doubt that our master intended to convey to us that included in this commandment is to understand the process by which existing things derived from Him, to the extent that this is within human comprehension.

There can be no doubt concerning this, for how could one assume that the call to know as here used means to *believe* in God's existence? The text would have stated that we have a positive commandment to *believe* that there is a God. But it is not written thus, it is written to *know*. This means specifically to attain *knowledge*, a comprehension of God in accordance with human intellectual capacity. And similarly did the Bible specify (Jer. 22:15): "Know the God of your fathers and serve Him." This is intended to teach us that to serve Him properly we must know Him, that is, know His *sefirot* and how He directs them, and His unity with them. This is the proper service, the unification of the Holy One, praised be He, and His *shekhinah*. This is alluded to in the Hebrew term for "serve Him," *avdehu*, which may be read as a composite of *avod*, serve, *hu* [in Hebrew the letter *heh*, or h, stands for God and the letter *vav*, or *u*, means "and" or "plus"], God plus, that is, the Holy One, praised be He, *and* His *shekhinah*. The term *da*, know, is to be read in the light of the statement (Gen. 4:1): "And Adam *knew* his wife Eve."

Apart from this, there are additional commandments that cannot be performed properly without knowing this wonderful Torah and wisdom —the love of God and the fear of God, two *mitzvot* enjoined on us in the Torah. Love is commanded in the verse (Deut. 6:5): "You shall love the Lord your God," and fear in the verse (Deut. 6:13): "You shall fear the Lord your God." If one should not realize the greatness and exaltation of His divine being, and how He is differentiated from other beings, and how other beings derived from Him, to a point of how He directs our lowly world — how will he fear Him?

The poor ignoramus thinks that God is an old man, because it is written that He sat as one ancient of days; that He had white hair due to His old age, because it is written that the hair of His head is like pure wool; that He sits on a wonderful wooden chair sending forth many sparks, because it is written that His throne is fiery flames (Daniel 7:9), that He has the appearance of fire, because it is written (Deut. 4:24): "The Lord your God is a consuming fire." There are other instances of such imaginings which the fool conjures up in his mind to a point where he endows God with corporeality falling into one of the traps that undermine religious faith; and he will not continue to fear Him, except according to his own conception of Him. But the enlightened person knows God's unity, and that He is devoid of the categories of corporeality, and that these may not be ascribed to Him at all. (*ibid.* 2:1, 2)

3. As to the appropriate time for commencing such study, I saw that this subject lends itself to a three-fold division. Firstly, there is the matter of preparing oneself to be fit to enter this holy domain. It is indeed true that it is not seemly that everyone who reaches out to robe himself in the holy garments in order to serve in the holy place shall come and so robe himself, God forbid. One must first remove from oneself the coverings of crude pride which impede one from grasping the truth, and direct his heart toward heaven so that he shall not stumble, and that he be not included among the sinful group we discussed in part 1, chapter 6.

Secondly, it is important that a person train himself in the method of profound textual analysis [*pilpul*] so that he be accustomed and skillful in detaching from a text the illustrative elaborations and this will enable him to reach the goal in this knowledge.

Thirdly, he shall dedicate himself to full acquisition of the laws of the Gemara, and the explanation of the commandments according to their simple meaning, as explained by Maimonides in the *Yad* [*Mishneh Torah*].

Fourthly, he should also accustom himself to study Bible, whether much or little, so that he be perfected with sound knowledge, with Bible and Mishnah, and he stumble not, and that he be not one of the group lost in error which we explained in chapter 6 [of part 1].

After this, a person is to cleanse his mind of the follies and pleasures of the times, to the extent possible nowadays, and then will the gates of wisdom open to him. And let not a person reading this assume that he is being offered advice, and he can reject our advice. Our words are well founded on the sound foundation of the teachings of our sages in many places.

Secondly, there is no doubt that a person will be unfit to pursue this knowledge unless, at the proper time, he marries, and cleanses his thoughts. Do not challenge me, because many did pursue this knowledge prior to this, for opinions are not all alike.

It is also necessary that a person reach at least his twentieth year, which brings him to the minimum of half the time fixed for the age of discernment [set at forty in Avot 5:24]. It is true that some desisted until they reached their fortieth year, but we do not agree with this, for many followed our view and they were successful. Despite this, everything should be dependent on the person's purity of heart, as we explained, and the *Zohar* alluded to this often, as in the case where a child expounded the mysteries of the Torah (*Zohar* II 29a).

Thirdly, as to the right time for engaging in this study, certainly it is easy to study any time in the day, but the time that is most conducive to understand matters in depth is during the long nights, after midnight; or on the Sabbath, for the Sabbath itself lends predisposition to it; and similarly on the eve of the Sabbath, commencing after midnight; and on the festivals, especially *Shavuot* [the festival of the giving of the Torah], for I tried it many times and found this a time of wondrous propitiousness; and on the days of *Sukkot* [Tabernacles], in the *Sukkah*, for there it is most conducive. The times here mentioned were tested by me, and I speak from experience.

As to the method of study: it is necessary that the student combine in himself fear and joy, as it is written (Ps. 2:11): "Serve the Lord with fear, rejoice with trembling." These two attributes should be joined by humility. These three attributes are needed for the following reasons: fear is needed lest one fall into error and thus commit sin, and also because one ventures into a perilous zone; joy is needed because study requires a clear mind, and, moreover, the study of Torah certainly depends on joy. But humility is the most important. It is for a person to say: What am I, what is my life, that I should study the mysteries of the divine Torah, as though it were an adornment to my garment, subjects that the Holy One, praised be He, concealed from creatures of flesh and blood? Who can speak about the attributes of the King, while the King listens, and not be ashamed? It seems to me that it is also necessary to add to those three, a concern about the sins committed during the vulnerable time of one's youth, and also remorse about the activities which are part of the flux of life, that serve as an obstructing screen. (*ibid.* 3:1, 2)

13.
Isaac Luria

Isaac ben Solomon Luria (1534–1572) is usually referred to as *haAri,* from the initials of the Hebrew words for "the divine Rabbi Isaac" (*haElohi Rav Yiẓḥak*). He was born in Jerusalem, but spent his early years in Egypt, where he began his studies in mysticism, concentrating on the *Zohar,* and the works of the early kabbalists. In 1569 he settled in Safed, then a center of Kabbalah, studying for a time with Moses Cordovero. He became the center of a circle of disciples to whom he imparted his unique system of kabbalistic thought. His saintly, ascetic life, and his seminal ideas, made him a legendary figure among his contemporaries, and he was said to have possessed the "holy spirit" and to have been vouchsafed the "revelation of Elijah."

Despite the fact that he died at the age of 38, he emerged as one of the most influential figures in the history of the Kabbalah. His grave has remained a place of pilgrimage to this day.

Apart from a number of mystical poems in idealization of the Sabbath, which bear his name in acrostic, Luria's only literary legacy is a commentary on the first few pages of the *Zohar.* It would seem that the profusion of his ideas did not lend itself to ready systematization, but his disciples sought to record from memory the substance of what he taught them. They sometimes differed in their renditions of what their master really believed but the work of Ḥayyim Vital is generally regarded as the most reliable. In fact, Vital sought to establish himself as the only authoritative source of Luria's views, but others continued to dispute him.

Luria's theory of creation through *ẓimẓum* is expounded in Vital's *Eẓ Ḥayyim.* It is often expressed in graphic language, bordering on the mythological. Thus he speaks of the "contraction" of the *En Sof* as though it were an actual physical process involving actual physical space and he uses geometric configurations in discussing the light. He is quoted as having cautioned that this was purely metaphoric: "Know that for the sake of comprehension we have been permitted to draw on analogies from the physical organisms. . . but you, enlightened one, cleanse your thinking to realize that in the supernal realm there is nothing physical, God forbid" (Vital, *Sha'arei Kedushah* 3, end).

A miscellany of Luria's personal traits, ritualistic practices and mystical beliefs was prepared by another of his disciples, Jacob Ẓemaḥ, under the title of *Nagid uMeẓaveh.* An adaptation of this work is found in the *Shulḥan Arukh shel haAri.*

THE CONTRACTION OF GOD

Know that before the emanations were emanated and the creatures created, the simple supernal light [of the *En Sof*] filled all there was [strictly speaking there was nothing, since this was before creation] and there was no empty area whatever, that is, an empty atmosphere and a vacuum. All was filled with that simple infinite light. It had no beginning and no end. All was simple light in total sameness. This is called the endless light.

When in His simple will it was resolved to create worlds and emanate the emanations, to bring to objective existence the perfection of His deeds, and His names and His appelations [which allude to His acts, like the thirteen attributes of His mercy], which was the reason for the creation of the worlds, then He contracted Himself within the middle point in Himself, in the very center. And He contracted that light, and it was withdrawn to the sides around the middle point. Then there was left an empty space, an atmosphere, and a vacuum extending from the precise point of the center.

This contraction was equally distributed around that middle empty point so that the vacuum was circular on all sides equally. It was not in the shape of a square with fixed angles because the *En Sof* also contracted Himself in a circular fashion in equal proportions on all sides. The reason for this was because the light of the *En Sof* is equally pervasive, and it was therefore necessary that it contract itself in equal measure on all sides. It is a well-known principle in the science of mathematics that no figure is as balanced as a circle, unlike the figure of a square with its protruding angles. This is also characteristic of a triangle, and other figures. Therefore, the contraction had to be in the form of a circle. . .

There was another reason for this. It was for the sake of the emanations that were due to be emanated thereafter in that vacuum, as mentioned earlier. By being in the form of circles, the emanations could all be equally close and attached to the *En Sof*; they could all receive in equal measure the light and the influences they needed from the *En Sof*. This would not be the case if the emanations were in the form of squares or triangles, or in other forms. . .

The purpose of this contraction was to bring to light the source of judgment, in order to make it possible thereafter for the attribute of judgment to act in the worlds. . .

After this contraction mentioned above, when there was left a vacuum, an empty atmosphere through the meditation of the light of the *En Sof*, blessed be He, there was now available an area in which there could be the emanations, the beings created, formed and made. (*Eẓ haḤayyim* 1)

WAYS OF PRAYER

1. It is wrong for a person to pray in a state of depression, but one is rather to pray in the manner of a servant who serves his master in joy. Otherwise the soul will be unable to receive the higher illumination through his prayer. Only when reciting the confessional of sin or when recalling his own sins is this permitted, but not when reciting the other prayers. Submissiveness is in order but it is to be expressed with great joy. (Jacob Ẓemaḥ, *Shulḥan Arukh shel R. Yiẓḥak Luria, Hilkhot Bet haKeneset*)

2. My teacher used to say that it is desirable for a person to consider himself the dwelling place and seat of the divine emanations, for man is made in the divine image. This is especially important during prayer, and

through this will his prayer rise and be accepted. The higher holiness will abide in him and thereby he will be able to unify worlds. (*ibid.*)

3. Know that there is no prayer which does not effect a complete renewal of the mind, for there is no prayer that does not engender a renewal of light and of divine influences. My teacher, may his memory be for a blessing, used to say that there is a great difference between the prayers recited on weekdays and those recited on the Sabbath, the festivals, *Rosh Ḥodesh* and *Ḥol haMoed.* Not only this, but even among the festivals themselves there is a difference between the effect of the prayers recited on *Pesaḥ* and those recited on *Sukkot* . . . Since the creation of the world there has not been a service that was in any sense identical with another service. (*ibid., Kavanat haTefillah*)

4. My teacher never raised his voice when reciting his prayers, not even the part of the service which is well established, like the psalm of praise, to show submissiveness before God, may His name be praised. Only on the Sabbath did he raise his voice slightly, in honor of the Sabbath. (*ibid.*)

5. My teacher used to recite the prayers from the prayer book and not orally. All parts quoted from the Bible he used to recite with the proper cantellation, and all parts quoted from the *Mishnah* he used to recite with a melody. (*ibid.*)

MORALITY

1. Before entering the synagogue a person is to take on himself the positive commandment of loving his neighbor. Then he is to enter. He is to direct his heart to love everyone among the people of Israel as himself. Thereby will his prayer ascend comprehending within itself all the people of Israel and it will be able to rise and it will be endowed with potency. Especially important is the love in our circle of colleagues. Each one must see himself as an integral part of the group. Our teacher, his memory be for a blessing, admonished us much concerning this. And if any one colleague should suffer affliction, or illness should befall any in his family, or among his children, he should associate himself with him in his grief and offer prayer on his behalf. He should similarly identify with him in all he does; and he should endeavor to include all his associates with him in this identification.

2. It was the practice of my teacher to recite in his prayer all the particularizations of sin as found in the confessional even though they did not apply to him. He maintained that each person, even when he was

not guilty of them, must confess them, especially since these prayers were couched in plural form. This is indeed how they should be recited —in the plural rather than the singular form: "We sinned," not, "I sinned." The reason for this is that the entire people of Israel is one individual organism. This is the secret of the mutual responsibility of all souls. (*Shulḥan Arukh, Hilkhot Bet haKeneset*)

3. I noted that my teacher was not particular about the clothes he wore. He used to eat little. Expenditures to meet his wife's needs he extended to her according to her wishes. He used to give charity with a glad heart and an open hand. At times he did not consider whether he was left with any funds for himself or not. My teacher also used to say that each *mitzvah* has its own letter among the twenty-two letters of the alphabet and when a person performs a *mitzvah* that letter shines on his forehead. . . and then it is absorbed within. But if he performed the *mitzvah* of charity, the letter pertaining to it does not recede quickly like the letters of other precepts, but remains on his forehead all week long, illustrating the secret meaning of the verse (Ps. 111:3): "And his righteousness [*ẓidkato*] endures always" [he takes *ẓidkato* in its meaning of charity and applies the verse to man rather than to God]. On purchasing objects pertaining to the performance of a *mitzvah*, like a *lulav* and *etrog* [for Sukkot], I saw that he gave the sellers whatever they asked of him. At times he placed the money before them and asked them to take whatever they wanted. (*ibid., Be'inyan haNadvut vehaVatranut*)

THE SECRETS OF THE TORAH

1. My teacher's comprehension of this knowledge proceeded along the following course: At first he studied the *Zohar*, and sometimes a week went by as he sought to grasp what he studied. He studied one subject many times in order to understand it in depth. He did this on many occasions. At times it was told to him that he still had not grasped that subject in its essence, and he continued to labor on this subject. Sometimes he was told the explanation of the subject, according to the interpretation of Rabbi Simeon bar Yoḥai [to whom the *Zohar* is attributed]. Sometimes he was told that this is how Rabbi Simeon bar Yoḥai understood the subject, but that he still needed to go more deeply into it. Then did the prophet Elijah reveal himself to him, and then he understood everything, the great and the small, of all kinds of knowledge. . .(*Shulḥan Arukh, Keri'ah beḤokhmat haKabbalah*)

2. My teacher used to expound matters of law, according to their literal meaning, each of the six days of the week. But then he used to expound secret meanings in honor of the Sabbath. (*ibid; Kavanat Talmud Torah*)

3. The study of the Torah must have its primary motivation to attach the soul to its source through the Torah, in order to complete the supernal tree [the order of *sefirot*] and to complete and perfect the supernal man. This is the reason for the creation of man and the goal of his Torah study. (*Nagid uMeẓaveh* 25a)

REINCARNATION AND IBBUR

1. "Thus shall you do with every lost object of your brother" (Deut. 22:3). Know that a person may at times be perfected through *ibbur* [a temporary joining the body of another person] and at times he may require *gilgul* [reincarnation], which is much more painful. The penalty for anyone who finds a lost object and does not return it is that he cannot find justification through *ibbur* after his death, but he must return it in a form of *gilgul*. And this is the meaning of the concluding section of the verse cited above: "You may not hide yourself." This refers to *ibbur* by itself, which involves being concealed in his neighbor's soul. He will require *gilgul* which is much more painful than *ibbur*. (*Shulḥun Arukh, Be'inyan Hashavat Avedah*)

2. If a person has not perfected himself by fulfilling all the 613 commandments in action, speech and thought, he will of necessity be subject to *gilgul* . . . Also whoever has not studied the Torah according to the four levels indicated by *p r d s*, which is a composite of the initial letters from the four words, *peshat*, the literal, *remez*, the allegorical, *derash*, the homiletical, and *sod*, the mystical, will have his soul returned for reincarnation, so that he might fulfill each of them. (*ibid., Keri'ah beḤokhmat haKabbalah*)

14. Ḥayyim Vital

Ḥayyim ben Joseph Vital (1542–1620) was a leading disciple of Isaac Luria and the principal popularizer of Lurianic mysticism. In 1575 ten of Luria's disciples entered a covenant in which they committed themselves to study Luria's theories only from Vital, and not to press Vital to reveal to them more of the kabbalistic secrets that he deemed proper and to refrain from disclosing those secrets to others. But there were, in fact, other Lurianic disciples who proceeded on their own to expound their master's teachings. Vital served as rabbi and head of a yeshivah in Jerusalem between 1577 and 1585, and later he served as rabbi in Damascus.

His most important work in exposition of Luria's thoughts is his *Eẓ Ḥayyim* (Tree of Life), which remains our chief source for the basics of the Lurianic system of Kabbalah. He also wrote a number of independent works, including the *Sha'arei Kedushah* (Gates of Holiness), which discusses the mystery of creation and man's central role in it.

Man's soul is engendered by the *sefirot,* without an intermediary, while his good impulse derives from the realm of the angels. The soul and the *sefirot* together constitute the person's true essence and they incline him to the good. His body and the evil impulse derive from the realm of the *kelipot,* and they incline him to evil. When man heeds the call of the good he releases potencies that are efficacious in the heavenly realm; he unifies the world of finitude with the world of the *En Sof.* By cultivating the disciplines of holiness, which Vital defines in strongly ascetic terms, man can attain to various forms of divine illumination.

Vital believed that, through practical Kabbalah, it was possible to "force" the supernal world to respond to human manipulation, but he cautioned against it, preferring the natural response which these would offer to the potency exerted by a life of holiness.

THE COVENANT

We whose signature appears below have covenanted to act as one fellowship: to serve the Lord, whose name be blessed, to pursue the study of His Torah day and night, according to all that our divine teacher, the perfect master and sage Rabbi Ḥayyim Vital, will instruct us, and we shall study with him the true wisdom. We shall be faithful and keep under concealment all that he will say to us, and we shall not press him unduly to reveal to us what he does not wish to reveal to us; and we shall not disclose to any outsider any secret we shall hear from him in the path of truth, nor of what he taught us in the past, and not even anything he taught us in the lifetime of our master, the great Rabbi Isaac Luria Ashkenazi. We shall even be constrained from disclosing without his authorization anything we heard from the aforementioned sage [Luria] directly, since we were enabled to understand those matters only through him, for he restored them to us. This commitment is made under a firm oath before God by the authority of our aforementioned teacher Rabbi Ḥayyim. It is to be in force from this day for a period of ten years.

Dated Monday, the 25th of the month of Av 5335 from the time of creation [1575] in the city of Safed. (Cited in *Zion,* 5th year Vol. 2, Jer. 1940, pp. 125f)

THE BEHAVIOR OF THE PIOUS

This section is devoted to a clarification of the standard of behavior of the *ḥasid* [pious person], in brief terms, so that a person may constantly have them in his mind. These are the choicest of the principles concerning which we are commanded, and they call for much vigilance. They are also of greater primacy than all the others, as I have made clear in the statements culled from the pearls of the teachings by our sages in the Talmud, the Midrash, in the tractate *Derekh Ereẓ*, the *Pirkei de R. Eliezer* and the *Zohar*. . .

The worst character traits which impede a person's cleaving to God are the following: pride, anger, impatience, a sorrowful disposition, hatred, envy, lust after bodily pleasures, the desire to dominate, the seeking after honor, the showing off of his good deeds before people. The opposite of these is humility in its extreme form.

One should shun anger altogether even at the members of his household, and he is not to show impatience in any degree. He is to be joyful even in times of affliction and he is to love all people including non-Jews. He is not to be envious of anything, for our days on earth are like a shadow that passes away. He is to hate and dismiss as trivial all worldly concerns, and is to find contentment in eating bread and salt. He is not to covet any of the vanities of this world, and run with all his strength from lording over others, which buries those addicted to it. Do not publicize your good deeds for you will thereby lose your reward for them and your share in the world to come and you will even be punished in *gehenna*.

Among the forbidden traits are these: speaking ill of another person, gossip, embarrassing another person, calling him by a derogatory epithet, mocking, dishonesty, flattery, deception, idle talk, slander, self-praise by tearing down others, sowing discord among brothers, exploiting the Torah for ulterior motives, and lewdness (*Sha'arei Kedushah* 2:5).

ON THE ATTRIBUTES OF MAN

The greatness of the soul has also been explained. It is a light engendered and drawn from the ten *sefirot* themselves, without an intermediary, and hence the designation (Deut. 14:1): You are children of the living God; they are in the category of the child who has an absolute link with, and derives from, his parent. This is the secret meaning of the statement in the Midrash (*Bereshit Rabbah* 47:8): The patriarchs are the chariot—it refers to the light of the ten *sefirot*, that rides on them without any intermediary. This, too, is the secret meaning of the verse (Isa. 49:3):

"Israel in whom I am glorified," for a person's garment is what adorns him, as it is written (Isa. 61:10): "He has covered me with the robe of victory, as the bridegroom bedecks himself with a garland and a bride adorns herself with her jewels." For the light of souls is a garment for the light of the ten *sefirot.* This, too, is the secret meaning of verse (Song of Songs 6:2): "My beloved went into his garden"—which alludes to this world—"to feed among the plantings and to gather flowers"; the initial letters of each word in the latter clause together spell *levush,* which means garment. He gathers the souls of the righteous who, by their good deeds in this world, are as fragrant as flowers; He gathers them to robe His light in them. This, too, is the secret meaning of the verse (Deut. 4:4): "And you who cleave to the Lord . . ."—it means a total cleaving with the light of the ten *sefirot.* It is otherwise with the other creatures. This is alluded to in the verse (Jer. 13:1): "As the girdle cleaves to the loins of a man so have I caused the whole house of Israel to cleave to Me."

The nature of the good impulse and the evil impulse in man has been clarified. They are two separate creations appended to man, in addition to his soul. They comprise a light from the light of the angels, which is called "the good creation," and a light from the light of the *kelipot,* called "the evil creation." The latter is external to the good impulse and serves as a shell (*kelipah*) around it. But the human soul itself is the most inward of all, and because it is inward it is also called "the essence" of the person, and for this reason does the person have the freedom to incline in any direction he desires, for he is greater than they. His basic inclination is toward the good impulse, for he is holy as it is and he is closer to it. But as for the body, its primary inclination is toward the evil impulse, for both derive from the evil side and they are also close to each other. This is why there is a conflict between man's material self and the soul, because, inasmuch as the soul performs the commandment only through the body, which is more inclined toward the evil impulse, it is very difficult to overcome it. It has thus been made clear that the soul has the freedom to incline toward the good impulse, but because of its dependence on bodily action, there is great difficulty in overcoming the evil impulse. Understand this well, so as to clarify why, after death, neither the soul nor the body by themselves are subject to punishment, until they are merged together, as in life.

We shall now try to answer the two previous questions: why was it necessary that man be created with a body, and an answer will also be given as to why the good and the evil impulse were created in him. We shall also account for the verses: "Give strength to God" (Ps. 68:35) and: "You have weakened the Rock who begot you" (Deut. 32:18).

At the inception of creation, all the worlds were created according to the order indicated previously, through the potency of the *En Sof*, by a simple act of will, as an expression of generosity and lovingkindness. Thereafter it was necessary to draw sustenance and vitality and abundance to all the worlds, to establish them firmly as at the time of creation, and no more. This is alluded to in the verse (Kohelet 3:14): "I have known that whatever God has made will endure always"; one cannot add or subtract from it, and as it is also written (*ibid.* 1:9): "There is nothing new under the sun," and (Gen. 2:2): "God completed on the seventh day all the work which He had made." All these refer to creation itself. But the continuity of their existence thereafter is dependent on their own action to sustain them. This is analogous to the case of a child who, when he grows up, no longer eats at the parents' table. However, the ten *sefirot* are not in need of any action, for the abundance they need to sustain them after their emanation flows toward them continually from the *En Sof*, for concerning the ten *sefirot* it is written (Ps. 5:5): "Evil cannot abide with You," and they are not dependent on any action to perfect them. But it is otherwise among creatures, in the category of souls and below, which are a mixture of good and evil; they are in need of action to perfect them. From another point of view, however, when there is diminuation of influences flowing toward creatures it appears as though, God forbid, there is a weakness in the ten *sefirot* that are not radiating influences toward them. Therefore does the verse state (Deut. 32:18): "You have weakened the Rock who begot you" [the usual rendering is, You were unmindful, but the Hebrew *teshi* means literally, "weakened," which is here applied to the *sefirot*]. The call for the opposite is expressed in the verse (Ps. 68:35): "Endow strength to God" [the usual rendering is, "Ascribe strength to God," but the Hebrew *t'nu* means literally, "give," and this verse is also applied to the *sefirot*]. Moreover, man himself, when healthy and clean, wants his garments to be distinguished, commensurate with his dignity. Therefore, the *sefirot* themselves seem as though weak in themselves, when the creatures are not perfected. This is implied in the verse cited above, Give strength to God, and in the verse (Isa. 49:3): "Israel through whom I am glorified."

For the reasons indicated it was necessary to create a man in whom shall be included all creatures and all emanations, who is to link all worlds, as mentioned before, to the very depth of the earth, for he is the closest to receive the influences from the ten *sefirot*. Then by the perfection of his conduct he will transmit the abundance from the ten *sefirot* to himself, and from himself to the angels and thence to the *kelipot* in order that whatever may be sifted out from them shall be perfected, as we shall explain when discussing the evil impulse. Then this influence is to be transmitted to the worlds themselves, "vessels" and bodies of each different world. But if, God forbid, he should sin, he will damage all worlds. Thus we have explained why man was created in this lowly world with body and soul, and with a good impulse and an evil impulse. (*Sha'arei Kedushah* 3:2)

ON ATTAINING DIVINE ILLUMINATION

After we have admonished a person in the previous section concerning the various levels of perception, as mentioned earlier, a person should not despair [about illumination by the holy spirit]. Commenting on the text (Judges 4:4), the *Tanna devei Eliyahu* stated: Let heaven and earth serve as my witness that whether it be man or woman, a Cuthite or an Israelite, male or female slave—the holy spirit rests upon each of them, to the extent that their behavior merits it. We have heard it with our own ears and seen it with our own eyes that certain chosen spirits in our own time attained to the stature of being illuminated by the holy spirit, and they foretold the future. Among them were men who attained levels of wisdom which had not been revealed in earlier generations.

In order not to discourage those who are inspired by the quest to hallow themselves I shall explicate some matters, disclosing a tiny measure [of this esoteric knowledge], and God, who is good, will not deny the good to those who walk with integrity. At first I shall explain certain aspects of perception, and in the next [lit. eighth] section I shall write, with God's help, about the proper behavior in each instance.

The choicest path is the one cited in the name of the *Tanna devei Eliyahu,* and it is the path followed by the saintly pietists of ancient times. It calls for a person to repent with great earnestness of all wrongs he has committed. Then he is to perfect his life by performing positive commandments and by directing his prayer toward their highest purpose, and by zealously pursuing the study of Torah, for its own sake, as an ox bows its head to the yoke, until his strength is sapped; and by confining himself to few pleasures, and little eating and drinking; and by rising at midnight or a little earlier, and by turning away from all unbecoming traits, and withdrawing from people, even from idle conversation. Then he is to cleanse his body by continuous immersion [in water]. He is to isolate himself for periods of time and contemplate the fear of God, putting the divine name YHWH before his eyes always, while making sure to empty his thoughts from the follies of this world;

and he is to be attached to God's love with great yearning. As a result of all these it is possible that he will merit to attain illumination by the holy spirit in one of the following ways:

One is, that he will draw on himself a supernal light from the source whence his supernal soul derives, as mentioned in the fifth section, and it will be revealed to him; and this is the full measure of the holy spirit.

The second is that by pursuing the study of the Torah or keeping a commandment, it will result in the creation of a real angel, as our sages said (Avot 4:13): Whoever performs one commandment acquires for himself one protagonist. But this is contingent on his performing it at all times, and with great devotion, in proper form; and then will that angel be revealed to him. In some holy books these angels are called *maggidim* [parton angels or sacred souls who communicate special teachings and guidance to worthy individuals]. But if he should not perform the commandment properly, that *maggid* will represent a fusion of good and evil, truth and falsehood.

The third is that as a result of pietistic practices, as mentioned earlier, the prophet Elijah will reveal himself to him, and the extent of the revelation will be in accordance with the level of his piety.

The fourth is the greatest of all and this is that he will be deemed worthy for the soul of some earlier righteous person to be revealed to him, whether it be of those that derived from the same supernal source as his or of another, because he performed some commandment in a perfect way as did that righteous person. Those who attain to this state will be revealed wondrous secrets of wisdom in the Torah; all this will be commensurate with their actions.

The fifth, and this is the lowest of all, is that he will see in his dreams events of the future and revelations of wisdom, close to the holy spirit.

The way here outlined is the right way, since by not applying oaths or pressuring the supernal powers, and depending only on the potency of his good deeds and his holiness, it is certain that the holy spirit in its purity will rest on him, without any evil admixture. It is otherwise when a person "forces" or utilizes the ways of "oaths" or invokes the coercive potency of special actions or prayers or "unifications" [special meditations on sacred names of God that were believed to have magical efficacy]. In such cases, if he should commit any error at all, it is possible that what will be disclosed to him will be mingled with the words of negative powers. (*Sha'arei Kedushah* 3:7)

15.

Judah Loew of Prague

Rabbi Judah Loew ben Bezalel of Prague (1512–1609), known as "Maharal miPrag," was one of the most colorful figures in the history of Jewish thought. He led an eventful career as a rabbi in Nikolsburg, in the province of Moravia (1553–1573), and in Posen, which seems also to have been his birthplace (1584–1588 and 1592–1597). His heart was drawn to Prague, which was a major center of Jewish culture and the home of his wife's family, but on two occasions the leaders of the Prague Jewish community rejected his candidacy for the office of the city's chief rabbi, in 1583 and again in 1592.

Rabbi Judah lived in Prague from 1573 to 1584 and again from 1588 to 1592 as a private citizen, doing his work in an unofficial capacity. Of independent means, he established his own academy where he taught many students his unique approach to rabbinic scholarship and his unique philosophy of Judaism. It was Rabbi Judah's outspokenness and innovative approach in many areas of religious thought which turned the leaders of Prague Jewry against him. But in 1598, seeking to mollify him in the twilight of his life, they elected him chief rabbi of Prague when the incumbent resigned.

Rabbi Judah's originality as a writer and thinker won him friends and admirers in the most sophisticated circles in the Jewish as well as the general community and many turned to him for guidance. He debated with learned Christian priests, and with apostate Jews who sought to demonstrate their loyalty to the new faith by slandering the old. In February 1592 he was received in audience by the emperor Rudolph II.

Popular folklore ascribed to Rabbi Judah the making of the *golem,* a robot animated by the ineffable name of God, and charged with various missions to protect the Jews against their would-be persecutors. This is, of course, legend; Rabbi Judah's writings are free of interest in the occult, but such legends indicate that he had become a beloved and highly revered folk hero.

Rabbi Judah's writings include *Gur Aryeh,* a study of Rashi's commentary on the Bible; *Derekh haḤayyim,* a commentary on *Avot* (the Ethics of the Fathers); *Tiferet Yisrael,* a philosophical study of biblical law; *Neẓaḥ Yisrael,* a study of the messianic hope in Judaism; *Be'er haGolah,* a defense of the Talmud against calumnies circulating in Christian circles; *Or Ḥadash,* a commentary on the book of Esther; *Ḥiddushei Gur Aryeh,* a commentary on several tractates of the Talmud; *Netivot Olam,* a popular exposition of piety and morals; and several sermons which he preached on various occasions.

His writings reveal a mastery of classic Jewish knowledge in rabbinics, philosophy, and Kabbalah, but he also showed extensive familiarity with current secular knowledge. The thrust of his writings was a call to cultivate inwardness in the religious life, to forge out of knowledge and ritual practice a ladder by which to ascend to God. In the exposition of these ideas he often referred to the teachings of the Kabbalah, but he had the art of transcending the esoteric linguistic symbols of the kabbalists, and distill from them lucid ideational content, charged with a noble spiritual sensibility. It is this which made him a figure of transition from the esotericism of the Kabbalah to the simple, popular mysticism one finds in Ḥasidism.

ON THE NATURE OF MAN

1. Man is endowed with a divine soul which distinguished him from creatures below him, but he must not deceive himself that he actually possesses this distinction, and say to himself, Even if I remain passive, without exerting myself, my intrinsic excellence and status will shield me and keep me in high station. Such thought is an abomination . . . for his

highest perfection is not in a state of realization . . . The differences between man and higher beings is that the higher beings are in a state of perfection and they do not need to bring their potentialities to self-realization, and the difference between man and lower creatures is that the lower creatures are not involved in the realization of potentialities, for whatever they were created with is beyond modification and in no need of self-realization. But man is in a state of potentiality and he is in transition toward self-realization . . . And he will never reach a state of full perfection but he must always toil to reach perfection and this is his highest excellence . . . For no matter what he will bring to realization, there will yet remain in him a measure of potentiality to be realized. (*Tiferet Yisrael* ch. 3)

2. Man is in a state of potentiality, and he was created for self-realization through the study of Torah and the performance of the commandments. It is for this reason that he is called *adam*, alluding to the name *adamah*, which means *land* . . . He is like the land which has been seeded with grain, a clean seed, and the land will bring the seed to fruition, until it will be an actual fruit. Similarly, the human body, which was created from the earth, has been seeded with the soul, which is pure and clean and free of base ingredients. Man is under a commitment to bring to fruition that with which he has been seeded; for this reason he bears the name *adam*. The Torah acquired and the good deeds performed are the fruit, as the verse suggests (Isa. 3:10): "Say of the righteous that it shall be well with them; they will eat the fruit of their labors." But one who does not activate his soul is called in Hebrew *bur*, a barren one, like a barren field . . . (*Netivot Olam, Torah*, 15)

3. All creatures were created because of the good inherent in them, and if the beings in existence did not have some good inherent in them they would not have been created. For whatever is not good in essence is unworthy of existence. And as has already been made clear, you must realize that all creatures depend on man, for they were created for man's sake. If man does not live up to *his purpose*, then all becomes void . . . Therefore man must achieve the good, which is his end, thereby justifying his existence, and when his existence has been justified, the whole universe has been justified, since all hinges on man. . . Therefore must a person cultivate good qualities. And what makes a person good so that one may say of him, "What a fine creature he is!" One requirement is that he must be good in relation to himself . . . The second category is that he must be good toward the Lord who created man, to serve Him and to do His will. The third category is that he must be good to others. For a person does not exist by himself, he exists in

fellowship with other people . . . And when a person acts with kindness toward other people there is a bond between him and his fellowman and thus is the person as God intended him to be. (*Derekh haḤayyim* on Avot 1:2)

4. One may also say that the meaning of the dictum: Be not evil to yourself [Avot 2:18, usually interpreted to mean, Do not regard yourself as evil in your own estimation], is that one must not commit acts of evil against oneself, that is, to afflict his body to a point of injuring himself. As we call a person pious who bestows good to himself, as it is written: "The pious man does good to himself" [Prov. 11:17, but the text is *ish ḥesed,* literally, a merciful man; Rabbi Loew reads it as though written *ish ḥasid,* which means "a pious man"], so we call a person who does harm to himself "a wicked man." Even in the case of fasting we say that one may not subject himself to pain and whoever does this is called a sinner. (*ibid.* Avot 2:19)

5. It is in order for a person to reject the pursuits of this world, that is those pursuits which are without merit . . . But the desirable pursuits of this world, though they are of a physical nature are desirable in the eyes of God and they lead a person to eternal life. (*ibid.* Avot 3:15)

6. Although it is improper for a person to be avid in pursuing wealth, it is in order that he make provision not to be dependent on people, because this is a defect in a person. A person's excellence is to be self-sufficient, and not to be in a state of want, for whoever is in want is not a complete person. He is surely an incomplete person when he is dependent on other people. It is for this reason that our sages said: Be a stripper of the carcasses of dead animals in the street, but do not be dependent on people (Pesaḥim 113a). Certainly it is embarrassing when one strips the carcasses of dead animals in the presence of people in the street. But to be dependent on others is a defect in the very being of the person. (*Netivot Olam, Asher* 2)

7. The Mishnah has criticized the reprehensible person who puts all his thoughts and aims upon this physical world. But Rabbi Eleazar (in Avot, ch. 3) criticized men who represent the opposite. They believe they must turn to reason exclusively and they deprecate everything which has any aspect of the physical. They desecrate the altar offerings in the Temple because they say God does not eat or drink and, therefore, there is no sense offering such things as sacrifices to Him . . . They despise the festivals because they say the holidays offer physical pleasure for man, in eating and drinking, and they claim that one does not achieve divine ends in this manner. They dissolve the covenant of Abraham [the rite of circumcision] and say it is despicable to think that God would make a

covenant with this organ which is a source of shame and dishonor . . . And they likewise disparage their fellowman by saying that man is a material creature and he is not of much worth. They also read improper interpretations into the Torah, treating irreverently the commandments which apply to bodily life, all because they pursue the intellectual and renounce the physical. These men for whom the physical world is of no value and physical deeds, even when they are good deeds are of no significance, who say that man's only interest should be the quest for enlightenment . . . will have no share in the world to come. (*Derekh haḤayyim* on Avot 3:15)

8. Said R. Joḥanan ben Rabbi Simeon bar Yoḥai: A haughty person is as offensive as though he served idols; and R. Joḥanan, in his own name, said: It is as though he denied the essence of our faith. (Sotah 4b)

You must realize that the proud of heart withdraw themselves from the authority of a higher sovereignty. One is only under the authority of the Holy One, praised be He, when one humbles himself. When he acknowledges his dependence he is under the authority of the Holy One, but when he is proud, it is as though he secedes from God's authority . . . and thus he said that such a person is as though he served idols. R. Joḥanan in his own name said that it is as though he denied the essence of our faith, for if man no longer acknowledges his dependence, there is no longer any center of sovereignty, and therefore it is as though he denied the essence of our faith. (*Perushei Maharal miPrag, Ginzei Rishonim*, Jerusalem 1958, I, on *Sotah* 46)

9. R. Yose said: Great is the rite of circumcision, for it supersedes the important commandment prescribing cessation of work on the Sabbath. R. Joshua ben Korha said: Great is the rite of circumcision for Moses was not granted one hour grace when he had neglected to circumcise his son (Ex. 4:24).

This is simple, for circumcision takes place on the eighth day, which is after the number seven, indicating the total transcendence of nature. Seven days correspond to the seven days of creation, and circumcision takes us beyond nature, and it is for this reason on the eighth day and it supersedes the Sabbath. Circumcision is a higher category than the Sabbath, for the Sabbath remains linked with the weekdays, but circumcision, which comes after seven, has no link with the weekdays. Similarly, the statement that Moses was not given one hour's grace when he neglected to circumcise his son follows from the same principle that circumcision is above time. Time is a category of life in our world, which is differentiated into the seven days of creation, as the text speaks of one day, the second day, until the completion of seven days, while circumcision is on the eighth day which is above time . . . Moreover, as we have already explained it, circumcision symbolizes the ideal *form* of man [in the Platonic sense, as opposed to matter] . . . and the ideal form is not subject to the relativities of time. (*ibid.*, on Nedarim 31b)

10. A sick person does not return to good health without being absolved of all his transgressions:

The explanation of this statement is that when one is restored to health it is as though he is created anew, and since he is returned to his original state he is absolved of his sins, for in his original state he was without sin. I cite as an analogy the tree that suffered injury in the winter so that it lost its foliage and the tree itself became damaged, but when it is restored from its illness in spring, then it once more draws strength from its roots and is renewed as it was originally. Similarly a sick person who was changed because of illness does not return to good health except by the potency of his higher state of being, a renewal of his original self, and thus his sins are purged away. . .

When a sick person returns to that state which restores him from damage to his body and the deterioration of his nature, he is by virtue of that new state of being also restored from spiritual damage. (*ibid.* p. 8, on Nedarim 41a)

11. A person in whom God created the *yeẓer hara* [the evil impulse] must endeavor to free himself from this passion. And even if one is righteous and pious he must not think to himself that this is an easy task. It is most difficult. This calls for a person to pray to God, praised be He, to free him from this passion, but by himself it is difficult to accomplish it . . . A prisoner cannot liberate himself from his imprisonment. He needs someone else to release him, that is God, praised be He, who will release him from his imprisonment . . . Though a person is opposed to *satan*, that is, the evil impulse, this opposition in itself will not enable him to prevail, without divine help. (*Netivot Olam, Koaḥ haYeẓer* 4)

STUDY AND PRAYER

1. The early generations set boundaries and specified times for educating a child according to his capacities: at five they introduced him to study Bible, at ten Mishnah, at fifteen Talmud. This was done to assign a child a task he will be able to cope with according to his nature, and whatever conforms to the child's nature he can accept . . . But the fools in these countries do the opposite of this. They teach the child a little of the weekly portion of the Bible and stop, the following week they

teach him a little of the second weekly portion, and when the year is ended he has forgotten his first lessons, and then the cycle is repeated the following year, and because his mind is more developed he teaches him more than what he did the previous year, and so he continues the third and fourth year, and so on. When he leaves off the study of Bible he retains nothing; he is as bare when he finishes as he was when he began.

There is another piece of folly in that they teach the Bible with the Rashi commentary. This practice developed with teachers in villages where books were lacking and they introduced this to take up the child's time, without serving the child any useful purpose.

Some introduce the child at once to the study of *Gemara*. The child mouths words without understanding the simple meaning of the subject . . . When the child grows up they assign him to the study of *Tosafot*, thinking foolishly that the study of *Gemara* and of *halakhah* will aid him. These people are stricken with blindness. It is only that the child's mind develops automatically, it is inconceivable that study not suitable for him and which was not adapted to his intellectual capacities should aid in his development.

There is no doubt that if he were left without any Torah education and began his studies later on he would accomplish in short time what he reached in his studies since their inception. Indeed, would that he mastered the text itself, and not reach out for the study of the supplementary *Tosafot*.

Moreover, the child will seek to climb the ladder to engage in useless pursuits, to spend his energies and waste his days and years by engaging in the vanities of *pilpul* [casuistry], to offer interpretations which do not accord with truth . . . Any person sensitive to the honor of God and concerned with the true study of the Torah must be grieved by this condition. It has reached a point that, because of our own failings, these conditions have left us without Torah, without wisdom and without the fear of God. (*Gur Aryeh, Va'etḥanan*)

2. One must not say that though Torah is eternal and the person who pursues it finds therein eternal life, it is nevertheless subject to change in some respects. The sages therefore said (Ḥagigah 3b) that the Torah is not "mobile," but that it stands fixed in one place. One must not infer from this, however, that there is no room for any diversity in the Torah, and that the teachings of the Torah do not permit of growth, but that they remain static. It is for this that the sages also added that the words of the Torah grow and increase, because the Torah is stirred by blessing. The text then adds that the Torah is under the authority of the assemblage of sages. This means that the opinions of the sages cannot be

uniform, and it is impossible for them not to have disagreement, as they are each endowed with a distinctive intelligence. There is more than one aspect in all things. Whatever we pronounce impure has an aspect that would tend to make it pure, and similarly what we pronounce as pure cannot but have some aspect that would incline it to impurity. People with different minds cannot see things in the same way, as we will make it clear. Therefore each one sees a particular aspect which corresponds to his particular mentality. Thus the text speaks of an assembly of sages, that is, that they sit in assembly and deliberate on the Torah. Though they are endowed with unique minds, they gather together, and in their togetherness are all divergent opinions represented. . .

As far as decisions in law are concerned, there is no doubt that one view may be more basic than another, even as in God's works, though each is a composite, one is not like the other, but may be more primary than the other. But one may not say that the less basic is of no value. It is not so. For one who listens to all views has comprehended the subject in all its diverse aspects. In this spirit one has studied the Torah as it is truly a composite of diverse aspects. (*Be'er haGolah,* p. 13ff.)

3. Even if the words spoken are against one's religion and one's faith, do not tell a person not to speak and to suppress his words. Otherwise there will be no clarification in religious matters. On the contrary, one should tell such a person to say all he wants, and he should not claim that he would have said more, had he been given the opportunity . . . Thus my opinion is contrary to what some people think. They think that religion is strengthened when one is forbidden to speak against religion, but this is not so. The elimination of the opinions of those who are opposed to religion undermines religion and weakens it . . . Through this [the confrontation of opposing views] a person authenticates the truth and reaches the full truth. One must not surrender to such views. Every man of valor who wants to wrestle with another and to show his strength is eager that his opponent shall have every advantage to show his real powers . . . But what strength does he show when he forbids his opponent to defend himself and to fight against him? (*ibid.* p. 151)

4. It is in order to study the wisdom of the nations. Why should one not study this wisdom which derives from God, since the wisdom of the nations also derives from God? It is He who imparted to them of His wisdom . . . It is proper for a person to study whatever sheds light on the nature of the world, and he is obligated to do so. Everything is God's creation, and it is in order to investigate it, so as thereby to understand the Creator . . . Our overall conclusion is that it is proper to study their teaching which will enable a person to answer anyone who raises

questions about their position, as our sages said. And if he should find any positive element in their teaching supportive of our faith, he should accept it. But whatever he may find in their teaching contrary to the Jewish faith, even in the slightest, or to the teachings of the sages, one must not pay attention to them. However, one must consider rationally how to respond to them, according to his intelligence. Thus he will be zealous and vigilant with all his faculties to clarify the truth. (*Netivot Olam, Torah,* 14)

5. Said Rabbi Judah in the name of Rav: What is the meaning of the verse (Jeremiah 9:11, 12): "Who is wise and understands this . . . Why is the land destroyed . . . ?" These questions were put to the sages and to the prophets, but they could not explain it, until the Holy One, praised be He, Himself offered the explanation, as the text continues: And the Lord said, Because they abandoned My Torah which I gave them, and they did not heed My voice, and did not follow it. But is not "they did not heed My voice" the same as "and did not follow it?" Said Rabbi Judah in the name of Rav: This means that they did not pronounce a *berakhah* [benediction] before studying the Torah (Nedarim 81a).

This does not refer to the verbalizing of a *berakhah.* No doubt they pronounced a *berakhah* in words. But the reference here is to the substance of the *berakhah,* which is the genuine love for and cleaving to God, to love Him for having given the Torah . . . The scholar's heart is attached to the Torah itself . . . and his love for the Torah becomes a factor displacing the love for God. For love permits of no duality and if you love one you cannot wholly love the other and therefore does the love for the Torah which is so precious to scholars influence them against offering the *berakhah* to God with fullness of heart . . . And this is what the text means: "And they did not heed My voice." It is a reproof against their attitude to the Torah because truly "they did not follow it" since they did not take the Torah with the due sensitivity as to its divine source. (*Tiferet Yisrael,* introduction)

6. Man, insofar as he is a physical being, is not one with God. Therefore, when he comes before God in prayer, he must shed all his bodily attributes, as though he is wholly spiritual. It is for this reason that Rabbi Simeon stated (Avot 2:18): Do not make your prayer a perfunctory act, that is to have your prayer become burdensome, due to your physical nature. In this light did the *Tur Oraḥ Ḥayyim* (*Hilkhot Tefillah* 98) write that the pietists known for their good deeds would isolate themselves during prayer to a point where they transcended their bodily nature and strengthened their spiritual selves so that they came near the state of prophecy. It is obvious that when a person rises in his

prayer to true devotion to a point where he cleaves to God, he thereby sheds his physical self which separates man from God, praised be He. The sage cautioned us properly that because man is a physical being he must be cautious not to allow his prayer to become perfunctory. (*Derekh haḤayyim* on Avot 2:18)

THE LANGUAGE OF THE TORAH

1. The statement in the verse: "God descended upon Mount Sinai" (Ex. 19:20) and other such statements, are expressions from a human perspective: thus was God, praised be He, experienced by man . . . This is the mighty principle on which are built great matters—that God is experienced relative to the recipient of the experience. We have elaborated on this extensively. And if you say, according to reason we cannot speak of God as descending, consider then that man is not wholly a creature of reason. It is for this reason that descent is ascribed to Him — as man experienced Him. There is no need to elaborate here.

We have also made it clear that the intention of those statements is not to suggest that it only *seemed* to people that He descended. This is not so, but it really was thus. For man He descended, and man formulates characterizations on the basis of his experience. This is a very important principle, and it is appropriate that one bear this secret teaching in mind at all times. And it is for this reason that we have all such expressions like "It grieved Him in His heart" [over the wrongdoing of the generation of the flood, Gen. 6:6], and "He was grieved because of the misery of Israel" (Judges 10:16).

All these characterizations are not true in God as He in Himself. As He is in Himself He is in His same state of perfection. It is only that He was thus experienced by man. When the generation of the flood did not do God's will and then He sought to destroy them He was conceived by man at that time in a state of sadness. And though in His domain there is joy, man conceived of His glory as in a state of sadness.

Similarly it said: "Awake, why do You sleep, O Lord?" (Ps. 44:24). Can sleep be ascribed to the Holy One, praised be He? But when Israel does not do God's will it is as though He sleeps. The characterization of sleep is from man's perspective; thus was God conceived by man . . . The conclusion of the matter is that there is no reason to reject such statements because they imply corporeality. All of it is written from man's point of view. (*Tiferet Yisrael,* 33)

2. Our sages said: A wise man is superior to a prophet (Bava Batra 12a). Thus the sages are the ones who bring the Torah to completion. Though it was given at Sinai through Moses who was a prophet of the Lord, nevertheless, because reason is higher than prophecy, the completion of the Torah is effected through reason which clarifies everything . . . All things were designed to be completed through rational man. The Torah came into the world like all things of nature, which did not come into the world completely clarified. Man with his intelligence is called on to clarify them . . . Accordingly, the sages said that everything must be perfected through man (Bereshit Rabbah 11:6) . . . The Torah which is rational, which was transmitted to Moses through prophecy, did not come altogether with its meaning fully clarified. Through the sages the Torah is clarified and the prophetic revelation is defined and authenticated. (*ibid.* 69)

3. Hell is described as fire because just as fire is a potent force, so is hell—which is the lot of the wicked—potent and formidable, and for this reason it is called fire. Its effect is called smoke because smoke is generated by the potency of fire. There is no doubt that hell—which is the lot of the wicked—extends its sway to this world, for hell reigns in this world also in many respects . . . And these matters are not at all physical, it is all a phenomenon of the mind . . . There is no doubt that hell—which is the severe fate meted out to the wicked—is the negation of existence. This is the meaning of hell: deterioration and destruction for a creature . . . The Torah is the affirmation of existence, hell is total negation. (*ibid.* 18)

16.
Moses Ḥayyim Luzzato

Moses Ḥayyim Luzzato (1707–1747) was another figure in the transition from Kabbalah to Ḥasidism. He was born to a well-to-do and learned family in Padua, Italy. He was given a well-rounded education in rabbinic as well as secular studies, but he was drawn to Kabbalah. A sensitive, mystically inclined disposition sent him to the quest for a more intimate knowledge of God and for more satisfying answers to the mysteries of existence. He even came to feel that he had been endowed with a *maggid,* a celestial spirit, that brought him new spiritual revelations. A considerable group of admirers clustered around him, but the rabbis in Central Europe were alarmed that this might prove a revival of the pseudo-messianism which had threatened the Jewish community in the movements launched by Shabbetai Ẓevi and Jacob Frank. He was excommunicated, and his writings were put under the ban. He sought refuge in Holland, and then in Palestine, but died shortly after his arrival in the Holy Land.

Luzzato wrote a number of works which entered the mainstream of kabbalistic literature. Although his most celebrated book, *Mesillat Yesharim,* avoids all kabbalistic allusions, it is permeated with the pietism which is generally associated with Ḥasidism. Indeed, the highest idea this book sets before the reader is *ḥasidut* (piety) and the hero of the virtuous life is called a *ḥasid* (the pious man). These terms are of course old, going back to biblical times, but Ḥasidism made them the core of its own religious formulation, and the terms are used in the same way by Luzzato This book has been cherished in all Jewish religious circles as one of the noblest expositions of Jewish piety.

PATH OF THE UPRIGHT

I did not write this book to instruct people in what they do not know, but to remind them of what is already known to them, and of what are for them well-established principles. You will find in most of what I say only what people generally know and about which they have no doubts at all. But as these matters are well-known and their truth apparent to all so is their neglect very common and they are often forgotten. Therefore, for the benefit to be derived from this book, it will not be enough to read it once, for it is quite possible that the reader will learn but little that is new after reading it, which he did not know before. The benefit will be derived from reviewing it again and again. Thus it will remind him of matters which people naturally forget, and it will bring to his attention his obligations which he has tried to evade.

If you will consider the state of mind among most people, you will note that the greater number of intellectually gifted and sophisticated people concentrate mostly on the speculative sciences and on subjects of great profundity, each according to his intellectual disposition and natural inclination. Some will invest their energies in the study of the natural sciences, others will place all their efforts on the study of astronomy and mathematics, and others on the arts. Others will move closer toward the realm of the holy, that is, they will pursue the study of the holy Torah, some the dialectical analysis [*pilpul*] of the *halakhah,* some the *Midrash,* and some decisions in law. But there will be a few among them who will regularly pursue the study of what constitutes perfection in the service of God, on His love and fear, on cleaving to Him, and on the other aspects of piety [*ḥasidut*].

These subjects are neglected not because they are not regarded as of fundamental importance. If you were to ask anyone, he would tell you that these subjects are primary, and that it is inconceivable for one to be truly enlightened who is not fully cognizant of them. The reason most people fail to pursue this study is because they regard it as commonplace and feel certain that there is no need for them to devote much time to it. The study of these subjects and the reading of books dealing with them is therefore left to those who lack the subtlety of intellect. It is these people that you will find zealously pursuing these studies. Indeed, if you see a person concerned with cultivating piety you cannot help but suspect him of being of limited intelligence.

The results of this condition are very bad both for the learned and the unlearned, for both lack true piety, and it is rare to find it among our people. It is rare among the learned because they neglect to study it, and the unlearned lack it because they do not comprehend it sufficiently. Most people, therefore, assume that piety hinges on the recitation of many psalms, on long confessions, difficult fasts, immersion in ice and snow, practices which cannot satisfy the intelligence, nor give one peace of mind. True piety, which is desirable and precious, is outside our comprehension, for this is clear: we cannot put our mind to whatever we are not interested in.

Though the basics of piety are rooted in the heart of every upright person, if he will not concern himself with them, he will see its elements and not recognize them, he will transgress them and not feel it, and not see it. Piety, the fear and the love of God and the purity of heart are not so innate that it becomes unnecessary to cultivate a pedagogy to acquire them and that people can reach them automatically, as they do the instinctive reactions like sleeping and waking, hunger and satiety, and all other responses which are implanted in our natures. Moreover, there is no paucity of factors that will obstruct a person's cultivation of them, but there is no lack of technique for overcoming these obstructions.

How therefore can we allow ourselves not to devote time to this study, to authenticate the truth of these principles and to learn the ways of acquiring them and enabling us to keep them fixed in our character? How can a person acquire this branch of wisdom unless he pursues it? Every wise man has realized the importance of the genuine service of God, and the obligation to practice it in purity, for otherwise it is not acceptable at all. It is rather despised, for "the Lord searches all hearts and He undermines the deviousness of all our thoughts" (I Chron. 28:9). What excuse shall we give on the day of Judgment if we have neglected this study and have ignored so important an obligation, which is the very essence of what God expects of us? Is it proper that we exert our minds in disciplines to which we are not obligated, in the dialectics of talmudic analysis which yield us no benefit, in the study of laws which are not relevant to us, while that which is our principal obligation to our Creator we leave to habit and allow it to become a habituated routine?

If we should not investigate what is the true fear of God, what are its implications, how we can acquire it, and how we can escape the folly of the world which causes us to forget it, it will be forgotten and gone from us, even though we are aware of its obligation. The same is true with the love of God. If we should not endeavor to fix it in our hearts with the help of all the instrumentalities which predispose us to it, how will we acquire it? Whence will we acquire the ecstatic attachment to God and His Torah unless we meditate on His greatness which inspires in us this attachment? How will our thoughts be cleansed if we do not make the effort to purge them of the defects which our bodily nature effects in them? And all those attributes of character which depend on cultivation and conditioning — who will perfect them if we do not attend to this task and concentrate on it carefully?

If we only investigated this subject seriously, we would grasp it in its authenticity and we would bestow benefits on ourselves, and we would be able to teach it to others and bestow benefits on them as well. This is what Solomon meant when he said (Prov. 2:4–5): "If.you seek it as silver, and search for it as a hidden treasure, then will you understand the fear of the Lord." It does not say, then you will understand philosophy, then you will understand astronomy, then you will understand medicine, then you will understand the laws, then you will understand the *halakhot* [the laws in the context of their talmudic discussion], but, then you will understand the fear of the Lord. Thus you see that in order to understand the fear of the Lord it is necessary to seek it as silver and to search for it as a hidden treasure. We thus have a confirmation of what we have been taught by our ancestors, and what every intelligent person knows in a general way.

Shall we find time for all other branches of study, and not allow any time for this subject? Why should not a person designate at least some time for reflection on this subject, if he should feel compelled to devote the rest of his time to other studies or pursuits? The verse (Job 28:28) declares: "The fear of the Lord, that is wisdom." The rabbinic comment on this suggests that this alone is wisdom. Surely wisdom presupposes study. The truth is that one needs much study to gain a true knowledge of those matters, and not to follow the imagination or deceptive interpretations, surely to acquire them and to gain mastery of them. Whoever will understand this subject will realize that piety does not consist of those elements that the foolish pietists imagine, but it involves true perfection and great wisdom.

This is what our teacher Moses taught us in the statement (Deut. 10:12–14): "Now, Israel, what does the Lord ask of you but to fear the Lord your God, to walk in His ways, to love Him, and to serve the Lord your God with all your heart and all your soul, to keep the commandments of the Lord and His ordinances, which I command you this day for your good." He included here all the elements of the perfect service which are acceptable to the Holy One, praised be He. These include fearing Him, walking in His ways, loving Him, sincerity of heart, and keeping the commandments.

Fearing Him is to feel a sense of awe before His greatness, to be in awe of Him as one is in awe before a great and austere king, and to be embarrassed before His greatness in every move, certainly when speaking before Him as in prayer or studying the Torah.

Walking in His ways embraces everything that has to do with moral character and the ways of perfecting it. This is what the sages meant when they said (Shabbat 133b): As He is merciful, so you be merciful. What this means is that a person should follow the principles of equity and morality in his character traits and his actions. The sages expressed this in the generalization that the right course for a person to pursue is one that is honorable in his own eyes and brings him honor from his fellow-man (Avot 2:1). This refers to one who pursues the true good, which results in strengthening the Torah and the spread of fellowship in society.

Loving Him means that the love for God be so firmly fixed in a person's heart that it ever inspire him to please Him, just as the heart is stirred to please his father and mother, and he should feel disturbed if God be displeased because of him or of others. This condition should fire him with zeal to do what he can to correct this and he should experience great joy in doing this.

Sincerity of heart means that he serve God with the purest motives, that is that His service be for its own sake, and not for ulterior motives. This includes the expectation that he be wholehearted in his service, and not vacillate or perform the *mitzvot* like one who acts out of habit. He is to give himself to this with fullness of heart.

Keeping the commandments means what it says, that is the keeping of all the commandments in all their details and provisions.

All these principles call for detailed explanation. I noted that our sages summarized these virtues in a different order, more detailed and better graded according to the pedagogy needed for their cultivation. This is stated in a talmudic passage cited in various places, one of them in the tractate Avodah Zarah (20b): Thus did R. Pinḥas b. Yair state: The pursuit of Torah leads to vigilance, vigilance leads to zeal, zeal leads to cleansing, cleansing leads to restraint, restraint leads to purity, purity leads to piety, piety leads to humility, humility leads to the fear of sin, the fear of sin leads to holiness.

I composed this book according to the levels of virtue cited in the talmudic statement, in order to teach myself and to bring to the attention of others the conditions of the proper service, in graded order. I shall explain each in its various aspects, how it may be cultivated, what are its obstructions and how to avoid them. I shall read it, and anyone else who may find it profitable in order to learn the fear of the Lord our God and that we shall not forget our obligation to Him. In reading this book and meditating on it, it will recall to us our responsibility, which our physical nature prompts us to neglect. And may the Lord guide us and watch us from error, and may the prayer of the poet, beloved of God, be realized in us: Teach me Your way, O Lord, I shall walk in Your truth, consecrate my heart to fear Your name. Amen, may this be His will. (*Mesillat Yesharim*, introduction)

17. Kabbalists and Liturgists

Mystical religion is a living experience rather than a structured tradition. Mystics cherish tradition as a holy path their ancestors travelled but they are not content to remain within the formalisms of a groove followed by others. They therefore seek some way of offering personal testimony of their own encounter with God. Mystics have enriched the tradition with commentaries in their own style, stressing their own distinctive insights, but they have also added original chapters that eventually became part of the traditions. This phenomenon is illustrated most dramatically in the area of the Jewish liturgy.

We have noted previously that *merkabah* mysticism, as exemplified in the *Pirkei Hekhalot Rabbati,* was the source from which a number of important prayers in the synagogue liturgy derived. The Kabbalah was similarly a rich source for liturgical innovations. The best known contribution of a kabbalist to the liturgy is the *Lekhah Dodi* by

Solomon ben Moses haLevi Alkabeẓ (1505–1576), which became part of the Friday night service. It hails the Sabbath as a prelude to the messianic redemption. In many cases, the contributions of the kabbalists remain anonymous but they were all stirred by the same emotions—a yearning for God, an ecstatic joy in experiencing His presence, the endeavor to acclaim His work whether in nature, or in the history of the people of Israel, or in the Torah He entrusted to His people. These liturgists wrote commentaries on old prayers; they added prefatory meditations before reciting the old prayers or performing a *mitzvah*; they added some devotional composition from an older source to the liturgy; but they also wrote original compositions of their own. The Safed School of kabbalists were the most active in these liturgical innovations. The most important sources for the kabbalistic contributions to the liturgy are *Sha'arei Ẓion,* a miscellany of prayers by Nathan Nata Hannover, a disciple of Ḥayyim Vital, which was first published in 1662, and Isaiah Horowitz's *Sha'arei Hashamayim,* published in 1717.

The kabbalistic additions to the liturgy are sometimes couched in the esoteric idiom of kabbalistic mysticism. Thus on putting on the *tefillin* a person is to recite the following: "Exalted God, may You grant me wisdom out of Your *wisdom,* discernment out of Your *discernment,* and in Your mercy may You perform great things for me. In Your *might* may You frustrate my enemies. And may You pour from Your good oil on the seven branches of the candlestick in order to extend Your goodness to Your creatures." The reference to wisdom (*ḥokhmah*), discernment (*binah*), mercy (*ḥesed*), and might are of course allusions to the *sefirot* by those names. The fourth *sefirah, gevurah,* is sometimes rendered as sternness, but the more general meaning of the term is might. The allusion to "good oil into the seven branches of the candelabrum" is a prayer that the divine influences may reach the seven lower *sefirot,* which direct the destinies of God's creatures. But many of the kabbalistically inspired prayers are written in a lucid style and speak directly to the heart.

In addition to *Lekhah Dodi,* we include here a devotional prefatory prayer before putting on the *tefillin*; *Berikh Shemeh,* a selection from the *Zohar* recited before taking the Torah from the ark; and *Yedid Nefesh,* a hymn of longing for God which is recited in some synagogues at the onset of the Sabbath, ascribed to the well-known kabbalist Eleazar Azikri. These prayers have become part of the liturgy albeit with certain interesting variations in the text. The *Berikh Shemeh* prayer, in the original text of the Zohar, also had a line in which the worshipper prayed for "male children who will do Your will." This line is retained in the version given in Horowitz's *Sha'arei Hashamayim,* and in many other early versions. The prefatory prayer for putting on the *tefillin* appears in two slightly varying versions, one in Hannover's *Sha'arei Ẓion* and the other in Horowitz's *Sha'arei Hashamayim*. The version as it appears in the current liturgy is a synthesis of the two. A section deleted from the current version, which does appear in Horowitz's text, reads thus: "I put the *tefillin* on the hand to signify the bringing of all the idolators (*akum*) under the authority of the Lord, the lower manifestation of the *shekhinah,* and on the head to signify the bringing of all the idolators under the sovereignty of the higher manifestation of the *shekhinah*. Thus it is written (Ps. 97:9): "For You, O Lord, are supreme over all the earth, You are exalted above all other gods."

LEKHAH DODI

Come, O friend, the bride to meet,
Come, O friend, the Sabbath greet.

"Keep" and "Remember" were fused in one word
When the voice divine at Sinai was heard.
The Lord God is One and One is His name,
In Him is our glory, in Him our fame.

O come, let us meet the queen of the days,
The Sabbath yields joy in all of her ways,
The last of God's work but first in design,
The Sabbath foreshadows blessings divine.

Thou holy city, thou shrine of the King,
Enough of thy grieving, come now and sing.
The Lord will redeem thee, lift up thy face,
The Lord will restore thee again to His grace.

Shake off the dust and rise from the mire,
Come and bedeck thee in festive attire,
Thy redemption is near; thy weeping let cease,
The Lord will fulfill thy yearnings for peace.

Arise, O arise, for come is thy light,
The darkness is lifted, gone is the night;
Awake, awake, sing the song of the free,
See all thy homeless returning to thee.

Why art thou downcast, why dost thou moan?
The Lord His glory upon thee has shone,
Thy foes He vanquished, He humbled their pride,
Thy God has loved thee as bridegroom his bride.

In freedom renewed, again thou wilt thrive,
Thy land will blossom, thy youth will revive.
God's deeds we will know and ever acclaim,
Chanting our praises to His holy name.

We greet thee, O Sabbath, crowned by the Lord,
We hail thee rejoicing, in common accord,
We are the faithful who bask in thy light,
We welcome thy day; we welcome thy night.

MEDITATION BEFORE PUTTING ON THE TEFILLIN

In the act of putting on the *tefillin* I desire to fulfill the commandment of my Creator who instructed us to put on the *tefillin.* As it is written: And you shall bind them for a sign upon your hand, and they shall be for frontlets between your eyes. Within the *tefillin* are inscribed four chapters of the Torah, which proclaim the absolute unity of God, and remind us of the miracles He wrought for us when He took us out of Egypt, and declare His sovereign power over all things in heaven and on earth.

He instructed us to put the *tefillin* upon the hand in remembrance of His mighty arm, with which He delivered us from bondage of Egypt; and opposite the heart, as a token of our duty to devote the impulses and emotions of our heart to His service, praised be He. We put the *tefillin* on the head, as a token of our duty to devote the mind, with all its faculties, to His service, praised be He.

And may my observance of the commandment of the *tefillin* draw unto me sacred influences and holy thoughts, and guard me from every inclination to sin, in deed as in thought, that I may freely serve the Lord as it is in my heart to do. Amen

BERIKH SHEMEH

Be praised, O Sovereign of the universe, and praised be the law by which You govern all Your creation. May Your love ever abide with us, and may You reveal to us in Your holy sanctuary, Your redeeming power and Your truth. In mercy heed us when we call, and grant us and all our dear ones a good life, among all the righteous who know Your peace.

You nourish and sustain all creatures. They are all under Your sovereignty. You rule over kings, for all dominion is Yours. We are the faithful servants of the Holy One, praised be He, before whom and before whose glorious Torah we bow at all times.

We place our trust not in any mortal man, or in any angelic being,[1] but in You, O God of Heaven. You are the God of truth; Your Torah is truth; Your prophets are prophets of truth; and You abound in deeds of goodness and truth. In You do we put our trust and to You do we chant our praises.

May it be Your will, O Lord, to open our hearts to Your Torah, and to fulfill the worthy desires of our hearts and the hearts of all Your people Israel, for good, for life, and for peace. Amen. (*Zohar*, II 206a)

YEDID NEFESH

Heart's beloved, merciful Father, draw me to Your service,
I yearn for You as the stag yearns for water,
Let me bow down before Your splendor,
Your friendship is my choicest delight.

Glorious One, light of the world, my soul pines for You,
Heal me by letting Your light shine on me,
Then I shall be strengthened and restored,
I shall serve You always.

Eternal One, show mercy to Abraham's child,
How long have I sought You!
My God, my heart's desire, take me into Your presence,
Hide not from me, delay not.

Reveal Yourself, O beloved, shelter me,
Let the earth be radiant with Your glory,
Hasten, O beloved, it is time,
Take us into Your grace, as in days of old.

---

1. The Hebrew is *bar elohin*, literally, "a divine son," perhaps an allusion to the Christian belief.

THE RISE OF ḤASIDISM

18. *Israel Ba'al Shem Tov*

The founder of Ḥasidism was Israel ben Eliezer Ba'al Shem Tov (1700–1760), often called simply the "Besht" (i.e. *B*a'al *Sh*em *T*ov). He was born in Okup, Podolia, a province of Russia. We know little of his life that has not been embellished by legend. He had a difficult childhood, and was orphaned at an early age. Raised through the good offices of the community, he gained a good command of classic rabbinical texts, but he showed little inclination for formal studies. A deeply sensitive spirit, he discovered inner meanings in the classic texts themselves and their hidden, immanent light shone brightly for him. He loved to roam the woods where he discovered God's word in the panorama of nature and in the human heart. He was stirred by a profound longing for God, and in moments when he felt close to God he experienced a rare joy which he sought to share with others.

For a time he served as a teacher's aid, and he loved to gather the little children about him and he would enthrall them with his songs and stories. There was a certain charisma about his personality, and people were readily drawn to him. He loved the common people and instructed them through parables and allegories, stressing the cultivation of closeness to God through love and devotion and through sincere prayer, rather than through the rigid disciplines of talmudic study, which was the conventional way of Jewish piety. Legends spread about him, and the common people began to idolize him as a leader who could convey more than knowledge. They found in him inspiration, and strength distilled by a deep religious faith, and even the secret potency to perform miracles. But even among the learned there were many who sought a deeper, more emotionally satisfying faith and they, too, joined the growing ranks of his followers. His adherents became known as *ḥasidim,* "zealots," because they were zealous in serving God, and were not content with the formal piety of outward conformity to the commandments.

The Besht left no writings of his own, but his views have been preserved in the form of quotations in the works of his disciples. He did write a will, but it exists in different versions and its authenticity has been questioned. His thought was dominated by several basic concepts which are often stressed in the teachings of the mystics. He called on people to place the focus of all their pietistic acts on the inner light which is immanent in the action, rather than on its outer formal expressions. He had a profound faith that the divine abides everywhere and that total evil is therefore an impossibility. He opposed the tendency to asceticism and advocated a joyous disposition as a more acceptable approach to God. He stressed the duty of the *ẓaddik,* the righteous person, to withdraw from a piety based on the quest for self-perfection and to descend to the common people in order to raise them toward a higher level of holiness. It was this emphasis which proved crucial in the transition of Jewish mysticism from a spiritual pursuit of an elitist group to the mass movement that it became in Ḥasidism.

The will, from which selections are included below, comprises the basic teachings of Ḥasidism. God is the center of life in the faith taught in this document, and serving Him involves a renunciation of worldliness and a total commitment of one's thoughts and emotions to the great quest for experiencing God's nearness. The sense of cleaving to God, *devekut,* is life's highest goal, but it is to be pursued not for the person's own gratification, but as a disinterested act of loving God; its highest motivation is to be the desire to please the Creator. By orienting his life to God, man becomes impervious to suffering; he can overcome depression and maintain equanimity even if he occasionally succumbs to worldly pressures. He can live in the world and share in its involvements without severance from the divine source where he has anchored his life. Whoever achieves this is a *zaddik*, a righteous person, but there are two kinds of *zaddikim*, one higher than others. The higher is not content to embrace God's nearness as a private boon. He also seeks to influence others to follow the same goal.

THE WILL OF THE BESHT

This is the last will and testament of Rabbi Israel Ba'al Shem, peace be on him.

One must be wholehearted in God's service, praised be He; it is to be a genuine service. The primary rule is not to be forgetful of one's responsibilities. It is particularly important to study each day a lesson in morals, whether much or little, and to strive constantly for the cultivation of good character traits and proper norms of behavior. One must not allow a single day to pass without performing some *mitzvah*, whether a minor or a major one. The principle involved is stated in Avot 2:1: Be as careful [*zahir*] in performing a seemingly minor precept as a major one. The Hebrew term for "careful," *zahir*, can also mean "shine." This is to suggest that the soul is to shine and be illumined through a minor as well as through a major precept, for God seeks the heart.

"I have placed the Lord always before me" (Psalms 16:8). The term for "placed," *shiviti*, reminds us of the term *shaveh*, which means "equal." The statement may then be taken to mean: Whatever may happen, whether people praise him or disparage him, it should be all the same to him, and similarly with reference to all other matters. Likewise concerning food, it should be all alike to him, whether he eats delicacies or other foods, since the evil inclination has been purged from him. No matter what happens, let him say: This surely emanated from God, and if it is agreeable to Him it is agreeable to me. His entire concern should be for the honor of God, but it should be of indifference to him what happens to his own person. This is a very high attainment.

A person should serve God with all his strength, for all our faculties are intended for God's service: God wants us to serve Him in different ways. At times, for example, a person may be engaged in conversation with people, and then he cannot study, but he should still cultivate his attachment to God and focus his mind on God's unity. Similarly, when a person is on a journey and is unable to pray and study, as is his custom, he must serve Him in other ways. This, moreover, should not grieve him, for it is God's desire that we serve Him in diverse ways, at times in one way and at times in another. The coincidence of his being on a journey or of his involvement in conversation was to illustrate that he might serve God in a different way.

The great principle is this: Commit your works to the Lord and Your plans will be established. Whatever happens, let him consider that it derives from God. Let him see to it that he entreat God, praised be He, that He always provide what He knows is for his best and not what seems good to man according to the calculations of his intellect, for it is possible that what seems good to him is, in fact, to his detriment. But let him commit all his affairs and his needs to Him, praised be He.

His thoughts should cleave to the heavenly realm, and he should not eat or drink to excess, nor seek pleasures. He should not concern himself with the affairs of this world but try in all matters to detach himself from the physical, for by centering his attention on this world, he accentuates his material nature. The sages cautioned us, the object of sight is preserved in memory and memory stimulates lust. It is similarly written concerning the tree of knowledge that it was "attractive to the eye and good to eat" (Gen. 3:6); it was attractive as a result of being seen.

He should see himself as belonging to the heavenly realm, and all the people residing in this world should seem as of little importance, for this entire world is like a grain of mustard against the heavenly realm; and it should be all the same to him whether people like or dislike him, for their likes and dislikes are of no consequence. Similarly he is to pay little attention to his bodily lusts which are a continuation of the original temptation with which the serpent tempted man.

It is written in the *Zohar* that one must show friendship for the poor. He is to consider himself as a poor person and always speak gently and imploringly, as one who is poor. He is to try and withdraw his mind from all else, and focus on the *shekhinah,* thinking only of his love for her, and of his desire that she cleave to him. Let him ever say to himself: When will I be worthy that the light of the *shekhinah* abide with me? If some worldly lust assail him, he should put it out of his mind, and disparage that lust so that it will become hateful and loathsome to him. He is to incite the good impulse to combat the evil impulse and its temptations, and thus will he subdue it. He should not be disturbed if he does not feel any worldly desires. On the contrary, he should rejoice that he was privileged to overcome his desires for the sake of the Creator, praised be He. When our sages spoke in praise of one who rejoices in suffering (Shabbat 88b), they had in mind one who does not pursue his lust even in his thoughts, but disparages it, thereby subduing the evil force. The *Zohar* similarly defined the biblical idealization of the person who is pure in heart (Psalms 24:41), as one whose heart's desire does not follow the multitude.

The great principle to pursue is equanimity. This means that it should be of indifference to him if he be considered a person of little knowledge or as one who is knowledgeable in the entire Torah. The means for attaining this is *devekut,* cleaving to God, for the preoccupation with *devekut* leaves one no time to think of such matters, being constantly concerned with linking himself to the realm on high, to God, praised be He. In whatever act he performs in the service of God he is to consider that he thereby brings delight to his Creator, praised be He, and not for his own benefit. Even if in fact he himself derives pleasure from the service of God, his motive should not be for his own gratification.

A person may not think to himself that he is greater than his neighbor because his service has reached the level of *devekut,* for he is only like other creatures who were formed to serve God, and God who endowed him with intelligence also endowed his neighbor with intelligence. In what sense is he better than a worm, since the worm also serves God with all its strength and intelligence? Indeed the person is only as a worm, as it is written (Psalms 22:7): "I am a worm and not a man." If God had not given him the capacity for reason he would have been able to serve Him only as a worm. Thus he is no greater than a worm, certainly not than other people. He must see himself as a worm, and look upon all other little creatures as companions in the world, for all are creatures, and they have no other strength than what God endowed them with. This should always be in his mind.

If he should find himself tempted to commit any transgression, let him recite the verses which caution against this transgression, with the prescribed cantellation and punctuation, with fear and with love for God, and it will depart from him. And if he should find himself lusting with some evil emotion, let him recite six times the verse in which God is quoted as promising the Israelites the power to overcome the Canaanites and the other nations inhabiting the land they were to enter, with all his strength, with fear and love for God, and it will depart from him. Let him instead link that emotion with the Holy One, praised be He. Thus if he should find himself drawn to love what is evil, let him condition himself to love only God, and let all his efforts be directed toward this end. If he should find himself drawn toward anger, which is a form of evil, fear, deriving from the attribute of sternness, let him overcome his impulse, and fashion out of this attribute a vehicle for the service of God, praised be He. If he should hear any one preaching with fear and love for God, let him cling to his words and identify himself with the preacher.

The reproving words will turn to him into thoughts and his lust will depart from him.

First and foremost he must be vigilant that every gesture in his acts of service to God be free of ulterior motivation, God forbid. This requires considerable sophistication. It is very profound, and who can attain it? There is no other choice, but that this concern be at all times in his memory, and he must not be distracted from it, even for one moment. This is one of the matters which becomes invalid by turning one's mind away from it. This is important, and there is more. A second strategy is to be careful at all times to immerse himself in a pool of water for ritual purification. His mind is to focus on the intention appropriate to the place of purification. This three-fold strategy will not be easily evaded. He must avoid melancholy, but his heart should always be joyous in God.

He should cultivate the quality of fervor. He should rise from sleep with fervor for he has been renewed and has become a new person, and is capable of creating, and resembles the Holy One, praised be He, who created worlds. Whatever he does, he is to perform with fervor, for all his acts can be of service to God. In all he sees he is to remember the Holy One, praised be He; if it is something he loves, he is to remember the love of God, if it be something he fears, he is to think of the fear of God. He is to say to himself: I am separating good from evil. This is what is meant by effecting "unifications," with the good being directed to the divine service.

Sometimes the *yeẓer hara* [evil impulse] deceives a man by telling him that he committed a grave sin, whereas he only performed a minor infraction, or no sin at all. The intention of the *yeẓer hara* is to lead the person to a state of depression, and his depressed spirit will distract him from serving God. It is well that a person be wise to this deception, and tell the *yeẓer hara*: I will not be disturbed by this infraction about which you pursue me, for your goal is to distract me from serving God, and you are lying; and even if what I did is in some respects sinful, it will be more agreeable to my Creator that I do not allow myself to be disturbed over my infraction to depress me and inhibit me from serving God—on the contrary, I will serve Him in joy, for this is my guiding principle: my goal in serving Him is not to benefit myself but to bring delight to Him, praised be He. Thus, even if I do not perturb myself over the infraction you mention, God will not be angry with me, since the reason I do not allow myself to be perturbed is that I be not distracted from His service even for one moment. This is the general principle in serving the Creator, that a person guard against being depressed, to whatever extent he can.

Weeping is very bad, for a person needs to serve with joy. Only if one cries out of joy is it very good.

This is how one must condition himself in looking at things. If he suddenly found himself gazing at a beautiful woman, let him say to himself, How did she become this way? If she were dead she would not have this face, she would in fact be repellent. How then does she come to look this way? Obviously it comes to her because of a divine potency diffused in her which endows her face with color and beauty. It thus turns out that the source of beauty is in the power of God. Why then should I cling to the part, it is better that I attach myself to the life-endowing source of all worlds where all beauty resides. Similarly, in looking at any physical object, like a vessel, let him reflect whence does the vessel acquire its beauty and form? The raw material is base matter, the beauty and form is a spiritual element which establishes its identity, and this, too, is part of the divine. Similarly, when eating let him consider that the agreeable taste of that food also derives from a spiritual essence, and the good taste is also a living potency; the "inanimate" also has a living potency, for we see that this "inanimate" object has endurance. We thus find that the life of God abides in all things.

"The righteous shall blossom like the palm tree, he shall grow tall like a cedar in Lebanon" (Ps. 92:13). It is to be noted that there are two types of *ẓaddikim,* both fully righteous, but with this difference. One constantly cleaves to God, praised be He, and he performs the service incumbent on him, but he is righteous only for himself, and for no one else; he does not influence others by means of his righteousness. He is compared to a cedar tree which, as the rabbis observed, yields no fruit. He is a righteous man by himself, but he bears no fruit, in the sense of influencing others toward the good path and thus contributing to an increase of righteous people in the world. This he does not do, but he grows in personal stature and enhances his own merit. The second type of righteous man is compared to a palm tree which bears fruit. This is meant in the analogy of the verse: He "shall blossom like a palm tree." He extracts the precious substance from the crude matter and causes the good to thrive in the world. This is what the rabbis alluded to in the statement (Berakhot 34b): The ground on which a penitent [*ba'al teshuvah,* literally, a master of penitence] stands, the fully righteous are not worthy of standing. This refers to the second type of *ẓaddik.* He is a master of penitence, for he causes the penitents to turn toward the good, and brings many back from transgression. He stimulates penitence in the world. His merit is many times greater than that of the first type of *ẓaddik* mentioned earlier, though the latter is also fully righteous.

19. The Maggid of Mezhirech

Rabbi Dov Baer, the direct successor of the Besht, who bore the title "The Maggid of Mezhirech," was born in Lukatch in 1704. As a child he revealed extraordinary ability in his studies and his father, who was himself a teacher, sent him to the renowned talmudical academy in Lvov to immerse himself in the study of Torah. Like his father, he also became a teacher, conducting his own *ḥeder* in a village community. He also served as a *maggid,* or popular preacher, in several Polish cities. At the same time he was drawn to mysticism and became a devotee of the Kabbalah. After the Besht appeared, he became his devoted follower, and it was the Besht himself who selected him to be his successor. He left no writings but his views were later recorded by his disciples, especially by Shlomoh of Lutsk in several works, including *Maggid Devarav leYa'akov, Or Torah,* and *Or Emet.* But many of his views, almost in the same words, also appear in the writings of others, especially Menahem Mendel of Vitebsk. On the other hand, some of his views are also found in writings ascribed to the Besht himself. He died in 1773.

The dominant concept in the thought of the Maggid is the omnipresence of God. He is immanent in all things; the existential world is a kind of robe worn by His indwelling presence. But God's presence in all things is in various levels of confinement. He is the inner reality of all things, but the inner essence is surrounded by a peripheral realm which pursues its own course, often in alienation from the divine element. The Torah itself is beset with the same dichotomy. Its inner essence is robed in stories, commandments, admonitions and exhortations. Man's limited powers of comprehension necessitate these particularizations.

It is man's vocation to reunite the creation with the Creator. He does this by focusing his life and all the worldly elements he encounters on the divine dimension. He expresses this by the motivation which inspires his actions. The lowest of deeds, when motivated by an ultimate purpose related to the service of God, becomes an act of unification. Without such motivation, even prayer and even Torah study become a lower service, and fail in their intended purpose. When man makes himself a channel for uniting all things with God he transforms his world. His perspective raises all things toward the good, and evil is nullified. His service has efficacy in the higher realms, disseminating harmony in the divine order; and it achieves man's commitment—to bring delight to his Creator. Such a person has become selfless, he has transcended his ego and became part of God, but in that act of renunciation of self he has risen to the highest reaches which is attainable by man.

The highest type of service man can reach is cleaving to God. But in his present state man cannot remain permanently on this high level. He reaches it but then recedes from it. Indeed it is this oscillation which invests the upward thrusts with joyous excitement. A static service could not generate the enthusiasm which is characteristic of piety at its best.

This transformation of man will reach its apex in the messianic age. God's light will shine in him unencumbered by the peripheral crust. He will discover meanings which he cannot discern in the present state of his obtruseness. All existence will have been reunited with its Creator. The wayward child will have returned to his divine home.

GOD'S PRESENCE

1. In every movement God is to be found, for it is impossible to make any move or utter any word without the might of God, and this is the

meaning of the verse (Isa. 6:3): "The whole earth is full of His glory." (*Maggid Devarav leYa'akov* 41)

2. "The whole earth is full of His glory" (Isa. 6:3). Even in idolatry there are holy sparks . . . as it is written (Nehemiah 9:6): "And You animate them all." God has done this to form a basis for reward and punishment . . . Though the whole is pervaded by His glory, one must, nevertheless, serve Him in the essence of His glory and not through that in which He is robed. (*ibid.* 132)

3. A person is to consider that the divine realm from which speech emanates speaks through him, and without it one cannot speak, as it is written (Psalms 51:17): "O Lord, open Thou my lips." This refers to the *shekhinah.* Similarly there can be no thought except through the divine realm of thought. He is only like a *shofar* that emits whatever sound is blown into it, and if the person sounding it were to withdraw it would not bring forth any sound. Similarly, if God did not act in him, he would be unable to speak and to think. (*ibid.* 154)

TRANSCENDING THE PHYSICAL

1. It is written in the Talmud (Ketubot 5a): The work of the righteous is greater than the creation of heaven and earth. The explanation for this is that while the creation of heaven and earth brought into being something from nothing, the righteous make nothing from something. From all things they do, even the physical, like eating, they raise up holy sparks, and similarly from all other things. It is in this sense that they make from something nothing (a no-thing, non-material essence). (*Maggid Devarav leYa'akov* 9)

2. "And Rachel arrived with the flock" (Gen. 29:9). It is written (*Zohar* I 153a) that Jacob was drawn to Rachel because of her beauty. On the face of it this is incomprehensible. The true meaning is that it refers to the "heavenly" Rachel. On seeing this Rachel, Jacob became attached to the heavenly Rachel, for all the beauty of this lower Rachel derived from the heavenly Rachel [in the Kabbalah Rachel is identified with the *shekhinah*]. We are to interpret similarly Joseph's reaction to the wife of Potiphar. It is written (Gen. 39:11): "And he came into the house to do his work." This is interpreted (Sotah 36b) to mean that he was ready to yield to her, but he desisted when he saw the image of his father. It is known that the wife of Potiphar made great efforts to appear attractive to him, as it is written (Yoma 36b): The garments she wore for him in the morning she did not wear in the evening, all in order to

seduce him. But the righteous Joseph did not seek this type of beauty, his encounter with this beauty stirred him to seek the heavenly beauty which is associated with his father [each of the patriarchs was associated with a different *sefirah*: Abraham, love; Isaac, sternness; and Jacob, the mediating element which is beauty]. And thus we interpret the statement (Gen. 39:12): "And he fled, and he went outside." He fled from this physical beauty and was stirred to go outside, that is, outside of this world, and he attached himself to the heavenly beauty. (*ibid.* 23)

3. When a person is in pain—let him attach himself to the Creator, praised be He . . . and he will not feel the pain. (*ibid.* 57)

4. It is because the soul is robed in a body that the higher realms seem small. In truth they are very large, and as one transcends the material confinements of the body he will see in his wisdom that these realms are very great. (*ibid.* 67)

THE TORAH

1. For a new Torah will go forth from Me [an allusion to Isaiah 51:4. The word "new" is an interpretive interpolation, suggesting that a more spiritual level of the Torah would be in vogue in the messianic age. Cf. Leviticus Rabbah 13:3, and Scholem, *On the Kabbalah and its Symbolism*, p. 75.] The Torah is a complete organism including skin, flesh, sinews [*gidin*], and bones, [*aẓamot*]. The skin is represented by the external sense of the Torah; flesh refers to its deeper meaning, as the term is used in the Talmud (Eruvin 21b); whoever probes the teachings of the sages enjoys the taste of meat; sinews refers to admonitions of reproof, as the term is used in a talmudic comment (Shabbat 27a) on Ex. 19:9: "And Moses spoke," this means that Moses spoke to them words as hard as sinews [the term for "spoke," *vayaged*, is similar to the term for sinews, *gidin*]; bones, the Hebrew *aẓamot*, which has an affinity with the word *eẓem*, designating essence, refers to the essence of the Torah which has not yet been revealed. The entire Torah is an aggregate of events concerning righteous men—Adam, the patriarchs, and Moses—who caused His *shekhinah* to rest on their works. But the Torah's light in itself will not be revealed until the coming of the messiah and the inner light itself will be understood. This is what is meant by "a new Torah will go forth from Me." (*Maggid Devarav leYa'akov* 6)

2. It is written: "Open my eye and I shall behold the wonders of Your Torah" (Psalms 119:18). This refers to those elusive worlds which are concealed in the Torah. This is to be read in conjunction with the

statement: God created the world with [that is, according to the principles embodied in] the Torah (Midrash Bereishit Rabbah, I). It is the same Torah as we have it. However, it is robed in each world according to its state, while in its essence it remains unchanged. Thus we can understand the teaching that the patriarchs and Noah studied Torah. It means that they comprehended the Torah as it is in itself, though it was not at that time robed in the garments as at present. These are a kind of sheath for the Torah. In this sense we interpret the statement: In the hereafter God will withdraw the sun from its sheath (Avodah Zarah 3b). It means that the Torah will then be understood as it is in its essence, without its robes. At the present state of man, we would be unable to bear its brilliance; not every mind would be able to bear it. The righteous, each one to the extent that he has emancipated himself from the physical, is in a position to comprehend it. (*Or Torah, Vayera*)

THE TRUE SERVICE

1. Do not make your prayer presumptuous [the term "presumptuous" is a rendition of the Hebrew *keva.* The text is from Avot 2:18, where the term is usually rendered "a set routine," but the word may also be used in the sense of "to rob," or "overpower"]. This means that a person must not pray for his private concerns; he is rather to pray that the *shekhinah* be redeemed from exile. In this sense we understand the continuing injunction in Avot: . . . but offer your prayer as a plea for mercy and graciousness before God. One is always to pray before God, that is to say, on behalf of the *shekhinah.* Similarly the *Zohar* (*Tikkunei Zohar,* 6:22a) calls those who pray on their own behalf rather than on behalf of the *shekhinah* "dogs, insolent ones who scream, 'Give, give.' " It is thus that we are to interpret the verse (Psalms 27:4): "One thing have I asked of the Lord, this do I pray for" ["one thing" and "this" in the Hebrew are feminine in form]: I have asked and prayed before You on behalf of the *shekhinah* [a feminine form for the divine presence], to mend the damage which was effected by sins. (*Maggid Devarav leYa'akov* 13)

2. Even if one performs a *mitzvah* but does not direct it for the sake of God, that is, he performs it for some ulterior motive, he thereby effects estrangement, heaven spare us. For, as taught in the *Zohar* (III 43a), the Torah and God are one, and if one performs a *mitzvah* properly, this *mitzvah* becomes one with God, one holy essence, constituted of one spiritual reality. If, however, one performs it improperly, he fashions an

obstructing shell around this *mitzvah* so that it cannot unite itself with the holy essence of God. (*ibid.* 14)

3. The world was created, if we may use the term, to be an ornament or a source of pleasure to God, through man's performing the commandments, in that He commanded and it was done. This means that the most important factor in bringing pleasure to God is when man directs his mind, and feels enthusiasm to bring delight to God, that is, to do His will. The service itself is not primary, for at times a person may study because this is his nature, he likes study. It is like a person engaging in business because he has a desire for it. The essential factor in performing the commandment is the enthusiasm . . . but enthusiasm by itself is without vessels in which to clothe itself. It must, therefore, clothe itself in deeds. (*ibid.* 142)

4. A person must regard himself as nothing [*ayin*], and dissociate his ego from everything, directing his prayer, in all its petitions, on behalf of the *shekhinah.* Then he will be able to rise above time, that is, to the divine realm of thought, where all things are alike, life and death, the ocean and the dry land. (*ibid.* 159)

5. When a person attaches himself to God, then all the worlds below Him are united with God through him. Thus a person who is endowed with vitality through eating and wearing clothes, includes in himself the inanimate, vegetation, animal and rational life, and they are all united with God through him. But it is most important that he cleave to God. If he should not believe firmly that his speech and his action and his cleaving to God has effects in the heavenly realm, then he will indeed accomplish nothing. Faith is a mighty principle. There are many people who feel love and fear for God but effect nothing because they lack a firm faith. (*ibid.* 188)

6. Know what is above you [Avot 2:1; literally, "what is above from you"]. This means, know that whatever occurs above derives from you. (*ibid.* 208)

7. There cannot be constant cleaving to God, praised be He. This state is reached but soon we relapse from it. It is comparable to fire. At first, if one should blow on it, it will be extinguished, but then the flame is enhanced thereby; and the fire itself rises and recedes and wavers. Enthusiasm [for God] operates the same way. We reach it but then recede from it. A constant pleasure would not be pleasurable. (*Or Torah, Ekev*)

8. "When you enter the land your God gives you as an inheritance . . . you shall take some of the first fruits of the soil . . . and go to the place which the Lord your God will choose to establish His

name" (Deut. 26:1–2). These verses, by way of allusion, teach a person how to behave in this world, so that he might merit the life of the world to come . . . "When you enter the land"—when you wish to enter the higher realm . . . to possess it always, not requiring to go through the round of reincarnations . . . you shall behave in the following manner . . . You shall direct all your "takings" and your "doings," whether in eating or in any other acts, toward the first cause of all, the divine wisdom . . . and your entire objective shall be to raise the holy sparks to their source, to the highest divine realm. This is the divine service to be rendered by man in this world . . . The text continues to advise us that we are not to limit this act of "elevation" only to physical objects, the inanimate, vegetation and animal life, but even to spiritual matters, that is the study of Torah. This is referred to in the statement, "which the Lord God gives you." It refers to the Torah which was given as a gift . . . You are not to say: Since I study the Torah and perform the commandments which are absolutely holy, they remain holy in themselves even without *kavanah,* proper intention. Do not say this. On the contrary, especially in matters involving holiness, you must have proper intention and pure thoughts and sincere words . . . If you should act thus, you will ascend from level to level, upward, toward the place where God "has chosen to establish His name," He will surely cause His *shekhinah* to abide with you . . . and you will merit eternal life. (*ibid., Ki Tavo*)

9. "The words of his mouth are iniquity and deceit, he has stopped to be wise, to do good" (Psalms 36:4). This means that the evil impulse has stopped [his victim] to be wise, to do good. Surely the evil impulse does not incite a person not to study at all, for he knows that he will pay no attention to him, for if he should not study he will not enjoy any esteem among people, and he will not be regarded as a learned man [*lamdan*]. But the evil impulse incites him not to study a subject that will lead him to the fear of God, such as moralistic works, or the *Shulḥan Arukh* code, which would enable him to know the practical aspect of the law. Instead it tempts him to devote himself solely to the study of the *Gemara,* with all the commentaries. Thus the evil impulse stops a person "to be wise, to do good." This refers to its dissuading him from the kind of study which can bring a person the real good, that is, the fear of God.

Another way of explaining the verse: "The words of his mouth are iniquity and deceit, he has stopped to be wise, to do good." We must note that there are two types of people: one is wholly wicked, he is knowledgeable about God but he intentionally rebels against Him; the second has been deceived by the evil impulse and it appears to him that he is wholly righteous, and people, too, regard him as righteous. In truth, however, the latter person, though he studies regularly and prays and indulges in acts of penance—all his labors are in vain, because he is not attached to God, praised be He. He lacks the proper faith calling for constant cleaving to God, he does not know the essence of what religious devotion consists, that it demands study and prayer and the performance of good deeds, with proper intention. The difference between the two is this—that the wholly wicked person may find healing for his affliction, when a thought of penitence should stir in him and he should return to God with a full heart . . . but the second is beyond help. He is blind and cannot see the greatness of God, praised be He, and the way to serve Him. He seems righteous in his own eyes, and how then can he do penance? The reason for all this is, that when the evil impulse tempts a person to commit transgression, it generally induces him to think that he has acted righteously, so that he may never turn back. This is alluded to in the verse: "The words of his [i.e. the person duped by the evil impulse] mouth are iniquity and deceit." The evil impulse has duped the person to regard the transgression he has committed as a righteous act, why then should he stop "to be wise, to do good"? (*ibid.*, Psalms 36:4)

THE MASTER

1. "Speak to the priests, the sons of Aaron, and say to them: None shall defile himself for any soul [*lenefesh*, usually understood in this context as dead body] among his people" (Lev. 21:1). This is meant to teach us that when the priest arises to reprove his people, he must not be moved by pride or some ulterior motive, for thereby he injures and defiles his soul. In this sense we are to understand the term *lenefesh*: he is to be cautious not to injure and defile his soul. In this sense, too, we interpret the phrase "among his people," it means when he is among his people and reproves them. (*Maggid Devarav leYa'akov* 27)

2. The righteous are like a planted tree (Kiddushin 4b). We understand it thus: just as when we plant anything in the ground, it draws all the vitalities from the earth into the seed and it bears fruit, so does a *ẓaddik* draw into his soul holy sparks from everything in the world and he raises those sparks to the Creator, praised be He. (*ibid.* 44)

PENITENCE

1. "Those who seek the Lord shall not lack any good" (Psalms 34:11). Why shall those who seek the Lord not lack any good? Because whatever happens seems good to them, and they are content with little. And it is by virtue of their merit that the world is sustained. (*Maggid Devarav leYa'akov* 216)

2. I heard another reason why a penitent is greater [than a wholly righteous person]. It is because he has experienced the passion of sin and when he repents and pursues the study of the Torah and keeps the commandments, he does everything with great enthusiasm and desire since he knows the nature of enthusiasm. The wholly righteous person never experienced this.

My teacher offered one more explanation. For the wholly righteous person the performance of good deeds and the study of Torah have become a habit, and he cannot pursue them altogether with enthusiasm. But for the penitent it is a new experience. Moreover, if he should not perform everything with attachment he will fall from his high station. Therefore, he must necessarily serve God with great enthusiasm. (*Or Torah, Toledot*)

3. Our sages said: A person should attach himself to the attributes of God: as He is merciful so you be merciful, etc. (Shabbat 133b). This will become more comprehensible if we compare it to a fountain in a high place, at a distance from a person's fields. If he wants to water his fields from this fountain he must prepare a broad enough channel through which the water is to flow. Certainly he must see to it that there be no break or hole in this channel or any obstruction to the flow of the water. If he should be lazy and not attend to this, his labor will be in vain: the waters will not reach his field. . . The point of the analogy is self-evident. The attributes of God are the thirteen ways of His perfection, they constitute the living fountain that bestows mercy to all worlds. The person who cleaves to God's attributes must first of all attend to the channel, which is the man himself, for it is he who serves as the channel bearing the divine influences to all worlds. Therefore, must a person check his own impairments, that his good action not be corrupted by alien thoughts or ulterior motives. (*ibid., Ki Tisa*)

4. Everything emanates from God, praised be He. This includes the thoughts which lead a person to penitence. The initial awakening is from above, as we are told in the *Zohar* that God calls us each day: Return you wayward children. But who heeds this call? It is known that from

God's call an angel is formed and this angel enters the heart of the Jewish individual and stirs in him thoughts of penitence. (*ibid., Koraḥ*)

Man generally fears punishment [consequent on sin] rather than the sin itself. But God, if we may use the term, fears and is grieved lest a person commit sin. He does not fear the punishment which will befall the person as a result of it. On the contrary, the latter is an act of His mercy, of His healing, for he punished him to cleanse him of his sin. This is how we understand the text (Deut. 10:12): "What does the Lord ask of you but to fear the Lord your God?" He asks that one's fear be like His fear, praised be He. (*ibid., Ekev*)

20.
Menahem Naḥum of Chernobyl

Rabbi Menahem Naḥum ben Ẓevi (Twersky) of Chernobyl (1730–1798) was born in the town of Garinsk, in the province of Volhynia, in Russian Poland. Orphaned at an early age, he was raised by an uncle. He received the traditional Jewish education in rabbinic studies, which focused on the Talmud and its supplementary literature, but this did not satisfy his inner yearnings. His heart was drawn to mysticism, and he soon became a devotee of the Lurianic Kabbalah. But not only did he adopt Luria's theosophy, he also began to emulate his way of life. He was drawn to asceticism; he fasted twice a week and refrained from eating meat and drinking wine on weekdays, limiting this indulgence only to the Sabbath.

A dramatic change occurred in his life when he came into contact with the new Ḥasidism launched by the Besht. He abandoned his ascetic practices, and adopted a more positive type of piety, which made room for joy and shunned morbidity and self-inflicted pain. Man's greatest need, he felt, was to draw closer to the holy spirit within himself, and thus to become part of the Infinite. He derided scholars who lacked deep piety, which alone leads man to the highest good. The truly great spirit, the *ẓaddik,* was one who sought to inspire the masses and lift them to a higher life. He became one of the small band of followers and disciples who served as the Besht's emissaries in disseminating his teachings among the people and travelled far and wide as an advocate of the new movement. Rabbi Menahem Nahum's modesty, his simple lifestyle and his deep love for the people helped him in this endeavor.

The selections included here are from his works *Me'or Einayim* and *Yismaḥ Lev.*

THE TRUE SERVICE

1. If one comes to defile himself he is given an opening, if he comes to purify himself, he is helped (Shabbat 104a).

The act of purification is attained through raising oneself, with the element of the divine that inheres in him, toward the source of all, toward God, His name be praised, to become attached to His divine being, thereby bringing the part into union with the whole, the Infinite. The effect of this union is to make the light of the Infinite manifest in him, since the part has now been merged with its source. Certainly one's acts in the divine service become an aid in this process, for God's name, praised be He, thereby is introduced into him, and no greater aid can be accorded a person.

It is otherwise, however, with "one who has come to defile himself." He is given "an opening", for one who seeks to defile himself disrupts the unity between the Lord of existence, and His *shekhinah,* the dimension of divinity that abides in the world below, he severs himself from the Source, the Creator, praised be He; and it is as though he has excluded Him from himself. This is suggested in the very word for a violation of a commandment, the Hebrew *averah,* which may be read as a composite of *avar ya,* meaning literally, "God has passed away" from him . . .

Though God's presence in the commandments is not visible to the naked eye, they link us with ties of love to the Creator, praised be He. The divine presence, and the light of His influence, are present in the commandments, in a state of concealment, and this is the portion of the righteous.

How different is the consequence of a violation of the commandment, God spare us such a fate. God withdraws from the one who has chosen this course, and then he is given an open road to follow the whims of his heart; for the light of the divine influence has departed from him. (*Me'or Einayim, Bereshit*)

2. God commanded Abraham to leave his native land and go toward a land He would show him; here He promised He would make his name great. As stated previously, it was necessary for him to descend from his station and to seek fellowship with those he was meant to uplift, enlarging the domain of holiness, and spreading the love of the Creator in the world. He was to do this by directing the misdirected loves toward their divine source . . . And it is incumbent on us to serve God as our ancestors did . . . to purge all thoughts of their evil direction, but to redirect them toward the divine service solely. (*ibid., Lekh Lekha*)

3. When a person comes before the heavenly tribunal he is asked: Did you conduct your business faithfully (*be'emunah*, literally, "with faith"). Did you appoint time for the Torah? (Shabbat 31a)

The thrust of the question is whether, while conducting business, he maintained his faith in the Creator, praised be He, and in the Torah, and whether his transaction was conducted according to the teachings of the Torah, which is called *emunah*, faith. If so, then such a person has appointed all his time for the Torah, even the time not spent in study. This is what is meant by the statement (Avot 2:2): It is good when the Torah is studied together with the pursuit of a worldly occupation. It is good when the worldly occupation is pursued within the norms of the Torah. This means that one must altogether avoid wrongdoing; then he will be able to do good.

On the other hand, if one seeks to do good without prior avoidance of wrongdoing, to conduct even his worldly affairs for the sake of the Creator and not for his own pleasure, he has not spurned evil and he will not be able to attain to the level of doing what is truly good. This is alluded to in the verse (Psalms 36:5): "He has placed himself on a path which is not good, he does not despise evil." One remains on a path which is not good, if he does not despise what is evil. Such wrongdoing is very despicable, but the evil impulse rationalizes it. One must altogether renounce wrongdoing, then it will become possible to do good. (*Yismaḥ Lev, Shabbat*)

4. The attainment of the state of cleaving to God, praised be He, is designated as "tasting," as it is suggested in the verse (Psalms 34:9): "Taste and see that the Lord is good." It is analogous to a pleasant taste

felt on eating good food—it is impossible to convey this to another by telling him, unless he tastes it for himself, for taste cannot be appreciated unless one experiences it for himself. . .

However, a person must not assume that when he is engaged in studying Torah or in praying or in the performance of any other commandment, then he is close to God, and through these he can experience Him, but when he is engaged in earthly pursuits, in eating and drinking, or in meeting other worldly needs, he has turned aside from God. This is not so, as it is suggested in the statement (Prov. 3:6): "In all your ways, you shall know Him." In all pursuits one is linked with the life of the Creator, praised be He. This is what David alluded to in the Psalm (Psalms 116:9): "I shall walk before the Lord in the worlds of the living." Even in the pursuits of worldliness he pledged that he would remain linked with life, that is, the life of the Holy One, praised be He. (*Me'or Einayim, Likkutim*)

5. Rabbi Eleazar haKappar said: Envy, lust, and the pursuit of honor withdraw a man from the world (Avot 4:28).

The Hebrew term which means world, *olam*, may be related to the term which means concealed, *ne'elam*. This alludes to the presence of a divine element in all things, but in a state of concealment. Even in the traits of envy, lust, and the pursuit of honor, there lies hidden a divine element enabling one to draw closer to the Creator, praised be He.

Lust, for example, can take the form of inspiring a person avidly to study the Torah and to serve God, and with like avidity to pursue all the commandments. Envy can be similarly directed, in accordance with the teaching that envy among scholars is a stimulant to wisdom. The pursuit of honor can be turned into a solicitousness for the honor of God's great name.

Through such conduct one enters the sphere of *olam*, the Holy One praised be He is the hidden presence in him, and in his actions. But one whose conduct is otherwise becomes "a disrupter who effects disunity among friends" (Proverbs 16:28), for he separates the things of the world from the Creator, praised be He. Then it is as though for him there is no God.

This is alluded to in the verse (Deut. 31:18): "I will surely hide my face in that day for all the evils they shall have done." The term "surely hide" is a translation of the Hebrew *haster astir*, which literally means "hide, I will hide"; a double hiding is alluded to here: a rejection of God's providential care, and an alienation from God Himself.

This in a sense is the admonition that "envy, lust and the pursuit of honor" withdraw a person from the world [*olam*]. They withdraw him from the sphere of *olam* which designates the world when it is inwardly pervaded by Godliness. (*Yismaḥ Lev, Avot*)

THE TORAH

1. There are four levels of understanding the Torah: *peshat* [the simple meaning], *remez* [allusions], *derush* [the inferential], and *sod* [the mystical]. The first level is called *peshat,* which means literally to disrobe, because even the simple meaning of the Torah can be grasped only by stripping it of the gross garments in which the Torah is robed. There are all kinds of garments in which the Torah is robed, from crude to subtle, so that even on the seemingly simple statement there is a thick garment, and he who wishes to understand even the simple must remove the thick garment, and then he will understand. The more he strips the Torah of its garments the more he will discern, until he will be able to glimpse the allusions [*remez*], the implied inferences [*derush*], and the mysteries [*sod*]. This is the real meaning of *peshat*—it is an act of stripping the garments.

For be it remembered that the goal of the Torah is to "unite the Holy One, praised be He, and His *shekhinah,*" that is to say, to link the divine element inherent in oneself, the dimension of divinity abiding among earthly beings, with the whole, the Infinite, praised be He.

This is the secret meaning in prefacing the performance of every commandment with the declaration: For the sake of uniting the Holy One, praised be He with the *shekhinah* [a liturgical practice among many *ḥasidim*]. It is a suggestion of union. Through the performance of the commandment we are to unite ourselves, with the divine element abiding in us, to the whole, as is implied in the verse (Deut. 32:9): "The Lord's portion is His people." We are literally a portion of the divine, and it is through the Torah and the commandments that we are to link the portion called the *shekhinah* which abides in us with the source. If one fails to do this he causes estrangement between intimates.

This spiritual union is analogous to the physical union between husband and wife, bearing in mind that countless differences separate the two. The analogy is suggested in the verse (Job 19:26): "Out of my flesh I shall see God." Just as in the physical union there is a need to disrobe, so in a spiritual union is there a need of stripping garments. The Torah has indeed been called a bride, as it is written (Deut. 33:4): "Moses commanded us a Torah, an inheritance of the house of Jacob." The Hebrew word for inheritance, *morashah,* has an affinity with the word which means betrothed [*me'orasah*]; try to understand this. All this can be accomplished if prior to his engaging in the study of Torah one has attained to the fear of God; this is the gate of entry, as is well-known. Without the fear of God preceding, the Torah will not reveal herself from behind her garments, and one will not glimpse the real truth of the Torah, as it is written (Psalms 111:10): "The beginning of wisdom is the fear of the Lord." Before one can attain wisdom, which is the truth hidden in the Torah, one must possess the fear of God. (*Yismaḥ Lev, Shabbat*)

2. It is well-known that there is a hidden light in the Torah, it is called the "inwardness" of the Torah, its soul . . . That which everyone can perceive is the body of the Torah, but there is a soul in its inner being, and it is of this that the verse speaks when it declares (Psalms 19:8): "The Torah of the Lord is perfect."

It is also concerning this inner light that it is written (Sukkah 52a): If this despicable one [the evil impulse] has encountered you, drag him to the house of study, if he is as rock, he will be softened, if he is as iron, he will be melted. For we see many who study Torah, yet do all kinds of evil deeds after their study. But clearly the suggestion is for an exposure to the hidden light of the Torah, but not everyone is worthy of attaining this.

The Torah is like a mirror in which a person only sees himself as he is. If one is gross by immersion in the physical, his life being an admixture of good and evil, he will also see particularities in the Torah, the pure and the impure, the fit and the unfit, the allowed and the forbidden; and to the extent that evil will dominate in him he will see a like reflection in the Torah, and he will find precedents in the Torah to support his permissiveness and his disposition to evil.

One must purify oneself, to remove from oneself his "filth" so that his grossness will not impede him from seeing the brightness of the Torah, and then he will discern the inner light, which overcomes all splits and is wholly good. All this is gained through reverence for the Creator, praised be He, by becoming attached to Him in truth, provided, of course, one has previously departed from evil. But though one has not attained this level he must continue to study according to his capacity; and a wise man persists in seeking the inner essence of everything. (*ibid., Pesaḥim*)

3. Said Rabbi Judah in the name of Rav: A person should always pursue the study of the Torah and the fulfillment of the commandments even if not for its own sake, for from the study not for its own sake he will be drawn to study it for its own sake (Pesaḥim 50b).

This is to be understood thus: The wisdom embodied in the Torah is infinite, as is well known, and it therefore follows that its pursuit "for its own sake," is also infinite, for as one ascends the levels of its mastery, one's mind expands and he comes to know how to embrace the more subtle concepts. It is for this reason that a person is characterized as being constantly a "goer" (Jer. 2:10); as he progresses toward higher levels he can grasp more of the inner light of the Torah. The latter is what we would properly call a study "for its own sake," while the level attained previously is then turned into the category of "not for its own sake," as compared with the new level one has now attained. This goes on always; it is a progression without end; and you must understand this.

It is in this sense that the text says one must "*always* study even if not for its own sake." On the face of it, it is strange that the text projects the possibility of studying always "not for its own sake." Does it not assure us that at some point we will be drawn to study for its own sake? But it is as we indicated, the Talmud admonishes us that a person must not be static in his studies, but that he must always grow from level to level so that, in comparison to present attainments, the previous will always seem as "not for its own sake." (*ibid.*)

21. Menahem Mendel of Vitebsk

Menahem Mendel of Vitebsk (1730–1788) was born into a family of early followers of the Besht. His father was an intimate of the Besht, and he himself visited the great master. His primary teacher in Ḥasidism was the Maggid Dov Baer, the Besht's successor. Rabbi Menahem Mendel was part of a great circle of early followers of the Besht, including Rabbi Abraham of Kalish, Rabbi Israel of Polotsk and Rabbi Shneur Zalman of Lyady, who became the founder of the Ḥabad School in Ḥasidism. The influence of this circle evoked the opposition of the Gaon of Vilna, and Menahem Mendel was part of a delegation that sought to prove to him that his opposition was groundless, but the Gaon refused to receive them. To avoid controversy, he and a group of some 300 followers left for Palestine, settling in Safed and Tiberias. His published writings include in one volume *Peri haAreẓ, Peri Eẓ* and

Likkutei Amarim; some of his comments are also found in *Or haEmet* by the Maggid of Mezhirech, and some have been attributed to the Besht.

The ideas expressed by Menahem Mendel are within the general range of ḥasidic thought, but some of his concepts are of singular interest. He stressed the need for single-minded service of God; that this involves total submissiveness to His will, and a near nullification of one's own notion of what is good for him; that the good found in the world below is only a dimension of the divine which inhabits it, so that the real good which transcends it, and which is to be sought—is God; that man's acts of divine service should have as their highest motivation that they give "pleasure" to God, as a father takes pleasure when his child orders his life wisely; that one's worldly involvements are to be diminished as much as possible so as not to impede the continued cleaving to God, which is man's true happiness; and that there is a need to beware of the feelings of depression because of occasional lapses from the righteous path.

Noteworthy among his teachings is his defensiveness about the study of Torah and his attitude to asceticism.

The study of Torah, which is regarded as the highest good in conventional Jewish piety, is regarded by Menahem Mendel as only a second best—because it interrupts cleaving to God! We are even given a strategy for mitigating the perils which inhere in study: it is periodic interruptions for meditation on God which is the higher goal.

It has sometimes been asserted that Ḥasidism was opposed to ascetic practices. This is not altogether true. It opposed depression and sought to turn the act of divine service into a joyous experience. But ḥasidic piety often included many ascetic practices, particularly fasting. In the teaching of Menahem Mendel this is recommended often as an expression of remorse for wrongs done, and as a means of curbing one's natural impulses, which are identified with the "evil impulse."

THE TRUE SERVICE

1. When a person performs any act of holiness, such as fulfilling a commandment, or studying Torah, or praying with full cleaving to God, to a point of detaching himself from his earlier attachment to the mundane, becoming altogether insensitive to it—such a person has fulfilled the exhortation (Zech. 3:4): "Remove from him the filthy garments . . . and I will dress [him] in festive attire," for he is now robed in a holy spirit . . . Similarly when he takes on himself the *mitzvah* of the

Sabbath or Ḥanukkah and turns all his thought, his entire self into it, nullifying all his previous feelings—this is called real union with God, for the robes of the commandments then surround him, without any obstruction . . . and the Torah and the commandments are divine, in their very essence, as is well known. Through them God unites Himself with him, and he thereby enjoys, in a certain sense, a taste of the world-to-come. This is alluded to in the statement of the liturgy, that those who "have tasted thereof [of the Sabbath] have attained to life," for it is impossible to enter upon the higher life and light of the world-to-come unless one has tasted it in this world. But it is quite otherwise when one pursues the Torah and the commandments out of habit, without attachment to God. Thus we are admonished to prepare ourselves in this world, through the Torah and the commandments, so that we may merit to enter the palace. We are commanded to keep them in a manner that will qualify us to enter the world-to-come, which is the palace, and not allow them to become a routine prompted by habit. (*Peri haAreẓ, Vayeshev*)

2. It is reported in the Ethics of the Fathers (4:1): Ben Zoma taught: Who is wise? He who learns from all men.

The category of a wise man refers to one who absorbs himself in the contemplation of wisdom to a point of self-effacement. All his dispositions, his knowledge, his analytical powers, his intellect—all are focused on the quest for wisdom, and the only expression that is retained of his physical self is the desire for nourishment. All the rest of himself is dedicated to the contemplation of wisdom. He becomes like one of the early masters who were oblivious to day and night, for many a day, once they had been absorbed in wisdom, which involves the shedding of the physical.

Such a person is called a wise man. This is supported by the interpretation of the verse (Job 28:12): "Whence will wisdom be found," as it is expounded in many writings. The Hebrew term for "whence," *me'ayin,* also may mean "from nothing." This means that wisdom may be found only where one has effaced himself to a point of nothingness . . . We may further clarify this theme by referring to the statement of King Solomon (Ecc. 7:23): "I said I would seek wisdom, and it was remote from me." In other words, the more that a person seeks wisdom, the more he is reduced to nothing, in comparison to the greatness of God, and he is literally nullified because of his smallness and his remoteness from the divine. In contemplating the splendor of the Creator, praised be He, because one remains immersed in the physical, whatever he may grasp, even the most subtle and refined of perceptions, is still entrapped in the physical, as compared with what God's being really is. This is what Solomon meant by saying "and it was still remote from me." A person of such uprightness can literally turn over worlds . . .

The person called a wise man has already been characterized as one whose entire probing is focused solely on God, and all his knowledge, all his faculties—they are all focused on Him. Certainly such a person learns from all men, and from every source of wisdom or reverence; he is unconcerned as to the nature of the person or the object through whom knowledge is conveyed to him, since he is not concerned with himself and he has transcended his physical self. This is what Ben Zoma referred to in giving us the definition of a wise man as one who learns from all men.

The substance of the matter is that a person should efface himself altogether, with total abandon, both body and soul, to be ready for obliteration in sanctification of God's name, praised be He, both in this world and in the hereafter, in every conceivable manner, and under all circumstances. His yearning is to be centered only for God through intense concentration on the greatness of the Creator, praised be His name, as the prophet Jonah tells us (Jonah 2:3): "From the belly of the netherworld I cried out." Even from hell, from the netherworld, he turned to God. For of what consequence is it to him what his state is, whether he had never been born, or whether having been born he had perished like a beast, since he has become totally indifferent to himself by contemplating the greatness of the Creator, praised be His name, and all his desires are centered only on one goal—that God's name be magnified and exalted, and His divinity become manifest. (*Peri Eẓ, Kedoshim*)

3. This is the great principle: a person must always be single-minded in his service of God . . . for through many thoughts a person becomes confused in serving Him. He must consider that God abounds in all things of this world and that all things done by the desires and strategies of man really derive from God, and that even the slightest occurrence in this world is ordained by His providence; and since all derives from God it should be of indifference to him whether an occurrence is in accordance with his desire or not, for he knows that this is best for him, even if it turned out contrary to his desire.

He should consider that all existence in all realms of being is as nothing in comparison to Him, for they all came into being in the finite zone where He "contracted" His infinite light, and they were formed in response to His one utterance. Therefore, why should one be drawn to the delights found in these worlds, which embody only one divine utterance? It is preferable to attach oneself to what is beyond those worlds, to the Creator, praised be He, who is the essential reality and not to what is peripheral to Him. This is what the *Zohar* wrote: The righteous are meritorious because they know to direct their love above, toward the heavenly King, and not toward this world and its vain desires, for all these worlds are destined to perish. He should always seek to attach himself to the Creator, praised be He, with absolute love, loving Him more than anything in the world, since everything good in this world has its source in Him, praised be He; and he should say to himself: I desire always to do His will, to give Him pleasure and to serve Him always; and his mind should always focus on Him, on the divine realm. This need is hinted in the verse (Lev. 21:12): "And he shall not depart from the sanctuary."

When one needs to discuss worldly matters he must realize that he is descending from the divine realm. Like a person who leaves his house but is set on soon returning to it, and at the very time of leaving reflects on when he will return, so must he always have his mind set on the divine realm which is his true home. This is alluded to in David's admonition to his son, Solomon, before his death (I Kings 2:2): "I am about to depart on the way of all the earth." He saw himself like a person who sets out on a journey while his heart was focused on returning to his home as soon as possible. In addition he is to consider that the essence of the person is God and His *shekhinah,* and as we are told that the angelic beings "ran and returned (Ezekiel 1:14), so must he behave similarly, to attend to his worldly matters but immediately to return to his house and to his place, to God, following his discussion of worldly matters by resuming his earlier concern with the Creator, praised be He; and this is a very great attainment. And he must first purify his soul so that it will be constantly attached to the higher realm, to Him, praised be He.

While studying, a person must interrupt himself each hour in order to attach himself to God, praised be He. During study it is impossible to remain attached to God, for not every mind is capable of studying in a state of fear and love, as demanded in the *Zohar* . . . Nevertheless, he should study regularly, for study refines the soul, and the Torah is also a tree of life to those who hold fast to it, and if he should cease studying, he will lack the intelligence needed to cleave to God, praised be He, as it is written (Avot 2:5): An empty-headed person cannot be sin-fearing, nor can an ignorant person be pious. Even if he is knowledgeable already, we cannot regard the time of study as worse than the occasions when the spirit grows sluggish or when one sleeps, when one is similarly unable to cleave to God. Moreover, if he should remain idle, the evil impulse will incite him to alieen thoughts and evil lusts and vain pursuits, as an outlet for his energies, for the mind is always active and is never at rest.

Certainly if he had the capacity to envision in the wondrous wisdom of the Torah the power of God which is immanent in all creation he would recognize that the mercy of the Creator, praised be He, and the blessings released by His influence never cease, and he would cleave to Him with absolute love and with longing to do His will and serve Him and to commit all his faculties toward the sanctification of His name, and to devote his actions to God alone, without sharing them with any other goal. This was the way of early ḥasidim, whose thoughts were turned on God exclusively. This would be as good as study, and perhaps better, as the authors of *Hovot haLevavot* [Baḥya ben Joseph ibn Pakuda] and *Shenei Luḥot haBerit* [Isaiah Horowitz] stated. The latter put it thus: "Cleaving to God is seven times greater than study." But in our generations would that we could cleave to the Creator, praised be He, during the three daily prayer services, and while reciting the prescribed benedictions on partaking of foods and other bodily enjoyments! If we should give up study we shall be doubly deprived. However, he should not study continuously without any interruption . . . He should take a break during study to contemplate the greatness of the Creator, praised be He, in order to love Him, and to fear Him, and to be embarrassed before Him, and to yearn for the performance of His commandments; and he should not contemplate many diverse thoughts, but be single-minded as we have written earlier.

When one commences serving God, he must not be overly punctilious about everything he does. This is of the evil impulse's doing to induce fear in a person that he is not doing enough. Thus he brings him to depression, and this is a very bad trait and a hindrance to the service of the Creator, praised be He, as is well known. Even if a person should stumble over some sin, he should not allow himself to be overly depressed. This will destroy his entire edifice, and induce in him callousness, and then he will go beyond the boundary and he will be distracted from God's service. What he should do is sorrow over the transgression, and feel shame before the Creator, praised be He, and cry and plead with Him, to remove the evil he had done. But then he is to resume his rejoicing in the Creator, praised be He, since he has felt full remorse, and is resolved not to return to such folly again. And though he knows with assurance that he has not made restitution through this, because of many impediments, he must not allow himself to remain in a state of depression; he is rather to consider that the Creator, praised be He, who knows our innermost thoughts, is aware that his intention is to do the best, but he is unable to do so; and he must strengthen himself to rejoice in the Creator. (*Likkutei Amarim* 14a-15a)

4. In assuming a fast a person is to meditate on the following: Woe is me! As a result of my lusts and my miserable quest for honor, I have angered the Creator, the supreme King. Therefore, do I wish to fast to subdue the evil impulse, and my lusts and my desire for honors . . . In order to fulfill the commandment to do penance I am prepared to afflict myself so that I may serve God, praised be He, in truth, and with fullness of heart, in fear and in love, and thereby to bear witness to His unity. Therefore, do I wish to afflict myself and to sacrifice myself before Him.

Woe is me! Of what value is my offering . . . His glory fills the earth, and all worlds were created by His command, and all things are as nothing compared to Him. I, a miserable sinner—I can only ask that He enable me to offer Him many sacrifices. It is for me to be happy that through me some pleasure has been effected for the Creator, praised be He, and I am also to find happiness in the fact that He gave us a means for subduing the evil impulse. I desire to afflict myself because I angered the Holy One, praised be He, and His *shekhinah,* so that I may mitigate their suffering. Woe is me! Of what account is this affliction in comparison with the pain I caused them for many years.

I can only ask that He grace me with His great kindnesses to take account of this affliction to lessen the pain of the *shekhinah,* and that He remove the "shells" which obstruct me; and that I effect the removal of the "shells" from the *shekhinah* so that, cleansed, she will be reunited with her spouse, the *sefirah tiferet,* in a perfect unity. . .

I am confident that He who created all worlds out of nothing in comparison to whom all that has being is as nothing, and who provides for them their sustenance and their life—that He will surely be able to give me added strength and watch over me to save me from the evil impulse . . . If He should not help me the evil impulse will distract me from everything; he will tell me that I am too weak and I will become ashamed of my mental capacity and I will be unable to serve God as is fitting; he will seduce me with all kinds of seductions. I can only ask that as in His great mercy He inspired me to afflict myself and He helped me, so may He also help me this day and guard me against all impediments.

I desire to fulfill the commandment to be holy. May He in His mercy give me added strength to serve Him, and that I fall not ill because of His service and may He spare me from ulterior motives, and may the potency of the *shekhinah* be enhanced through my self-affliction. And may He help me so that people be unaware of what I do. I am not afraid of any weakness because of my fast, for even without this many people suffer illness. Moreover, the *shekhinah* supports the sick as it is written (Psalms 41:4): "The Lord will strengthen him on the bed of sickness." In His mercy God will also strengthen me. (*ibid.* 15b)

5. A person should consider that the glory of the Creator, praised be He, fills the universe, and that His *shekhinah,* His presence, is always with him . . . that He is the Lord of all things in the world and can do with them what He desires, that it is improper to depend on anyone or anything else, but on Him; and one is to consider that just as he looks on physical objects so does he, in his mind, look on the *shekhinah* which is with him. This is the divine service of a lower level.

At other times he will be able to discern in his mind that there are above him many other heavens, and that he finds himself on the lowly earth; and that all these worlds are as nothing compared to Him, praised be He, who is the *En Sof,* the Infinite; and that He "confined" Himself, so as to make room in the vacuum formed by His withdrawal for the creation of the worlds. Though he understands this with his mind, he will be unable to ascend to the higher realms. This is what the prophet (Jer. 31:2) meant when he said: "From the distance God appeared to me"; he saw God at a distance. But when he reaches the level of the higher service, and strengthens himself and rises in his mind above all heavens in one swoop . . . this is the complete service. (*ibid.* 17a)

22.
Shneur Zalman of Lyady

Rabbi Shneur Zalman (1745–1813), the founder of the Ḥabad movement in Ḥasidism, was born in Liozna, White Russia. As a young child he studied under a kabbalist, a certain Rabbi Issachar in Lubavich; and he later continued his education in Vitebsk. His fame as a child prodigy brought him to the attention of the Russian governor of the province who sought to have him enrolled in the Academy of Sciences in Vitebsk. He pursued his general rabbinic and mystical studies in Vilna and Mezhirech, where the successor of the Besht, Rabbi Dov Baer, maintained his court. Soon recognized as the most gifted of Dov Baer's students, he was asked to head the ḥasidic movement in Lithuania, then a center of opposition to Ḥasidism. He sought to influence the Gaon of Vilna to mitigate his opposition to Ḥasidism, but the latter refused to see him. He was persecuted by the opponents of Ḥasidism, who resorted to slandering him before the government authorities as a subversive influence in the country, and he was jailed twice. He set out for Palestine where he hoped to escape the conflict, but later returned and settled in Lyady, where he served as rabbi and as a focus of ḥasidic thought.

His own version of Ḥasidism was actually a kind of synthesis with the normative rabbinic tradition, because he emphasized the importance of talmudic study, and was not content to base the quest for closeness to God on faith and emotional stirrings alone. Similarly, he did not demand of everyone the total annihilation of the natural inner drives and a love for God to reach the level of ecstatic intensity. These may be attained by the select few, thanks to a special grace of God. The goal for which all can strive is to be a *beinoni,* a person of intermediate disposition, who feels the lower stirrings, who has not attained an ecstatic love for the highest, but who has enough potency in the divine dimension in his nature to keep his lower impulses under control and to direct his active life in obedience to God and His law. The extremist demands which Ḥasidism generally made of its devotees fostered a lack of faith in the common man about his ability to reach the goal of piety by his own efforts and this led to an over-dependence on the role of the *ẓaddik,* who became a virtual intermediary between God and man. Shneur Zalman, by moderating his demands on the devotee, defined the role of the *ẓaddik* in more moderate terms as well. He was seen in terms closer to the classic conception of the rabbi, as a teacher and a guide but not as a channel of divine grace.

His writings include a running commentary on the Pentateuch, *Torah Or,* which is based on Genesis and Exodus, and *Likkutei Torah,* on Leviticus, Numbers and Deuteronomy; and the *Tanya* or *Sefer Shel Beinonim,* where he develops his version of ḥasidic thought, which has become the basis of the Ḥabad or Lubavitch movement in Ḥasidism.

THE VOCATION OF THE JEW

1. The purpose of establishing the tabernacle was to cause the divine presence to abide in the Jewish people, as it is written (Ex. 25:8): "They shall build unto Me a sanctuary and I will dwell in their midst" [literally, "in them"], and as it is also written (Jer. 7:4): "The Temple of the Lord, The Temple of the Lord, the Temple of the Lord, are these." This is to be understood in the light of the statement of the sages (*Tanḥuma* on Ex. 25:8): The Holy One, praised be He, told Moses, Make me a sanctuary because I desire to abide with My children. On the face of it, this is strange, because even without man, God is declared as having said (Jer. 23:24): "I fill the heaven and the earth." But the abode meant here referred to the disclosure of His divinity, and this could be accomplished

only by lowly man; the lowly does not refer to place . . . but only to the lowly in terms of quality and stature. . .

The perception of God in this world is in great concealment and limitation, and darkness covers the earth; and God wanted an abode in the sense of having a center for revealing His divinity to illumine the darkness. This could be effected only through the Torah and the commandments . . . This establishing of an abode and this revelation of the divine involves curbing the influence of the evil force, which is the evil passion; and after the curbing of evil we turn darkness to light. The area where evil is to be curbed is in our five faculties: sight, as we are told (Isa. 33:15), that the favored of the Lord "shuts his eyes from seeing evil," and similarly, with hearing, speech, action and thought . . . Thus one reaches the state of turning his five faculties, including his thought, into vessels of the light of the Infinite, praised be He. This is involved in calling the children of Israel the Temple of the Lord. In other words, through keeping the Torah and the commandments the children of Israel were to become the Temple, a vessel to make manifest the name of God. It is likewise in this sense that we are to understand the promise that if they would build a sanctuary, God would dwell in them. (*Likkutei Torah, Pekudei*)

2. The goal in the creation of man is that he might make himself submissive to God. This is to be explained thus: the descent of the divine potency through many stages of self-limitation was to serve as a prelude to its return upward, so as to transform darkness to light; and it is for this role that God created man on earth. Since this world is the lowly realm, covered with darkness, and there is need for many lights to illumine the darkness, God created man whose vocation is to serve as a light, and as a candle, as it is suggested in the verse (Prov. 20:27): "For the soul of man is a candle of the Lord." Man illumines the world with the light of the divine Name, revealing it from its concealment, thus transforming darkness to light. In this sense we are to understand the call to Abraham (Gen. 12:2) to "be a blessing." He was to spread blessing throughout the earth; and it is similarly written of the children of Israel (Isa. 61:9): "They are a seed blessed by the Lord." The terms for blessing and blessed, *berakhah* and *berakh,* suggest the words *mavrikh* and *markhiv,* which mean "to graft" or "to merge," and this defines their role as a source of blessing. They were to spread the influences from one world to another, from the world of concealment to the world of disclosure. Thus would the divine realm be disclosed. Those who effect this disclosure are the Jewish people. They are the seed that discloses the Lord; and as the soul of man is a candle of the Lord, the multitude of

souls are a multitude of candles. The extent of the darkness determines the number of candles burning in souls that are needed to overcome it. . .

The disclosure of the divine must be "with all your heart," with the two hearts, the inner and the outer . . . The inner heart reveals the divine impact through excitation felt over the awareness of His being, that He is beyond comprehension . . . This is the hidden love in man's nature, but its effect is visible always. The "outer heart" means that the love spread, curbing the evil impulse and in the end redirecting that impulse to serve a positive end. At first we are to curb it, as is suggested in the verse which defines the man worthy of being in God's presence as "he who shuts his eyes from seeing evil" (Isa. 33:16), and we have a similar admonition (Nu. 15:39): "not to stray after your heart and after your eyes." This expresses a desire that the outer world reveal its divine dimension, for the term *olam* which means world suggests the word *elem,* which means concealed, it hides the divine light, and one must curb the evil impulse to make the light manifest. The next step is to convert the darkness to light. This means that the passion of one's bodily nature which is bent on lusting after all kinds of lusts shall be redirected from its worldly disposition, to yearn for God, praised be He . . . Thus will he fulfill the call to love God with his whole heart. (*ibid., Vaetḥanan*)

LEVELS OF PERFECTION

1. When the divine soul asserts itself in a person to battle against his animal nature to a point where he vanquishes the evil in him . . . but the evil is not transmuted into good, he is called an incomplete *ẓaddik,* or *ẓaddik vera lo,* "a *ẓaddik* in whom there is evil" [literally, a *ẓaddik* who suffers evil]. This means that some small measure of evil persists in him, but it is subservient to the good because it is so limited in scope. It appears to him that he has vanquished it and it is gone, but in truth, if all the evil in him had been altogether overcome, it would have been transmuted into good . . . A complete *ẓaddik* is one who has transmuted evil into good so that he is called *ẓaddik vetov lo,* "a *ẓaddik* in possession of the good" [literally, a *ẓaddik* who enjoys good, or happiness]. He has totally removed the evil facade from the evil experience, despising the cravings for the pleasures of the body solely, and ignoring the service of God. These cravings are rooted in the demonic, and whatever derives from the demonic the complete *ẓaddik* hates with an absolute hatred because of his great love for God and His holiness, a love that distills

profuse delights . . . For the two are antithetical, as we are told (Psalms 139:22, 23): "I have hated them with absolute hatred; they have turned into my enemies; search me and know my heart." Great as the love for God is so great is the contempt for the demonic and the hatred for evil, for contempt is the opposite of love, as much as is hatred.

The incomplete *ẓaddik* does not hate the source of evil with an absolute hatred and therefore he does not show absolute contempt for the evil deed; and because his hate and contempt for these is not absolute, there remains a lingering of some love for them and some craving for their pleasures. The filthy garments, the outer facade of evil, have not been removed from his cravings, and thus he has not become actually good. He still has some affinity for those filthy garments, except that it is minor and inconsequential; and for this reason he is called a *ẓaddik* in whom evil has been reduced to subservience and has in effect been nullified. It is for this reason too that his love for God cannot be regarded as absolute; he is accordingly called an incomplete *ẓaddik*. . .

The excellence of the complete *ẓaddik* was acclaimed by Rabbi Simeon bar Yoḥai who declared: See the people who are worthy of standing before God, and they are few! They are called, literally, *benei aliya*, "the sons of on high," because they transform the evil and raise it toward holiness . . . (*Tanya* 10)

2. The middle course is attainable by every person, and every individual should try to reach it. Everyone can at all times pursue the middle course. The person who pursues the middle course does not despise evil, which depends on the heart, and the times are not always conducive to such feelings. But such a person is called on to depart from evil and do good, that is, by his behavior, in deed, word, and thought. Here a person has the freedom of choice, and one can act, speak and think even in defiance of the heart's cravings. When the heart craves some physical pleasure, whether permissible or forbidden, one can distract himself from it by telling his heart: I do not wish to be wicked for even one brief hour, I do not want to be estranged from God's oneness under any circumstances, remembering the admonition (Isa. 59:2): "Your iniquities separate you from God." On the contrary, I want to unite my breath [*nefesh*], spirit [*ruaḥ*], and soul [*neshamah*] with Him by robing them in the three vestments of action, speech and thought, all centering on God and His Torah and the commandments. I want to do this out of the love for God hidden in my heart as it is in the heart of all Jews who are called "lovers of His name" (Psalms 5:21). Even the least significant among them is ready to sacrifice himself for the sanctification of God's name, and I am surely not inferior to him. It is only that the

latter yielded to folly and it seemed to him that despite his particular transgression he still retained his full status as a Jew, and his soul had not been separated from the God of Israel, forgetting his love for God hidden in his heart. I do not wish to be a fool like him to deny the truth.

It is quite otherwise with matters that depend on the heart, as demanding that one feel absolute contempt for evil and absolute or at least relative hatred for it. This cannot be effected, truly and sincerely, without a mighty love for God, in the category of "love with delight," akin to the delight in God to be experienced in the world to come. This is what our sages alluded to in the prayer: May you attain your hoped for fulfillment in this life, and the culmination thereof in the world-to-come (Berakhot 17a). But not everyone merits this. This is a kind of gift of divine grace, as is suggested in the verse: "Your priesthood is a service to which I have called you as a gift" (Nu. 18:7) and as explained elsewhere. It is in this sense that we are to understand the statement attributed to Job: *You created* the righteous (Baba Batra 16a). It is likewise mentioned in the *Tikkunei Zohar* [Introduction]: Many different gradations of Jewish souls come into the world: *ḥasidim*, mighty men to control their passions, masters of the Torah, prophets, etc. and *ẓaddikim*, etc. Note the text there.

Thus we can understand the talmudic statement (Niddah 30b) that an oath is administered to each person on birth: Be righteous and be not wicked. On the face of it, it seems strange that after having administered an oath to be righteous it should be necessary to add that he is not to be wicked. However, it is not within each person's privilege to become a *ẓaddik*, as it is not within his free choice truly to find delight in God and altogether to despise evil. It is for this reason that he is abjured at least not to be a *rasha* [a wicked person]. This is within a person's free choice. Everyone can dominate the lusts in the heart and control his passion so as not to be wicked even for a brief moment by adhering to the double admonition to "depart from evil and do good" (Psalms 34:15). The true good is Torah, that is the study of Torah, which is the equivalent of all other commandments.

Nonetheless a person must devote time to devise a strategy to condition himself to truly despise evil . . . Thus it is with all the delights of this world—a wise man sees that in the end they will rot and turn to worms and refuse. On the contrary, let him delight in God, praised be He, by contemplating the greatness of the Eternal, to the extent of his capacities. Even though he is aware that he will not reach this to its ultimate depth, but only by approximation, it is for him to do what he can in fulfillment of the oath to be a *ẓaddik*. Beyond that it is for God to do what seems right to Him. Moreover habit dominates in every sphere and becomes second nature. If he should habituate himself to despise evil, it will, to some extent, become truly despicable to him. Similarly, if he should accustom himself to delight in God by meditating on His greatness, the self-induced inspiration will evoke heavenly inspiration. Possibly he will reach a point where a higher spirit will stir him and he will be granted the privilege that the spirit emanating from some *ẓaddik* enter him, enabling him to serve God with true joy, as we are admonished: "Rejoice in the Lord, O righteous" (Psalms 97:12). Then will be truly fulfilled the oath administered to him to be righteous. (*ibid* 14)

3. We may now understand the verse (Mal. 3:18): "Then will you return and distinguish between the righteous and the wicked, between one who serves the Lord and one who does not serve Him." The difference between one who serves God and the righteous is this: the term "who serves" is the active present, it refers to one who is engaged in the service, which consists in waging active resistance to the evil impulse, to overcome it and vanquish it from one's life, so that it should not vest itself in the organs of the body. It is indeed an arduous labor constantly to struggle against it. This is the service of the person of medium stature.

The righteous, however, is designated as a servant of the Lord, which is a descriptive title, like the term "scholar," or "king." The latter designates one who has already become a scholar or king. Similarly in our case, the term "servant of the Lord" characterizes one who has ended the battle with the evil impulse and has vanquished it, and has purged his heart of it.

There are also two levels of service among persons of medium stature: one who serves God and who does not serve Him. But even the latter is not wicked, for we are dealing with one who never committed any transgression, even the slightest, and he has also kept all the commandments within his capacity, especially the study of the Torah, never discontinuing his studies. His only failing is that he does not actively combat his evil impulse to overcome it with the help of the light of God which illumines the divine soul abiding in the brain that in turn controls the heart, as mentioned earlier. This passivity stems from the fact that his passions do not distract him from the study of Torah or the service of God, and he faces no need to combat them. This is found in the person who by nature is zealous in his studies, as a result of a hereditary disposition, being somewhat withdrawn by nature or he has no need to resist sexual lusts because he is frigid by nature, and similarly indifferent to other pleasures. Such a person does not need to concentrate so much on the greatness of God to generate in his mind a sense of the knowledge and the fear of God to act as a deterrent to his transgression of any prohibitions, or to inspire in him a love of God, to cleave to Him, by heeding the positive commandments, especially the study of Torah. He is content with the concealed love that is in the heart of all Jews, who are described as "lovers of God" (Psalms 69:37). Such a person is not to be regarded by any means as one "who serves," for this concealed love is not his achievement or the result of his service; it is part of the ancestral legacy in possession of all Jews, as we explain later. . .

We may, in the light of this, understand the statement in the Talmud (Ḥagigah 9b), that "one who serves God" is one who reviews his lesson a hundred and one times, and "one who does not serve Him" refers to a person who reviews it one hundred times only. In those days it was customary to review a lesson one hundred times . . . Therefore, the one hundred and first time, which is beyond what one has been habituated to do from one's youth, is as great and even surpasses all the others, to qualify such a person to being called "one who serves the Lord." In order to overcome his habitual pattern it was necessary to arouse in himself the love of God by contemplating His greatness . . . This is the true service for a person of medium stature. (*ibid.* 15)

FEAR AND LOVE

1. It is necessary always to remember the fundamental principle involved in serving God, and it is this: though the fear of God is the motivation for withdrawing from evil, and the love for Him the motivation for doing good, it is not enough to invoke love alone for the doing of good. At the very least, one must first evoke the natural fear hidden in the heart of every Jew not to rebel against the King of kings, praised be He, that it be activated in his heart and mind. This is effected by contemplating the greatness of the *En Sof,* the Infinite, praised be He, and His kingdom which embraces all worlds above and below, who pervades all worlds and surrounds all worlds, as it is written (Jer. 23:24): "Do I not fill heaven and earth? says the Lord." Yet He ignored the worlds above and below, to focus His dominion on His people Israel, and particularly on him, for each person must say, For my sake was the world created; and he himself will thereby accept His sovereignty to serve Him and heed His will, with every manner of service performed by a servant . . .

One must concentrate on this thought ever more deeply, according to his mental capacities, and in accordance with the time available to him, before studying Torah or fulfilling a commandment, as before putting on his *tallit* and his *tefillin.* He should contemplate how the light of the Infinite, praised be He, who surrounds all worlds and pervades all worlds, the supernal will, is robed in the letters and in the wisdom of the Torah or in this *tallit* or these *tefillin,* and that in the act of reading the Torah or putting on the *tallit* and *tefillin,* he draws the divine light toward himself, enabling the fragment of divinity in himself to be embraced and absorbed in the light of God, praised be He . . . This bears with it the commitment to direct his wisdom and understanding toward God's service exclusively. . .

Even if after all this, awe and fear fail to arise in his heart, since he has mentally accepted God's kingship and sought to cultivate His fear, and he has done these sincerely . . . then the Torah he has studied and the commandment he has performed are regarded as a full service, as the service rendered by any servant for his master and king. It is otherwise if one studies Torah and performs the commandment out of love alone, in order to cleave to Him through His Torah and His commandments. This is not the service of a servant . . . A person must serve God on two levels, as a servant and as a son . . . and one cannot reach this state unless one attains, as a preliminary, the higher fear.

The failure to feel a sense of fear and embarrassment before God due to one's insensitive nature . . . remains a complete service since his intention is to serve the divine King. The call to fear God and to serve Him are two commandments in the order of 613 commandments, and one is not dependent on the other. Moreover, such a person also fulfills the commandment to fear God by the act of invoking this fear mentally, for at that time he at least experiences the fear he would experience if an ordinary person, not the king, were to see him about to commit an improper act . . . except that this is called the lower fear and the fear of sin, which precedes the acquisition of wisdom and the higher fear, the sense of embarrassment before God. But without any fear at all, with love alone, one cannot soar toward the heights, as a bird cannot fly with one wing; fear and love are our two wings.

Similarly fear alone is one wing, and one cannot fly with it. Such service is called a servant's service, but there is also the need for the service of a son, to bestir the hidden love dormant in the heart, to activate it in his mind, at least, to invoke to memory his love for God, and his will to cleave to Him; and this must be his goal in studying Torah and performing the commandments—to link with God his divine soul and spirit, in all their garments in which they are robed . . .

With such preparation of surrendering oneself to God, one is to begin the morning prayer . . . and similarly, with such preparation he is to begin to study his regular lesson after prayer; and during the day likewise he is to begin a period of study with the same preparation . . . Should he continue to study for many hours he must contemplate these preparatory thoughts each hour at least . . . But his entire motivation in surrendering himself to God through the Torah and prayer, by uniting the divine sparks in them with their source must be only to please God, praised be He; it is analogous to the pleasure felt by the king when his only son has returned to him from captivity and imprisonment. (*Tanya* 41)

2. "How beautiful and how pleasant are you, O love with delights" (Song of Songs 7:7).

There are two kinds of love for God. One is "love with delights." This is a state of wondrous delight in God, with a great, a mighty joy, the joy of the soul to the very limits of its strength, in experiencing that God is good and wonderfully pleasant, a veritable foretaste of the hereafter in this world. This is alluded to in the verse (Ps. 97:12): "Rejoice, O righteous, in the Lord." One cannot attain this by effort, like the fear of God . . . which depends on arduous effort, as one who searches for a great treasure . . . But this great love with delights descends on a person as a grace from above, without him preparing or striving for it. But it comes only after one has labored to reach the fear of God which is induced by contemplating His exaltation, in such measure corresponding to the state of his soul. Then the love of God comes to him by itself to be united with the fear of God. . .

The second level of love for God is the soul's yearning to cleave to God, to be included in the source of life. The nearness of God is her good, and she desires it; and it is painful for her to be separated from Him by a barrier formed by worldly involvements. This love is hidden in the heart of every Jew, even the wicked, and this is the source of the feelings of remorse. But because this love is hidden, in a kind of exile in the body, the *kelipah*, the evil power, can dominate it, and this is the folly which leads man to sin. Man's service to God consists therefore in overcoming the evil power altogether, to banish it from the body, from thought and speech and action, and he will then be able to release the prisoner from captivity, so that this hidden love shall become manifest in all one's faculties, primarily in his mind and in his thoughts . . . As the mind contemplates God, according to his intellectual capacity and the state of his culture, how He is the life of all life, and the life of his own soul in particular, he will naturally desire to cleave to Him and to be near Him, as the son always yearns to be near his father and as fire always tends to rise upward; and the more he will contemplate this desire in his mind, the more it will extend to his mouth and to all his organs, leading him to study the Torah and to practice the commandments, through them to cleave to God, for the Torah and the Holy One, praised be He, are one.

It is concerning this yearning, in active manifestation, that the verse (Ps. 42:3) states: "My soul yearns for God, for the living God." It is analogous to a person yearning for water but he is as yet without feeling any pleasure in it. It is also concerning this love that we pray for God's help to take it out of its imprisonment, that it alone fill the heart, and that her rival by which we mean the worldly lusts, shall not enter the house, but that she herself be mistress of the household, dominating her rival and banishing her from thought and speech and action. One may not be able altogether to banish her, but let her at least become the hidden one, in a state of exile and subservience to her mistress, the head of the house, to serve only for necessary pursuits solely, such as eating and drinking, as is alluded to in the verse (Prov. 3:6): "In all your ways acknowledge Him." (*Iggeret haKodesh* 18)

PENITENCE

1. The Torah commands us to serve God "with all our heart," and the sages defined this to mean that we are asked to serve with both impulses, the good and the bad. This means that we are to love God with the love of a penitent. Penitence is not a state confined to one who committed specific transgressions, God forbid. It is a state to which all are invited, for penitence [*teshuvah,* literally, "return"] means the return of the soul to its divine source, whence it emanated, from where all life unfolded, from God Himself. The soul descended from its glorious abode and became robed in the physical, so that no matter what noble spiritual perceptions she reaches, once robed in the physical, these perceptions are all subject to the limitations of time and space. There is thus a need for the soul to return, through crying out to God in protest against her confinement, as we are told (Psalms 107:6): "They cried unto the Lord in their trouble." The term for trouble, *ẓa'ar,* really means narrow, it refers to an outcry against confinement, against being placed within a boundary. It is this sense, too, that we understand God's declaration (Ex. 20:2): "I am the Lord your God who took you out of Egypt." The term for Egypt, *miẓrayim,* suggests *miẓar,* which means that which confines. Through the bitterness felt over the opposite state does the love for God arise all the more mightily, to become reunited with the light of the Infinite, praised be He. This parallels the greater worth attached to the

light if it comes after darkness. It is for this reason that our sages said (Berakhot 34b): Where a penitent stands, even the fully righteous are not worthy to stand. (*Torah Or,* Vayeḥi)

2. This should be made known as a basic principle. The effort to win a victory over one's evil impulse is analogous to seeking a victory in a physical contest, as when two wrestle and each seeks to fell the other. If one be lazy or slow he will be easily defeated, even if he be stronger than the other. One cannot defeat the evil impulse in a state of laziness or slowness induced by sadness or stupor, but only if one acts with zeal inspired by a joyous nimbleness, a heart that has been freed of anxiety, worry and sadness. As to the statement (Prov. 14:23): "In all sadness there will be some gain," which suggests that some gain accrues from it, the text implies, on the contrary, that sadness in itself is not of advantage, but that it might be instrumental in bringing about some advantage. This refers to the true joy in God which comes after periods of sadness at specially designated times, when one has experienced the pangs of remorse, through which the spirit of impurity and of evil has been broken, removing the obstructing wall that separates one from God.

I will now advise you as to how one may purge his heart of sadness and anxiety over worldly matters, even over concerns about children, health and sustenance. Everyone knows the talmudic admonition (Berakhot 54a): As one praises God for the good so should one praise him for evil. This is interpreted to mean that one should accept affliction with joy even as one accepts what is manifestly good, for even the former is for good, except that this cannot be discerned by the eyes of a mortal. It comes to us from the world where God's graces are in a state of concealment which is higher than the revealed world . . . Thus it is written (Ps. 94:12): "Happy is the man whom God reproves." It is for this reason that the sages (Shabbat 88b) applied the verse (Judg. 5:31): "His lovers will be as the sun going forth in its might," to people who rejoice in their affliction. They rejoice because they love the nearness of God more than all the life of this world. . .

As to sadness over the state of one's piety, one must devise strategies how to rid oneself of it. Needless to say that this needs to be done if it occurs during an act of divine service, since one must serve God in joy and gladness of heart. But even a person involved in the affairs of the world, if he is seized by sadness and worry over the state of his piety while engaged in some worldly pursuit, it is certain that the evil one is conspiring to incite against him some lust later on, for otherwise, why should he be seized with genuine sadness because of his state of love for or fear of God, precisely when engaged in some worldly pursuit? If he is seized by sadness while serving God, whether in studying Torah or reciting prayer, or if he is assailed by it at some other time, he must remember that this is not the proper time for genuine sadness, even because of concern over serious offenses.

For such concern one must set aside appropriate times, when one's mind is at ease, to think of the greatness of God whom one has offended so that he might thereby experience true remorse. We have defined elsewhere the appropriate time for this. We have also made it clear that at such designated times, immediately after experiencing deep remorse, one's sadness will immediately vanish and he will be fully confident that God has forgiven him; and this is the true joy in God which comes after sadness. (*Tanya* 26)

THE MASTER

1. My beloved, my brothers and friends, out of my hidden love for you do I bring you open rebuke. Come, let us reason together. Remember the olden days, consider the past generations. Has anything like this ever happened in the past? Where, in any of the writings of our sages, the early or the later masters, did you find this practice of [going to the Rebbe] to seek help [*ezah*] concerning mundane matters? Such counsel was not sought even from the early talmudic sages, like the *tannaim* and *amoraim*, for whom there were no hidden mysteries and who were knowledgeable concerning the celestial realm . . . In truth all human affairs except Torah and reverence for God cannot be discerned except by prophets, but the sages have no inkling concerning these. . .

But I shall declare the truth to those who heed what I say. Love upsets the order of things. It would be a kind of blindness not to see the truth. They are moved by a great concern for the body to be able to serve God with it with great enthusiasm, because they love God. Therefore, are they upset by bodily afflictions, God spare us and be merciful, and they cannot submit to them in love. They thus become mentally disturbed and go from city to city to seek counsel from distant place, instead of turning to God, to return to Him in humility, to accept His chastisement in love, "for it is whom the Lord loves that He chastises" (Prov. 3:12). This is analogous to a merciful, wise and righteous father who strikes his son. It is not appropriate for a wise son to turn his back and run to find an intercessor with his father, who is merciful, righteous and pious. It is rather for him to face his father directly, to bear his chastisements in love, thereby to enjoy the benefit thereof all his days. (*Iggeret haKodesh* 22)

23. Mordecai of Chernobyl

Rabbi Mordecai (Twersky) of Chernobyl (1770–1837) was a son of Rabbi Menahem Nahum of Chernobyl and a son-in-law of another renowned master in Ḥasidism, Rabbi Aaron of Karlin. When his father died, he succeeded him as the head of the community, conducting his leadership in affluent style. His followers took upon themselves an annual contribution, collected by special emissaries, for the maintenance of their Rebbe. He was popular among the general populace and his circle of followers grew ever larger.

His teachings reveal great depth and his adherents also included many who were learned in the Torah. We have a collection of his teachings in the volume *Likkutei Torah,* much of which is written in the familiar ḥasidic style of homilies based on specific biblical or talmudic texts. But this volume also has a series of seven didactic summaries of the hasidic way of life. They are written as simple directives, with little theoretical discussion or textual analysis, and offer us a succinct statement of basic values in ḥasidic piety.

A CHART FOR LIVING

1. The first principle is that a person must believe with full and firm faith that there is one God, who created all things out of nothing. We must believe this both by virtue of its being an ancestral tradition, and by virtue of its confirmation in knowledge. Both are alluded to in the verse (I Chr. 28:9): "Know the God of your fathers and serve Him" [the reference is to *knowledge* as well as to the tradition of the fathers]. A conscientious person must stake his life on this faith, for this faith is proclaimed in the first two commandments, "I am the Lord your God," and, "You shall have no other God," which were spoken by God himself [there is a tradition that only the first two commandments were spoken by God, while the others were communicated by God to Moses, who, in turn, communicated them to Israel]. It is incumbent on a Jew to assert himself against the pressures of his physical nature, to subdue it, and purify it, and then will his spiritual self shine in his physical frame, and he will become a "chariot" for God. These two commandments, "I am the Lord your God," and, "You shall have no other God," embrace within themselves the entire Torah.

When a person believes with a full faith that there is one Creator, the Cause of all causes, then he takes on himself the discipline of His Kingdom without forgetting it even for a moment and this illumines the inwardness of his heart every moment. Then it is resolved in his heart to commit all his strength to God, and faithfully to serve and love his Master, to fear Him, and to glorify Him, and to vanquish the evil tempter who seeks to estrange him from his Master, The Lord of all creation. He will be drawn to praise his Master with words of Torah and prayer, and the performance of the commandments, and to cleave to Him from the depth of his heart. He will be stirred by love to acknowledge His kingship, thereby to enlarge the area of holiness. Thus he will be attached to God always with a firm bond, and he will detach himself from the chains of his bondage to the follies of the time, and its delights, to which the evil impulse incites him. This is the goal of the admonitions of the evil impulse—to sever him from the true source of life, and to induce him to follow his bodily desires by arousing his physical passions, laziness and melancholy . . . anger at what runs counter to his will . . . the love of pleasure, and the pursuit of evil or other interests which are not totally dedicated to God.

As mentioned earlier, one must be a person of faith, and detach himself from evil, and attach himself to the Him who is "good to all, and whose mercies are over all His works" (Psalms 145:9). Thereby he will evoke God's mercy, strengthening him more and more in the fear of God, to take on himself the yoke of His Kingdom, praised be He. (*Likkutei Torah, Hadrakhah* 5)

2. It is an essential article of faith that God's glory, praised be He, pervades the whole earth, and that no part of it is devoid of His presence. When you confront the world, then you are really confronting the Creator, His name be praised. You must believe that He is present though you cannot see Him. It is analogous to your conversation with a person. When you speak to him, you are communicating with his soul, for when the soul leaves the body you cannot converse with him, he becomes like a silent stone. But while he is alive it is with his soul that you communicate, though you cannot see it. Thus it is with God, the Soul of all souls, who is likewise invisible.

When you study you must learn to attach yourself to each letter, the letters will enable your soul to ascend and link itself with the divine source.

Beware against depression whatever may happen, and have faith that all things are meant for your good, as it is suggested (Lament. 3:38): "The most High does not decree evil as well as good" [but only the good].

Beware of anger, flattery, falsehood, and if, out of habit, you tell a lie, be not bashful to tell the person that you told an untruth, until you will discipline yourself so that no falsehood will come from your lips.

Be careful about the company you keep, bearing in mind the admonition (Psalms 1:1): "Blessed is the man who has not walked in the counsel of the wicked, and has not stood in the path of sinners, and has not sat in the assembly of scorners."

Be careful to observe the Sabbath, and guard against idle talk on the Sabbath, but spend it in pursuing the study of Torah.

Recite daily eighteen chapters of the Mishnah without the commentaries, so that you will complete once each month all the six orders of the Mishnah. Make this your practice throughout life.

Do not flatter any person or envy any person, confess before your Creator all your sins, make certain that you have renounced your sins with a full heart, and pray from the *Siddur* word for word.

Give charity daily, whether much or little, in accordance with your means; but be sure that you practice this daily.

Rise to study during the night, for night time is meant for study. Also study a little at each meal, prior to reciting the Grace after the meal. Study each day the book *Reshit Ḥokhmah* ["The Beginning of Wisdom," a moralistic work by Elijah ben Moses de Vidas, a 16th century mystic], especially the chapter, "The Gate of Holiness."

Be alone one hour each day, to take stock of yourself, and ask forgiveness of the Creator, praised be He, for any offense you may have committed, whether in your youth or, surely, since growing up. Thus will you be in a state of penitence throughout life. (*ibid., Hadrakhah* 6)

24.
Naḥman of Bratslav

Rabbi Naḥman of Bratslav, a great grandson of the Beşht, was born in 1772 in Medzibezh, in the Ukraine. At an early age he sought a path of his own in ḥasidic piety: he loved nature, and in his lonely walks in the fields and the woods he felt the revelation of God as embodied in the wonders of creation. He yearned for the mystic aura of the Holy Land, and in 1798 he set out for Ereẓ Israel, reaching his destination a year later. But he remained there only a short time, returning in 1880 to Bratslav, which became a center of his brand of Ḥasidism. His independent spirit aroused fierce opposition against him within the ḥasidic world itself. This opposition was one of the factors that led him to leave Bratslav, and settle in Uman, where he died in 1810, after a protracted illness. His followers never selected a successor to their revered master, and they are sometimes called "the dead *ḥasidim*" because they continue to give their loyalty to a master who is no longer among the living.

The *Likkutei Moharan* [*Morenu Harav Rav Naḥman*], Rabbi Naḥman's major work, is not a systematic exposition of his thought but a series of homilies built around intricate interpretations of biblical and talmudic passages. However, the principle elements in his philosophy can be clearly seen in these homilies. In addition to formal discourses he formulated his teachings in allegories and parables, which he usually told in the Yiddish vernacular.

The great problem which agitated Rabbi Naḥman continuously was the tragic contrast between the high station to which man is born and the miserable reality characterizing his actual life. He is born to be a prince, to enjoy fellowship with God and thereby to enter into the bliss of eternal life. But he is alienated from his Creator, giving him a distorted perspective on the world around him. Trivialities disturb him; he focuses on the negative side of everything and sees himself as well as his fellow humans in a harsh light. People are like beautiful flowers which have not blossomed; the best part of their natures are dormant, asleep.

To help people discover their true identity we have the Torah and the commandments, of which the Jewish people have been charged to serve as custodians. The Torah will help them find their way to God and they in turn are to help the non-Jewish world find its way to God. But the Torah itself has an outer self and inner self, and one can study it on the surface and it will not touch his soul and wake him to the great light of God waiting to illumine his life.

The main channel for guiding man to find the light of God in the world and in the Torah is the rebbe, the master, who must be a person of great sensitivity, linked to God by great emotional attachment. He must be concerned with God's world and seek to redeem it, reaching out especially to those outside the realm of holiness, to non-Jews, to Jews who have strayed from their faith, to the common people who are without learning and without sophistication. The rebbe is a spiritual therapist who combines divine inspiration with an insight into human nature, and knows how to robe the truth in an idiom suitable to each person, according to his level of understanding. The rebbe consecrates his life to his vocation but sometimes he does not complete his mission in his own lifetime. But the efficacy of his ministry continues even after his death.

Indeed, there are many people who will not meet the goal to which they are called in their lifetime. They are given a second chance after their death, when their life's mission is carried on by others who come after them. This was expressed through the belief in the soul's reincarnation, which came into Jewish mysticism at an early period and which was reaffirmed by Rabbi Naḥman.

The goal of history is man's awakening from his lethargy to the realization of his true identity. The time of universal awakening is what we mean by the time of the coming of the messiah. Each person, by rising out of his own lethargy, by forging the ties that will link him with God, and by ordering his life with the divine light as his guide and compass, can help to bring nearer the day of the coming of the messiah.

Rabbi Naḥman was a gifted storyteller. His tales are sometimes enigmatic and difficult to interpret, but in many cases their meaning is rather obvious. They seek to awaken man from his spiritual stupor, from his melancholy over his spiritual growth. The motivation for these stories is well conveyed in the statement of his disciple Rabbi Nathan: "Since the teachings and the holy discourses and the like, on which he labored all his life, proved ineffective in bringing us back to God, he began to tell stories. In truth, there is in these stories a great power to awaken us toward God, praised be He" (Preface, *Sefer Sippurei Ma'asiyot*). Rabbi Naḥman's stories are collected in two volumes: *Sefer Sippurei Ma'asiyot* and *Sippurei Ma'asiyot Ḥadashim*. For the English reader, the most accessible collection of stories is Martin Buber's *Tales of Rabbi Naḥman* and Arnold J. Band's *Nahman of Bratzlav; The Tales* (Paulist Press, New York, 1978)

ON SERVING THE WORLD

1. Each person must say, For my sake was the world created (Sanhedrin 37a). Since the world was created for my sake, I must at all times concern myself with the perfection of the world, to overcome its deficiencies and to pray on behalf of the people in it. (*Likkutei Moharan* 5)

2. One cannot enhance the honor due God except through "the Torah of kindness," and this "Torah of kindness", according to our sages (Sotah 49b), is exemplified by one who studies Torah, with the view of teaching it to others. This is what glorifies Him, as it is taught in the *Zohar (Yitro* 69a). When those of the other nations come and acknowledge God, then is the name of the Holy One, praised be He, glorified, as was the case when Jethro testified (Ex. 18:1): "Now I know that the Lord is greater than all the gods." Thus, His glory is enhanced when people who are outside the circle of His holiness come within this holiness. This refers both to converts who embrace our faith, and to penitents who had also been outside. When one encourages them and brings them within, then one adds to His glory. (*ibid.* 14)

3. "O Lord, how many are my afflictions, many have risen against [literally, *on*] me" (Psalms 3:2).

Each one suffers according to the state of his soul and the level of his service to God. There is one who suffers because of troubles afflicting his children, a parent, or a neighbor. There is one of greater stature who suffers because of troubles which afflict the entire city. And there is one who is of very great stature and he suffers because of troubles which afflict the entire world. Each one bears on himself those for whom he suffers . . . But how is it possible for a physical being to bear on himself so many people? However, through suffering the body is subdued . . . the soul shines and is enhanced as a result . . . and the soul can bear on it ever so many people. This is the meaning of the verse: "O Lord, how many are my afflictions, many have risen on me." The more numerous my afflictions, the more people rise on me. Through this I bear many and raise them to their divine source. (*ibid.* 170)

4. When our faith is in a lowly state, false beliefs are strengthened . . . When we raise the condition of our faith from its lowly state, converts come to us . . . They either become converts in fact . . . or they only become converts in essence . . . and within their own faith as it is, they believe in the unity of God, the Creator, praised be He. This is prophesied in the verse (Malachi 1:11): "For from the rising of the sun to its going down My name shall be great among the nations, and in every place incense shall be offered in My name." (*ibid.* II 5)

5. Our goal is to draw the whole world to serve God in one fellowship . . . This is advanced in each generation to the extent that there is peace. When peace prevails among people they study and clarify to each other the truth. Thereby people are moved to discard the idols of falsehood and come closer to the truth. (*ibid.* 27)

6. The true function and chief ornament of our faith is in bringing the alienated close to it, fulfilling the prophesy of Zephaniah (3:9), that the time will come "when all people will call upon the name of the Lord." Even non-Jews will then draw close to the faith of Israel "to serve Him in one fellowship. . ."

The primary error of those who are alienated from God derives from the fact that the principal knowledge we have of God is by inference from the known to the unknown. Since on the face of it they see that the world is governed by the configuration of the planets they fall into a variety of errors. Some assume that everything is directed according to the workings of nature, and some believe that one must also worship the intermediary . . . that is, they believe in God but also in intermediaries . . . Thus they believe that commerce is the primary cause of earning a livelihood, as though without commerce God would be unable to provide for their sustenance. They similarly turn medicine into the primary factor in healing as though without medicine God would be unable to heal. But this is not so, the Holy One, praised be He, is the cause of all causes. And we are not dependent on intermediate causes, but must place our faith in God, praised be He, alone.

Through peace one becomes knowledgeable in answering the heretic in one's own heart . . . because heresy thrives in a climate of quarrels. Instead of meeting and communicating with one another so as to effect modification in thinking, each person holds on to his own views. Even if they should meet and hold discussions people will not change their views, because of the will to triumph in the argument . . . peace, engendering communication, would certainly lead to avoiding of idolatry and heresy which persist in each of them, and people would attain to a pure faith. (*ibid.* 62)

7. As long as idolatry persists in the world [God's] anger is turned on the world. This anger is reduced when idolatry is weakened and [former idolators] become converts. This was the ministry of Moses all his life, and even after his death. Thus he befriended the mixed multitude (Ex. 12:38) so that they might become converts. On his death he was buried opposite the idolatrous shrine *Beit Pe'or* (Deut. 34:5) so as to weaken idolatry and win converts. (*ibid.* 215)

THE WAY OF PENITENCE

1. A person is always in need of penance, for who can say, "I have cleansed my heart, I have purified myself from my sin?" (Prov. 19:9). Even when a person declares, in the words of the confessional, "I have sinned, I have been perverse, I have transgressed," he cannot do so with his full heart, without some reservation. It thus turns out that one needs to do penance for his original penance . . . After his penance, he certainly has a better comprehension of God, praised be He. Thus according to his present comprehension, his original one was gross, and he should therefore do penance for his earlier comprehension, for having thought of God in gross terms.

Whoever wishes to pursue the way of penitence must strengthen himself in his devotion to God, whether in a state of ascending or in a state of descending. These correspond to the statement (Psalms 139:8): "If I ascend to the heavens, You are there, and if I descend to hell, You are there." If a person should reach some high station, he must not remain there and be content with himself, but he must realize that it is for him to climb ever higher . . . The opposite is also true. If he should fall, God forbid, to some low estate, even to the lowest depths, he must never despair, but always seek God, and strengthen himself wherever he might be, in whatever way he can, for even in the lowest depths God may be found, and even there it is possible to cleave to Him . . . (*Likkutei Moharan* 6)

2. When a person wants to pray, he is assailed by all kinds of alien thoughts and obstructions that surround him, and he remains in darkness, and he cannot pray . . . But know that there are many doors in that darkness through which to go out, as the sages declare (Yoma 38b): Whoever seeks to defile himself, they open a door for him, and whoever seeks to cleanse himself, he is helped . . . It means that there are many doors in the darkness through which to leave, but man is blind and he cannot find the door. However, through truth, one is enabled to find the door, for the real light that shines is the Holy One, praised be He, as it is written (Psalms 27:1): "The Lord is my light and my help." Through falsehood one causes God to depart . . . but through truth the Holy One, praised be He, abides with him, as it is written (Psalms 145:18): "The Lord is near to all who call Him, to all who call Him in truth." When the Holy One, praised be He, abides with him, He, gives him light and helps him find his way out of the darkness which impedes him from prayer. (*ibid.* 9)

3. It is of the greatest importance to practice a regular period of withdrawal, to set aside at least an hour or more to be alone in a room or in the field, to speak his inner thoughts to God, imploring Him to bring him closer to His true service. This prayer and this speech should be in the vernacular, for in the holy tongue, Hebrew, one cannot express himself fully and the heart is not moved by such utterances, because . . . it is not our practice to speak in the holy tongue . . . But in Yiddish [Rabbi Naḥman uses the term *lashon ashkenaz*, the Germanic idiom], one can express all that is in his heart before God, such as remorse for past misdeeds, and pleas to be enabled from now on to draw close to God in truth . . . And one must be careful to do this regularly on a particular hour each day. But the rest of the time one must be in a state of joy. (*ibid.* II 25)

4. The primary value in weeping comes when it is inspired by joy. Even the remorse for misdeeds we experience is also of great value when it is inspired by joy, when one's rejoicing in God leads him to regret his past misdeeds . . . The Hebrew term for weeping, *bekhiyah*, may be seen as an abbreviation for the words that spell *beshimkha yagilun kol*

hayom, which means "in Your name they will rejoice all day" (Psalms 89:16). (*ibid.* 175)

5. There is a great difference in the fate of those who commit transgressions. If he feels an immediate stirring of remorse and turns in penitence, then he can easily retrace his steps for he has not yet travelled a great distance from the right path. For the transgressor turns aside from the right road to another road which is rough and from which many rough and deceptive by-paths branch out. When one begins to walk on this wrong road one strays on those by-paths until it becomes difficult to emerge from them.

The Holy One, praised be He, generally calls to a person immediately after He sees him straying from the road of good sense, summoning him to turn back. Each one He calls according to his condition, some He calls through a sign, some He calls literally, and some He strikes at, and this is the way He issues His call. Thus we are told that the Torah cries out: "How long will you fools love folly" [Prov. 1:22, but here it is wisdom rather than the Torah which is described as calling]. But in truth it is God Himself who calls them through the Torah, asking them to return to Him. Therefore, when one has not strayed too far from the right course he can easily return for he can recognize the voice, as he is familiar with it . . . He is like a lamb that has lost its way. If the shepherd calls it, immediately it will recognize his voice and then it will at once go back to him. But if it has gone too great a distance in its straying it has forgotten the voice, and even the shepherd has given up seeking it, since it has strayed from him a long time.

Similarly when one has, God forbid, remained a long time in his wrongdoing, and has wandered far from the right road to those rough and deceptive and confusing paths, it is difficult for him to turn back . . . and this is the meaning of the prayer (Psalms 119:17b): "I have gone astray like a lost lamb; seek Your servant, for I have not forgotten Your commandments." It is a plea to God to hasten to call him while he can still recognize the voice of the Torah and the commandments . . . for once a person has become hardened in wrongdoing, it is difficult to seek him. (*ibid.* 206)

6. Know that there are evildoers who struggle all their lives to uproot themselves altogether from God and His Torah. The dimension of holiness deriving from the holiness of Israel which persists in them, though they are evildoers, confuses them, and engenders in them thoughts of penitence and fear of the great Day of Judgment. As a result they do not enjoy their transgressions and their lusts. They desire ardently and weary themselves with the effort to bring their minds to total

heresy, so that no element of self-doubt appear to prod them back to the truth. But for this one needs very great exertion over a great many years, may God spare us from such fate. For the Judaism which retains its hold on them does not leave them at peace, and continues to confuse them. (*ibid.* 270)

7. When a person does not reflect on the real purpose of his life, what meaning is there to his existence? The soul always aspires to heed the will of its Creator, and when it sees that the person does not heed His will, praised be He, then it yearns desperately to return to its source. It tries to detach itself from the body, and this results in the person's illness. His soul force is weakened, because it seeks to dissociate itself from him since he does not respect its will. Its will is primarily that he heed the will of God, praised be He. (*ibid.* 268)

8. The Talmud states (Nedarim 41a) that the only real poverty is a poverty of enlightenment, and this is deserving of compassion . . . This type of poverty is encountered on an overall level and in particulars. An overall poverty is represented by a person who is unenlightened in the divine service. The one who is enlightened is obligated to enlighten him. The poverty in particular refers to the enlightened person himself, for there are times when such a person is without wisdom, and this is represented in what we call a "contraction of the mind," and he must endeavor to strengthen himself to reach an "expansion of the mind." On attaining an "expansion of the mind" all the severities of God's judgment are nullified and one experiences God's kindness and mercy . . . And if a person should be unable by his own efforts to attain an "expansion of the mind," a strategy that will prove helpful is to try and enlighten others, thereby effecting a stimulation in his own mind as well. (*ibid.* 106)

9. Know that *teshuvah* [usually rendered as "penitence," but a more literal meaning is "return"] means a return to the source from which one has been taken . . . and what is this source? It is the divine wisdom [*hokhmah,* the first of the *sefirot* bearing the divine creative potency] which is the source of all things, as it is written (Ps. 104:14): "With wisdom have You made them all." Therefore must every person guard his mind against alien systems of thought for only divine wisdom can lead one to perfection while other kinds of wisdom are futile, and are not real wisdom at all . . . And when a person allows alien thoughts, that is, alien systems of thought, to enter his mind, they diminish the holiness of his mind . . . and to such a mind are drawn evil and loathsome traits. . .

In addition to guarding himself against alien thoughts a person must continually renew his mind . . . for the renewal of the mind is the renewal of the soul; the mind is the soul . . . The renewal of the mind, that is, the renewal of the soul, can be accomplished through sleep . . . for when the mind is weary it is renewed through sleep.

There are different kinds of sleep. There is physical sleep which is relaxing to the mind. There is also a type of study which is called sleep, as compared to cleaving to God, and this is the literal study of Torah texts (*Zohar, Pinḥas* 242b; cf. *Bereshit Rabbah, Vayeẓei* 69). Our sages alluded to this in the statement (Sanhedrin 24a) that the verse (Lamentations 3:6): "He put me in dark places," refers to the study of the Babylonian Talmud. This corresponds to what is called *emunah,* simple faith. We may see an allusion to this in the verse (Psalms 92:2): "And Your faith in the night" [a rather free rendering of the original: "It is good to praise the Lord . . . to declare Your mercy in the morning, and Your faithfulness in the nighttime"], and in the verse (Gen. 1:5): "And the darkness He called night. A person who is constantly attached to the service of God and his mind grows weary because of the intensity of the attachment should study the plain meaning of the Torah. In the course of studying the plain meaning of the Torah his mind, that is, his soul will enter the real of *emunah,* where one is renewed each morning (Lamentations 3:23), and he will be renewed and reinvigorated from his weariness. And when the mind is renewed as in the beginning one is returned to the source whence one has been taken.

There is also a form of sleep which consists in directing one's business dealings in accordance with *emunah,* faithfully. This, too, corresponds to literal precepts of the Torah, for when a person transacts business in accordance with *emunah,* then his mind, that is, his soul, enters the realm of *emunah,* simple piety . . . and there it is renewed and invigorated from its weariness. This is the meaning of the statement of our sages (Baba Batra 175b): Whoever seeks to acquire wisdom should engage in the study of the laws governing commerce. It suggests that whoever wishes to renew his mind, that is, his soul, should study the laws governing commerce . . . This corresponds to the verse (Prov. 31:14): "She is like a merchant ship, she brings her food from afar." Through commerce, that is, through the literal study of the Torah, one brings one's food from afar, and effects his mind's renewal . . . for wisdom is characterized as distant. Thus it is written (Ecc. 7:21): "I said, I will acquire wisdom, but it is distant from me. . ."

And this is the significance of sounding the *shofar* on *Rosh Hashanah.* For *Rosh Hashanah* focuses on the level of man's sleep, as is well known. It focuses on man's business dealings in accordance with *emunah.* It corresponds to the literal study of the Torah, to the concern over laws governing commerce. The sounding of the *shofar* is to awaken one from sleep, which is a renewal of the mind, through an act of illumination. This explains why the face of the person sounding the *shofar* turns red. He has evoked lights from a higher realm. (*ibid.* 35)

10. For the most part, those who pursue the lust of money die in a state of indebtedness, and they have nothing. Even if they are not literally in debt, they are indebted during their lifetime to their lust, for they are so avid to earn money, that they drive themselves all their lives to great exertions . . . as though they had to make good a debt; this is a debt to their worldliness . . . It thus turns out that their wealth is not wealth for they do not derive pleasure from it . . . It is impossible to acquire abundance and earn a livelihood and acquire wealth that is true wealth, that is, wealth in a state of holiness, which means to be content with one's lot . . . except by breaking the lust for money. (*Likkutei Moharan* 23)

11. One cannot be receptive to the full benefits of divine providence until one breaks the lust for money, and this can be effected through charity . . . This state is an intimation of the time of the messianic revelation, when the avidity for money will cease as is suggested in the verse (Isa. 31:7): "In that day will man discard his idols of silver and his idols of gold . . ." As long as this idolatry of lusting for money persists in the world, hostility will persist in the world. To the extent that this idolatry will be repudiated will hostility also disappear . . . and lovingkindness will dawn for the world. (*ibid.* 13)

FAITH IN MAN

1. One must judge each person favorably. Even if a person be completely evil it is necessary to seek and find some good in him, wherein he is not evil. By finding some good in him and judging him favorably, one will indeed draw him to the side of merit and enable him to repent. This is in a sense alluded to in the verse (Psalms 37:10): "For yet a little while and the wicked is no more, and you will consider his place, and it will be gone" [in context, the verse means that destruction will soon overtake the wicked]. The verse cautions us to judge all people favorably. Though one notes a person to be completely wicked, one must seek out some good in him, wherein he is not wicked . . . By finding in the wicked person a little good, wherein he is not wicked, you will consider his place and it will be gone. This means that if you will consider his place and his condition, you will find that he is no longer in his earlier condition, for by finding in him some good and judging him favorably one will thereby truly withdraw him from the state of guilt to the state of merit.

One must similarly find some good in oneself. It is well known that a person must be careful always to be in a state of joy, and to keep away from depression. Even if a person, on confronting himself, should find that there is nothing good in him, that he is full of sin, and the evil impulse conspires to defeat him as a result of this by inducing in him depression and melancholy, he must not allow himself to be defeated by this. He must seek and find some good in himself, for how is it possible that he has not performed some commandment or some good deed in the course of his life? . . . For a person must find some good in himself in order to revive himself and bring himself to a state of joy . . . As a result of this he will truly withdraw from the state of guilt to the state of merit, and he will be enabled to repent. (*Likkutei Moharan* 282)

2. The evil impulse acts on various levels. In an inferior crude person, the incitements of the evil impulse are also lowly and crude . . . Whoever has any refinement at all regards this role of the evil impulse as folly and madness and he needs no special exertion of will to overcome it . . . But the evil impulse sometimes acts as a holy angel . . . as when he provokes sternness and condemnation of people. The enlightened person has to contend with the evil impulse on this level . . . and he must overcome it and mitigate the stern judgments so that he will see everything in the perspective of the good . . . This is illustrated by God's pronouncement against David (I Chronicles 22:8): "You may not build a house to my name because you have shed much blood." He did not "sweeten" his harshness and therefore he was not allowed to build God's house. And though the wars he waged were for God, nevertheless, in the highest, divine realm, where all beings are embraced in unity, in the *En Sof*, all is good and must be seen as good, without any place for condemnation. (*ibid.* 72)

THE MINISTRY OF THE MASTER

1. People find it difficult to understand why one must travel to the master, in order to hear the teaching from his lips, because, as they see it, one can study moralistic works. But this is of great value, for there is a great difference between hearing the truth from the master directly, and hearing it quoted by others in his name, and certainly if the one quoting it only heard from another, for it descends to lower levels the more remote it is from the master; and there is especially a great difference between hearing it from the master, and reading it in a book.

Man must refine himself. Each one can see himself by looking at the master's face, as if it were a mirror. Even if the master does not reprove him or preach to him, a person will feel immediate remorse for his deeds by merely looking at him. By merely looking at his face, he will see himself, as in a mirror, and note how he is sunk in darkness. (*Likkutei Moharan* 19)

2. One cannot comprehend God except through many "reductions," from cause to effect, from the higher concept to the lower, as we find in experience that one cannot comprehend a subtle concept except by robing it in a lower concept. Thus when a teacher seeks to explain to his pupil a subtle concept he must robe it in a lower, a lesser concept, so that the pupil might understand it. In other words, he presents to him prefatory statements, and less subtle concepts, thereby to explain to him the subtle concept which is his objective.

One must secure for himself a teacher who can explain to him so great a thought as the comprehension of God; for this one needs a very great teacher . . . And the more lowly one is and the more estranged from God, the greater a teacher he needs, one who is an artist in being able to reduce so great a thought as the comprehension of God in robes adapted to one as small and as estranged as he is. The greater the ailment, the greater the physician needed to heal it. (*ibid.* 30)

3. Every Jew exercises something of the role of a *ẓaddik* . . . as it is written (Isa. 60:21): "Your people are all *ẓaddikim* . . ." For there is in every Jew some precious element which is absent in his neighbor . . . and with the unique element in which he excels his neighbor, it is for him to influence, and illuminate, and stir the heart of his neighbor; and his neighbor needs to accept this influence from him, as it is written [the Aramaic translation of Isa. 6:3, as quoted in the liturgy]: "And they accept one from another." (*ibid.* 34)

4. There is a field, where trees and plants of indescribable beauty grow. Fortunate is the eye that has seen this. The trees and plants—these are holy souls in a state of ascending. There are many naked souls wandering outside the field, waiting, aspiring to be mended, so that they may return to their place. Even a great soul on which many other souls depend—when it occasionally strays from there, it finds it difficult to return. They all wait and yearn for the master of the field who may attend to their mending. Some can be mended only through another's death, through another's good deed or service.

Whoever wants to gird his loins and act as the master of the field must be of very great stature in firmness and courage, wisdom and righteousness. He must be a person of exceptionally great qualities. Some will not be able to complete their mission except by their death . . . Many afflictions and hardships will come upon him but through his greatness and his nobility he will withstand them, and attend to the needs of the field. . .

The master of the field constantly waters the trees and attends to their growth, and to their various needs; and he seeks to place them at a proper distance from each other, so that one will not trespass on the other. For at times one must keep at a distance from the most intimate, in order not to trespass on another.

The souls bear fruit when they do God's will. Then the eyes of the field's master shine . . . but when they fail to do good deeds then his eyes are darkened . . . When his eyes shine, then he can look into each one's eyes and lead him to his goal. He can discern in each one's speech, if he has not been fully mended, that he is still remote from his goal. Then he will lead him toward his goal. (*ibid.* 65)

5. A *ẓaddik* must be learned in the Torah and zealous [a *ḥasid*] in his good deeds. If he is not learned, then he is included in the condemnation of the sages: An ignorant person cannot be pious. But one who is only learned is nothing, for it is possible to be learned and a thoroughly wicked person at the same time . . . And whoever, in error, should think that learning in itself is primary is in the category of *Aḥer* [Elisha ben Avuyah, a sage of the Talmud, who became an apostate and was then called *Aḥer*, "another"], who violated all the essentials of our faith . . . If a *ẓaddik* should sometimes fall to a lower state, for as we know one cannot remain permanently in the same state, it would be wrong if he should desire to maintain himself on the level of learning alone; he should instead maintain himself in the cultivating of piety which remains with him from his earlier state. (*ibid.* 37)

6. This is the value of being close to the *ẓaddik*. Some people reach the level mentioned in Psalms 42: "My soul yearns for God, for the living God." When a person is very thirsty he drinks any water, even polluted water. Similarly there are people who are always thirsty for the divine service. They always engage in study and attend to God's service . . . even when it is not the proper time and even in violation of all rational considerations, because (Menaḥot 99b) there are times when the fulfillment of the Torah is served by voiding its precepts. The advantage of being close to the *ẓaddik* is that they prescribe the time and place for everything. (*ibid.* 76)

7. The person who listens to a discourse by a *ẓaddik* receives an imprint of his image, his mind and his soul, and the physiognomy of the

ẓaddik becomes fixed in his mind . . . but it becomes necessary to guard against forgetting. (*ibid.* 192)

8. At times it is necessary to give a person a certain medicine, but if the medicine should be given as it is, the patient would surely die. It then becomes necessary to dilute the medicine with other ingredients. Similarly, there are people to whom one cannot reveal the inner meaning of the Torah which they need for their healing, for the Torah is medicine . . . It therefore becomes necessary to robe the inner meaning of the Torah with other teachings of the Torah. At times some people will be unable to accept the inner meaning of the Torah even if robed in other Torahitic teachings. Then one must robe the Torah with stories from the secular world, so that they may be able to accept the therapy hidden therein. The Torah itself as it now exists is robed in stories because it would have been impossible to transmit it in its pure essence. (*ibid.* 164)

9. Even those who are remote from the *ẓaddik* receive vitality and illumination from the *ẓaddik*. He shelters them, like a tree, which has branches, bark and foliage, and all draw their sustenance from the tree. Even plants distant from the tree which do not appear to draw sustenance from the tree, do in fact draw from it. For the tree shelters them from the sun. Similarly the *ẓaddik* has the equivalent of branches, bark and foliage . . . And even those who are distant receive vitality from him by sheltering them like a tree. (*ibid.* 224)

10. One must seek out a true leader and draw close to him, for every true leader partakes of the spirit of prophecy. Though at the present time prophecy has ceased to exist, a leader must nevertheless be imbued with a different spirit, unlike that of the multitude, and it is as a result of this that he merits to serve in the role of a leader . . . And this unique spirit with which the leader is imbued is in the nature of the holy spirit, the spirit of prophecy . . . Therefore, all who come close to a true leader will be strengthened in their faith in truth and holiness . . . And one must pray to the Holy One, praised be He, to be deemed worthy of being close to a true leader in order to merit attaining a true faith in its fullness. (*ibid.* II 8)

11. The general principle is that the words in exposition of the Torah spoken by the *ẓaddik* or the words of prayer uttered by him may be called *Ereẓ Yisrael* . . . The ordinary conversation he holds with the general populace may be called a lower level [*pesolet*] of *Ereẓ Yisrael* . . . for it is not possible to link them with their divine source through the Torah and prayer alone—as they are alienated from the truth. When the *ẓaddik* seeks to raise the multitude who are far from the true teachings of the Torah, he must converse with them about ordinary matters and robe

the teaching in that conversation . . . Moreover, at times the *ẓaddik* himself falls from his heights, and when someone from the common people discusses with him worldly matters which he finds relaxing, he is then revitalized. The *ẓaddik* then returns to his heights and he can raise the common people to higher knowledge. (*ibid.* 81)

ON THE COMING OF THE MESSIAH

1. It is written (Ps. 139:5): "You surround me in the rear and in the front." There are matters which a person comprehends after many introductions; such comprehension is called "rear." But there is a comprehension which comes to a person through divine illumination, and this is called "front." Enthusiasm of the heart is generated by the stirring of the mind, for it is in the nature of all movement to engender heat. According to the swiftness of the movement of the mind is heat generated in the heart. Thus through the divine illumination which enlightens the mind swiftly so that one need not depend on any introductions the flame in the heart rises always by itself.

But such divine illumination can be attained only if one hallows his mouth, his nose, his eyes and his ears . . . It is they that activate the divine illumination . . . The mouth, the two nostrils, the two eyes, and the two ears correspond to the seven lights of the candelabrum in the sanctuary. And the candelabrum itself corresponds to the head, that is, the mind, and the face of the candelabrum is the divine illumination. . .

Eternal life is for God alone, He lives forever; and whoever merges himself in his source, that is, in God, praised be He, also enjoys eternal life . . . Similarly there is no perfection except in God, praised be He, and everything outside of Him is deficient, but whoever is merged in Him also enjoys perfection. The most important way of merging oneself in Him is through knowing Him . . . for the primary essence of man is his comprehension, and wherever one's reason is focused there one has his being; and when he has comprehension in the knowledge of God, he is literally in the divine realm, and the more one comprehends of God the more he is merged in his divine source. Whatever deficiencies a person suffers, whether affecting his livelihood, his children or health, and all other lacks—they all stem from a lack of knowledge.

It is true that there are people wholly deficient in knowledge but who nevertheless enjoy every good—in truth, whatever they possess is nothing. The opposite is also true. The one who is perfect in knowledge and nevertheless suffers deficiency—in truth his deficiency is nothing.

This is in accordance with the teaching of the sages (Nedarim 41a): If you acquired knowledge, what do you lack? And if you lack knowledge, what have you acquired? The basis of deficiency or perfection is the absence or presence of knowledge. . .

Similarly, anger and cruelty result from a lack of comprehension, as it is written (Ecc. 7:9): "Anger abides in the bosom of fools. . ." In the hereafter comprehension will be diffused, and all will know God, as it is written (Isa. 11:9): "For [with the coming of the messiah] the earth shall be full of the knowledge of the Lord as the waters cover the sea," and therefore there will be an end to anger. Thus it is written [in that same prophecy, Isa. 11:6]: "And the wolf shall dwell together with the lamb and the leopard shall lie down with the kid. . ." For presently the wolf and the lamb cannot dwell together because of their hostility, but in the hereafter they will be able to dwell together because hostility will cease as a result of the knowledge [of God] which will then be manifest. (*Likkutei Moharan* 21)

2. The original goal of creation was to make manifest God's sovereignty. As a result of the immense potency of the divine light, it was impossible to "receive it" and it became necessary to confine it in the realms of creation. This is the meaning of the verse (Psalms 145:14): "Your kingdom is the kingdom of all the worlds [*olamim,* generally translated "everlasting," also has the meaning of "worlds"]. It suggests that His sovereignty became robed in the worlds, so that it would be possible to receive it. And because there was no one else to accept the discipline of the divine kingship, the souls of the Jewish people appeared to take on themselves the yoke of His kingship. . .

The statement, "And the spirit of God hovered over the face of the waters" (Gen. 1:2), means that when one studies Torah, which is a metaphor for water, as is well known (Ta'anit 7a), then the spirit of God, the holy spirit, hovers over him and he draws it in his breath, for one cannot live without Torah . . . Thus when the heart of a Jew is afire with zeal for the Holy One, praised be He, his entire body might be consumed, but when he robes himself in the letters of the Torah or of prayer, he is shielded and rescued. The converse is also true. When one is afire with worldly lusts his whole being might be consumed, but on studying Torah or performing a commandment, he is shielded and rescued, and he can go on living.

And this is the state characterized as the coming of the messiah . . . when the kingship of God will be magnified and its light become diffused through the perfection of our behavior, then we shall be able to acknowledge our Creator above everything, that is, independently of all the worlds, not as at present, for at present He is known through His being robed in the worlds.

This is the significance of the verse (I Samuel 2:10): "And he will give strength to His king, and will exalt His anointed." When one will enhance the aspect of God's kingship then will His anointed one [the messiah] be exalted. Each person will bring to fruition his own messianic element, ascending from level to level, in slow stages, until God's kingship will become fully manifest; and this state corresponds to what we mean by the coming of the messiah. (*ibid.* 78)

3. A person must see to it that his life shall not be the factor which impedes the coming of the messiah. This calls for wholehearted penitence and a striving to perfect one's actions.

In every *ẓaddik,* if he is a true *ẓaddik,* there is a disclosure of the messiah. Though he is not the messiah in a literal sense, he partakes of the nature of the messiah, who is modeled after Moses. Thus the *Zohar* (*Bereshit* 25b) equates the messiah with Moses . . . for Moses offered his life in behalf of Israel. He had a true awareness of his own lowliness and of the importance and greatness of Israel, as the text (Nu. 12:3) states: "And the man Moses was more humble than any other man on the face of the earth." Because of this he offered up his very life for them. . .

There are people who are engaged in business and pursue the follies of this world, and in the midst of it all there occurs to them the thought of penitence, but they soon relapse to their earlier state. This corresponds to the vision of Ezekiel (I:2), who saw the life-giving divine element surging forward and then receding, it being without stability. Such a life is at times involved with the impure, and at times with the pure, at times with the permissible and at times with the forbidden. This corresponds to the state of the world on weekdays, but wholehearted penitence corresponds to the Sabbath, when everything is at peace, when he is liberated from those harassments . . . and evil has been altogether overcome. (*ibid.* 79)

THE GRAIN OF MADNESS

The king once said to his friend who was next in rank to the king: Since I am a stargazer, I see by the revelation of astrology that whoever will eat of this year's grain will go mad. Advise me, therefore, my friend: What shall we eat?

The next in rank to the king answered: This is my advice, my Lord King. Issue an order to prepare for us a supply of last year's grain, sufficient for our needs, and we will not eat from this year's crop.

The king then said: What good have you accomplished with your advice, my wise man? What will it gain us if we alone are sane and the rest of the people are mad? They will all say that they are sane and we are mad. And if you suggest that we prepare for others also of last year's grain, it will not suffice us.

What then is your advice, your majesty?

The king then replied, saying:

My advice, my friend, is that we have no choice but to eat of this year's grain and to go mad like everybody else. But my intention is that the two of us differ from other people in this, that we at least shall know that we are mad, while others will not be aware of it.

The one next in rank to the king asked: Tell me, your majesty, how will we accomplish this?

The king replied: This I can arrange. We will inscribe on our foreheads a mark of madness. And each time that I look at you and you look at me, we will know we are mad. (David Hadran, *Leket II, MeOlamo shel Rebbe miBraslav*, pp. 21f.)

TWO TURKEYS

The king's son once became insane and imagined himself to be a turkey. He removed his clothes and sat under the table naked, and renounced food, eating only grains and pieces of bones. The king tried all the physicians but no one could help him.

At last one wise man came to the king and said to him: I undertake to cure your son.

This wise man also removed his clothes, placed himself under the table next to the king's son, and gathered grains and pieces of bones and ate them.

The king's son asked him: Who are you and what are you doing here? The wise man replied: And who are you and what are you doing here? The king's son answered him: I am a turkey. The wise man replied similarly: I am also a turkey.

The two turkeys sat together until they became acquainted. The man then gave a signal to bring him a shirt, and after he put on the shirt he said to the king's son: Do you think that a turkey is not allowed to wear a shirt? He is allowed, and he does not thereby cease being a turkey. The king's son understood this and he also consented to wear a shirt.

After some time, the wise man signaled to bring him trousers; he put them on and said to the king's son: Do you think a turkey is not allowed to wear trousers? Even if he wears trousers he can still remain a real turkey. The king's son agreed and he, too, put on trousers, and then, following the wise man's example, he put on the rest of the clothes.

Then the wise man asked for regular food and he ate it, saying to the king's son: Do you think that a turkey is not allowed to eat good food? One can eat the best and remain a turkey as ever. The king's son followed him also in this, and he began to eat regular food.

Reflecting on the progress made so far the wise man then said to the king's son: And do you really think that a turkey must remain confined under the table? Not at all. A turkey may also go where he chooses, and no one has a right to interfere with him. The king's son understood this and accepted the wise man's advice. And since he now stood up and walked like a person he began to behave like a person.

Similarly the *ẓaddik* robes himself in worldly garments and behaves like ordinary people in order to draw them to God's service. (*ibid.*, pp. 22f.)

THE TRANSGRESSION

I dreamt that I was at home, and that no one entered my room. It was surprising. I went into another room, and there, too, I found no one. I went outside and saw many people standing in circles and whispering about me. This one mocked me, the other one laughed at me, a third one was insolent toward me; and even my friends were against me, some looking at me with contempt, and some whispering about me.

I called one of my acquaintances and asked him what it was all about. He answered: And how could you do something like that? How could you commit such a transgression?

I did not know what it was all about and why they ridiculed me. I asked that person to bring together some of my acquaintances. He left but did not return to me.

I reflected on what to do and decided to migrate to another country. When I came there I found there, too, people standing in circles and incited against me, because there, too, the facts were known.

I decided to live in a forest. Five of my acquaintances came to live with me in the forest. We lived there for some time. Whenever we needed food I sent one of my people to buy it. I asked him to *find out* whether the storm had subsided, but he answered: No, the storm is as great as before.

In the meantime an old man came and told me that he would like to discuss something with me. I followed him. Then he said: How could you do something like that, and were not ashamed of your ancestors, your grandfather, Rabbi Naḥman, and your great-grandfather, Rabbi Israel Ba'al Shem Tov? And how were you not ashamed of the Torah of Moses and of the holy patriarchs Abraham, Isaac and Jacob? And do you think you can remain here? All your funds will soon be exhausted, and you are a weak person, and what will you do? Do you think you will migrate to another country? Consider all the alternatives. If they will not know in that country who you really are, you will not be able to live there for you will not be able to earn a livelihood at your regular occupation; and if they should know who you are, you will not be able to live there because they will know what you did.

I said to him: This being the case, that I am such an outcast, will I have a share in the world-to-come?

He answered me: Do you think you will have a share in the world-to-come? Even in *gehinnom* there will be no place for you, because you caused such sacrilege.

I said to him: Leave me. I thought you would comfort me, but you cause me such great pain. Go, go. The old man went away.

I reflected: Since I am living here a long time I am prone to forget my studies. I asked the man whom I sent to purchase food to get me a book. He left but did not bring me a book, telling me that it is impossible for him to disclose for whom he needs a book, and secretly it is impossible to secure a book there. I was greatly anguished because I was a vagabond, and had no book and was prone to forget everything I knew.

The old man returned, with a book in his hands. I asked him: What do you have in your hands? I said to him: Give me the book. He gave it to me. I took the book but did not know how to hold it. I opened it but could not make out the words. They seemed to me written in a strange language and in a strange script. This caused me great pain. I was afraid that if my people will discover this, they, too, will leave me.

The old man again asked me to follow him so that he might talk to me. Again he began to reprove me that I committed such a great transgression, without being ashamed, that even in *gehinnom* there will be no place for me to hide.

I said to him that if one from the heavenly realm told me this, I would believe him.

He said to me: I am from there. And he proved to me that he was from there. I reminded myself of the incident which occurred to the Ba'al Shem Tov when he thought he had forfeited his share in the world-to-come and he said: *I love God without the world-to-come.*

I threw my head back in bitterness. When I threw my head back, all the great people that the old man had said I should have been ashamed of came to me, my great-grandfather, all the patriarchs, and they quoted to me the verse (Isaiah 4:2): "and the fruit of the earth is for pride and beauty." On the contrary, they said, we take pride in you. Then they brought all my people, and my son, all of whom had previously withdrawn from me, and they comforted me, because I had thrown my head back with such bitterness that even if one had violated the entire Torah, he would have been forgiven. (*ibid.*, pp. 81–84)

25.

Ẓadok haKohen of Lublin

Rabbi Zadok haKohen of Lublin was born in 1823 to a prominent rabbinic family. While still a youth he gained fame as a master of classic rabbinic studies. He also made impressive gains in his study of mathematics and engineering. He was drawn to the study of mysticism and Ḥasidism in 1847, and he left a rich collection of writings that constitute an important contribution to ḥasidic thought. He lived modestly, often in great poverty, consistently refusing rabbinic positions which were offered him. He earned his modest and uncertain livelihood from an old clothes shop which came to his wife by inheritance.

The dominant trend in his thought is the interpretation of all religious concepts in terms of inwardness: hell is the anguish experienced as a result of the sense of guilt felt after wrongdoing; angels are divine forces operative in the world and in the human heart; God speaks to us through the yearnings for the good which seem to arise spontaneously within us. He died in 1900.

PENITENCE

1. The remorse felt by a person because of any wrongdoing he may have committed is veritably the pangs of hell meted out for that transgression. It is for this reason that our sages stated (Berakhot 12b) that one who commits a transgression and is ashamed because of it will be forgiven, for he has already suffered the pangs of hell. It is an act of heavenly grace to be reminded constantly of one's wrongdoing so that one may suffer the measure of hell due him because of it. (*Ẓidkat haẒaddik* 57)

2. Every service performed by a physical act and all commandments which they fulfill have only one objective—to condition the heart to righteousness. The essence of all is the heart, for it is there that God, praised be He, abides . . . This is alluded to in the vision of Elijah (I Kings 19:12, 13) that God is to be found in the still small voice, rather than in the fire or the earthquake, for God's glory is not in the tumultuous, stormy phenomena, but in the still small voice, which expresses the heart . . . But at first he must act in a "stormy" manner, vigorously resisting the temptation to evil, as our sages counselled (Berakhot 5a): a person should always incite the good impulse against the evil impulse. However, this is not yet a true domination over it. The latter is attained when it is without tumult, as David said (Ps. 109:22): "My heart is wounded within me." The sages (TJ Berakhot 5:5) interpreted this to mean that he had slain the evil impulse by his fasts . . . Only thus is the full sovereignty of God established. (*ibid.* 68)

3. God calls to man each day, as it is written (Prov. 1:25): "Because I called and you refused to hear, I stretched out My hand and you did not heed." This call is in the form of thoughts that arise spontaneously in the heart, which engender a yearning for God, praised be He. This is effected through God calling to him; as the verse says (Prov. 27:19): "As in the water face answers to face, so the mind of man reflects the man" [what arises in the mind is only a response to a message from outside] . . . But a person must condition himself to hear God's voice which speaks to him and inspires in him thoughts of penitence, never to allow these thoughts to recede. Whoever allows himself to be diverted to the vanities of the world will not comprehend the divine influence. (*ibid.* 222)

GOOD AND EVIL

1. Let a person know that the very time when he stumbles over some sin is the occasion set for some good deed. If he proves worthy, he can

rise in that very time to very high stature. The gravity of the sin to which the evil impulse has incited him can become the very measure of the good that he can extract from it, if he should only turn this yearning toward the good. The deed of evil can become the source of good, the very opposite of that evil. (*Ẓidkat haẒaddik* 76)

2. All souls are linked to each other, as is alluded to in the verse (Deut. 32:9): "Jacob is the portion [the Hebrew *ḥevel,* which also means rope] of His inheritance." When all are held together by a rope, if one pulls toward the heights, all are pulled along and the opposite is also true. The latter corresponds to the statement (Ecc. 9:18): "One sinner effects the loss of much good." (*ibid.* 163)

3. One should be careful not to cause pain to any being, even if motivated by a desire to serve a good purpose. Thus our sages taught (Bava Batra 86) that Jeremiah's pronouncement (Jer. 30:20): "And I will punish all their oppressors," is meant to include collectors for charity. Adoniram, whom King Solomon appointed to exact tribute from the people, to force them to hew stones for the building of the Temple—surely there could be no greater *mitzvah* than this—was punished measure for measure: the people stoned him (I Kings 12:18). This tribute, called by the Hebrew term *mas,* indicated that it was in excess of a person's capacities . . . It is for this reason that the Sanhedrin fasted on the day they pronounced a death sentence, to seek atonement for what they had done (Sanhedrin 63a) . . . Their action fulfilled the precept (Deut. 13:6): "You shall purge evil from your midst." Nevertheless, this action caused pain in heaven, as it were, as it is written (Megillah 10b): God does not rejoice at the fall of the wicked . . . Certainly He does not rejoice at the pain suffered by the righteous, even if it is to effect some meritorious purpose. (*ibid.* 175)

4. The commandments and the good deeds a person performs, and surely the Torah he studies, generate virtuous thoughts in his heart, while transgressions committed have the opposite effect. This is expressed in the statement (Avot 4:2): one righteous deed pulls along another righteous deed, and one transgression another transgression . . . The term "pulls along" is to be understood on the basis of the teaching that every commandment performed effects the birth of an angel, that is a spiritual force . . . and it is this force which puts it into his heart to perform other commandments. (*ibid.* 241)

5. The glory of the Holy One, praised be He, pervades the entire world, but it is in a state of great concealment . . . When the heart of a person has been illumined by this perception . . . the statement of the

Passover *Haggadah* may be applied to him: He has taken us out of darkness to a great light. (*ibid.* 261)

THE NATURE OF MAN

1. As a person must believe in the Holy One, praised be He, so must he believe in himself. This means that he must believe that God is concerned with him, and that he is not a meaningless creature here today to be gone tomorrow, like the beasts of the field who after their death are doomed to oblivion. It is for him rather to believe that his soul derives from God, the source of life, praised be He, and that God takes delight in him when he performs His will . . . that God is pleased with his noble actions. (*Ẓidkat haẒaddik* 154)

2. A person's perfection consists in molding his life according to his conception of what perfection represents . . . for a person's comprehension and his wisdom are expressive of the very essence of his soul and life, every person has a unique core of being, as our sages said (Berakhot 58a) that people are distinctive from one another in their appearance, and the outer appearance reflects the heart's inwardness . . . Thus people diverge in their understanding of life. Therefore did our sages (Exodus Rabbah 52) interpret the verse (Ecc. 12:6): "Each person returns to his world," as meaning that each person has a world of his own . . . that he has a private world of his own. (*ibid.* 149)

THE TRUE SERVICE

1. One should offer only a brief prayer in a place that is distracting . . . It is better to pray less with devotion than more without devotion. This is true of all actions and at all time. (*Ẓidkat haẒaddik* 31)

LATTER DAY MYSTICS

26.

Ḥayyim of Volozhin

Rabbi Ḥayyim ben Isaac of Volozhin (1749-1821) combined eminence in talmudic scholarship with a profound mastery of the Kabbalah. In this dual interest he followed the tradition of his great master, the Gaon of Vilna, but like his master he was an uncompromising opponent of Ḥasidism. He felt deeply the reality of God as the inner light shining in all expressions of Jewish piety. But he was troubled by certain excesses in the ḥasidic theology and the ḥasidic way of life, especially by its overemphasis on pietistic and moralistic literature, at the expense of talmudic study. In his zeal to disseminate talmudic study, he founded the Volozhin Yeshivah in 1803, which became one of the most celebrated centers of talmudic study in East European Jewry.

His polemic against Ḥasidism was waged principally in his *Nefesh haḤayyim,* but this was at the same time a serious exposition of ethical and kabbalistic teaching. He also wrote a commentary on the Ethics of the Fathers, and a collection of responsa. The selections included here illustrate his opposition to Ḥasidism, as well as his positive disposition toward other expressions of Jewish mysticism.

THE PATTERN OF STUDY

1

I have resolved to write concerning the great obligation which rests on each Jew to study the Torah day and night and to elaborate a little on the precious nature of the Torah. I want to speak also in praise of the right-minded people who study the Torah in love, in order to bring delight to the Creator, praised be He, and of those who act in defense of the holy Torah, whose esteem has declined in the past. Especially in recent generations, due to our many sins, has its esteem fallen greatly, almost to the lowest depths, as we see.

This has resulted from the great burden of striving for a livelihood. It has also resulted from the tendency among many who seek God's nearness, but have chosen to spend all their time in studying moralistic works, without spending any time on the basic study of our holy Torah in biblical and halakhic texts. They have not yet seen the true light, the light of Torah has not yet shone on them. May God forgive them, for their intention was sincere, but this is not the way for gaining the illumination of the Torah.

The truth is that study of moralistic works is among the paths pursued by the upright. The early generations used to devote all their time to study the holy Torah; they concentrated on the rabbinic exposition, the study of the *Gemara*, the codes, and the *Tosafot* on the talmudic texts. Their hearts were afire with the love of our holy Torah, with a pure love and reverence for God. Their primary desire was to enhance the honor shown to the Torah, and to strengthen it. They raised many disciples in order to spread the knowledge of God in the world.

In the course of time—this is always the way of the negative impulse to be aroused against these godly people, who pursue the right path—these people were incited by an evil inclination. The result was that many of the scholars devoted themselves *solely* to talmudic dialectics and to nothing else. This was contrary to the statement in the Mishnah (Avot 3:21), that if there is no fear of God there is no Torah, and to many other admonitions of the sages, as will be shown later on, God willing. This excess brought a reaction from many great sages, leaders of the people, who always seek to redress abuses of our Jewish brethren. They acted to eliminate the stumbling from the path of the people of God, by bringing to them moralistic and ethical reproof; they wrote works on the fear of God, to refine the hearts of the people, so that they might pursue the study of the holy Torah, and the service of God, with pure reverence. But every rational person can understand that these men did not intend to effect a neglect in the core subjects of Torah study and to have people spend all their time on their moralistic works. Their objective was that the primary subject of study among the holy people should be the written and the oral Torah, and the legal decisions; this is the core of Torah study. They meant that one should in addition concern himself with the study of religious faith.

But in recent generations, due to our many sins, the opposite has occurred; the high has been brought low. So many have made the primary subject of their study, most of the time, works on religious faith and on morals; they maintain that is the major goal of a person's life always to pursue such studies, thus stirring the heart, to humble and break the power of his lusts, and train him in good behavioral dispositions; thus the crown of the Torah lies humbled in an abandoned corner! I saw with my own eyes one community where this practice has become so prevalent that in many of their study houses they have only moralistic books, but not even one complete set of the Talmud. They do not realize that this is not the way God has chosen, that this is contrary to His wish. It may soon transpire that we may not have a qualified scholar to decide problems of law. What will then happen to the Torah?

Who can remain silent in the face of such conditions and not proclaim to the God-fearing people, who revere His name, the proper path to pursue according to the teaching of the Torah? Woe unto us who will face judgment for the sin of neglecting the Torah, when He, praised be His name, will avenge her disparagement! Firstly I want to explain what is meant by pursuing the study of Torah for its own sake, what is meant by "for its own sake." This, too, is a result of the sin of many who fail to study the holy Torah, because they think that "for its own sake" means with great, uninterrupted cleaving to God. They are afflicted with an even more sickening evil, thinking that if one studies without cleaving to God, it is nothing, and of no value, God forbid. Thus if they find that their hearts are not disposed to reach this state, to have all their study with constant "cleaving," they will not even begin to study, with the result that the Torah is in a state of decline. In the course of our discussion there will be a clarification of the importance of the holy Torah and of the person who studies it properly. Toward this end it will be necessary to cite certain statements of the sages in the Talmud, the Midrash and the *Zohar* which discuss the wondrous excellence of the holy Torah, and of those who pursue its study, the greatness of their reward for doing so, and of the retribution for neglecting it. Though many of these statements are well-known, I have brought them together, to stir the hearts of those who want to attach themselves to God's Torah, praised be He, and to take shelter in His awesome presence.

2

As to the meaning of studying the Torah "for its own sake," clearly this does not refer to cleaving to God, as people generally think. Thus the sages declared in the Midrash that King David, peace be upon him, prayed that one who recited the psalms should be deemed as though he had pursued the study of the mishnaic tracts *Nega'im* and *Oholot*. This therefore shows that the diligent study of the laws of the Talmud is more highly esteemed by God, praised be He, than the recitation of psalms. If we were to hold that "for its own sake" means cleaving to God, and this alone is what is involved in the study of Torah, there could certainly be no more wonderful experience of cleaving to God than through the proper recitation of the psalms all day. Moreover, we have no way of knowing whether God consented to David's prayer, for we find no reference in the teachings of the sages to God's response to David's plea concerning this. Indeed, as far as cleaving to God, it could have sufficed to study one tractate of the Talmud, or one chapter of Mishnah in a state of cleaving to God. But we find that the attitude of the sages was otherwise. Thus they said concerning Rabban Johanan ben Zakkai that he did not neglect the study of Bible, Mishnah, *halakhah* and *aggadah*. This means that he never thought that he had satisfied the duty to study the Torah "for its own sake" with his past accomplishments in study, and he was therefore zealous to add to his studies each day and each hour . . . Logic also refutes this, for there are many laws in the Talmud whose grasp involves a concentration on the mundane aspects which they involve, and it is practically impossible at such time to remain in a state of cleaving to God.

3

But the truth is that the meaning of "for its own sake" means for the sake of the Torah. This is alluded to in the comment of the Rosh (Rabbi Asher ben Jehiel, 1250–1327) on a statement by Rabbi Eleazar bar Ẓadok

(Nedarim 62a): Perform the deeds for sake of their Creator and speak of them for their own sake. The comment of the Rosh is as follows: Perform the deeds for the sake of their Creator, or for the sake of God, who created all things for His sake, and speak of them for their own sake, that is, that all your discussions in the Torah shall be for the sake of the Torah, to gain knowledge and insight and not to be argumentative or boastful.

4

Certainly this does not mean that one needs no purity of thought or fear of God in the pursuit of Torah study. For we have a whole mishnah (Avot 3:21), which teaches that if there is no fear of God, there can be no wisdom. It is further stated (Yoma 72b): What is meant by the verse (Prov. 17:16): "Wherefore is there a price in the hands of a fool, to buy wisdom when he has no understanding?" It means, Woe unto scholars who study Torah but have no fear of God. In the Midrash (Exodus Rabbah, ch. 40) we have the statement that whoever is knowledgeable in the Torah but does not have the fear of God has nothing, for the Torah is safeguarded by the fear of God.

5

This is the truth, this is the true way God has ordained: Whenever a person has readied himself to study, it is proper for him to reflect before commencing, at least for some time, on the fear of God, in purity of heart, to confess his sins with deep feeling so that his Torah might be holy and pure. He is to aim to attach himself to God by the act of his study. This means to attach himself with all his strength to God's word, which is the *halakhah,* and thereby he will attach himself to God Himself since God and His will are the same, as it is written in the *Zohar,* and every law in the Torah represents God's will . . . Even if he is engaged in studying *aggadah* which has no bearing on law, he is still attached to the word of the Holy One, praised be He.

6

Thus it is appropriate for a person to prepare himself each time before beginning a session of Torah study, to reflect for some time on his Creator in purity of heart to stir in him the fear of God, to cleanse himself of sin with thoughts of penitence, so that he might attach himself to God and His will while studying the Torah. He is also to resolve to keep all that is prescribed in the Torah, the written and the oral, that he might discern the way to live on the basis of the holy Torah. Similarly, when seeking to clarify some point of law it is appropriate to pray that God may help him to come to a decision according to the true teaching of the Torah.

Similarly, in the course of studying, it is permissible for a person to stop awhile, lest the fear of God he took on himself before commencing to study begin to ebb, to concentrate again in the fear of God. This is in accordance with a further comment of the sages (Shabbat 31a): It is analogous to a person who said to his agent: Take up for me a *kur* of wheat to the loft, and he did so. He asked him: Did you mix with the wheat a *kab* of the preservative? He said: No. He said to him: It would have been better if you had not taken up the wheat. This is an allusion to one who is engaged in Torah study who must also mix with it the fear of God as a preservative that he might retain the Torah he has studied.

7

The truth is that a person who studies Torah regularly, for its own sake, as we have explained the meaning of "for its own sake" in chapter 3, need not invest much effort and time in studying books on the fear of God, so that this fear might become fixed in his heart, like the person who does not study Torah regularly. For the Torah itself will robe him with the fear of God even if he exerts but little time and effort. For this is the attribute of the Torah, as it is written (Avot 6:1): Whoever studies the Torah for its own sake attains to many merits . . . It robes him with humility and the fear of God. (*Nefesh haḤayyim,* Gate 4, ch. 1, 2, 3, 4, 6, 7, 9)

27.
Abraham Isaac Kook

Rabbi Abraham Isaac Kook (1865–1935) represents a climactic development in the history of Jewish mysticism. He was the heir of the hasidic tradition. The writings of the hasidic masters exerted a profound influence on his mind and their impact is discernible in his work. But there was a certain one-sidedness in Hasidism. Sometimes it neglected the discipline of talmudic learning. Its very stress on the spiritual had effected a certain alienation in the Jews from the world of reality. The stress on God's sovereignty had shrunk the zone of man's initiative. Man's role was to seek a vertical ascent toward God, by devotional prayer and meditation, by shedding the trappings of the material world. But the need to grapple with the problems of the world, to mold the world toward more humane ends, it was maintained, was not within man's scope.

There were positive as well as negative consequences to this position. As long as the Jews lived in a static society, in the rigid patterns of the ghetto, the transcendence of the physical enabled the Jew to create a substitute world for the real world which was intolerable and oppressive. In this substitute world of the spirit the mundane was not allowed to intrude, and the joy distilled by great faith sweetened life, and made it a joyous adventure. But when the thaw of modernism dissolved the rigidities of the old order and change was the order of the day, Ḥasidism became an obstructive factor, and inhibited change. Ḥasidism generally opposed the Zionist movement as human impertinence in "hurrying" the "end," an arrogant intrusion into what was clearly in God's domain, to redeem His people as and when He saw fit. And even when the Holocaust decreed by the Nazis had already written legibly its ominous signs on the wall, the masters of Ḥasidism refused to decipher its text, and failed to alarm their followers sufficiently concerning the impending tragedy. Some of that indifference to the existential realities of history is still manifest in many centers of Ḥasidism which have been reconstituted in the post-holocaust world. It expresses itself in a coolness, if not in open hostility, to the State of Israel.

Rabbi Kook liberated Jewish mysticism from this one-sidedness. He molded a new synthesis in which the yearning for God as a direct experience is pursued with unparalleled intensity, but in which God does not vanquish man, in which existential reality is not robbed of its cogency. In his thought, the physical and the historical are reinstated to a new dignity, not as competitive to the spiritual, but as the ground where the spiritual may have a new flowering. Indeed, all currents of Jewish and secular thought impinged on Rabbi Kook, and out of them all he molded a new mystical-philosophic system, that is still waiting to be discovered in the modern world.

Rabbi Kook's thought recognized a core of validity in all expressions of the life process, and he advocated a sympathetic openness to all thought as a necessary implication of our commitment to God who is the ultimate reality which inspires the universal expressions of life. At the same time he cautioned against the parochialism of embracing any fragment of life as though it were the whole. The most grievous proneness to parochialism he found in the religious community itself. Viewing the established religious system as an autonomous entity, abstracted from the rest of culture, tempts people into the illusion that one may cultivate piety as a self-contained system. One can never serve God in a vacuum of life. The true service of God is in the identification with the rhythms of the creative thrust emanating from God and endlessly seeking to engender and perfect life. It expresses itself in the surge to order life toward beauty, truth, righteousness and peace. It is by making oneself a channel for serving these values that one has entered into the divine rhythm pulsating through the universe. This is the closest we can come to relating our lives to God. Institutional religions, with a particular body of rites and doctrinal formulations, have their sole efficacy as channels of the "higher light," as aids in cultivating the sensibilities which will make us willing instruments in the service of divine ideals.

Rabbi Kook's published writings include four volumes on rabbinic law, a succinct formula of moral principle entitled *Midot haRe'ayah*, a collection of poetry, a treatise on the mysticism of the Hebrew alphabet, the cantillation and vowel signs, a treatise on penitence, two volumes of a commentary on the prayer book, three volumes of correspondence, three volumes of reflections on God and man under the title *Orot haKodesh,* and various occasional essays on problems in contemporary Jewish life. But the greater part of his work still remains in manuscript, and a definitive appraisal of Rabbi Kook's contributions as a religious philosopher must await the publication of all his writings. What has appeared thus far, however, clearly reveals him as a seer of great stature who added a most remarkable chapter to the history of Jewish mysticism.

The selections included here are from his three volume collection of letters, *Iggerot haRe'ayah;* the two volume commentary on the Prayer Book, *Olat Re'ayah;* the three volume meditations on the meaning of the spiritual life, *Orot haKodesh;* a collection of essays, *Orot,* which includes the collection called *Orot Yisrael;* a treatise *Musar Avikha,* "The Admonitions of a Father," which includes another treatise on morals called *Midot haRe'ayah;* an essay "Talele Orot" which was not included in any of Rabbi Kook's published volumes, but which was published in the journal *Tahkemoni* in Berne, Switzerland in 1910; and *Arpele Tohar.* The *Arpele Tohar* means "Clouds of Purity." It is a collection of meditations which was intended to be published in Jaffa in 1914, but was later withdrawn from official circulation.

A LETTER

Greetings of peace to the renowned scholar, celebrated for wisdom and piety, our master Rabbi Eleazar haKohen Bihovsky, may he live to a long and good life, Amen.

Your precious letter, written with the zeal of a sensitive Jew, reached me, and though I am always ready to associate myself with the God-fearing people in any measure they project to strengthen the Torah, especially here in Ereẓ Israel, I am compelled to remind those engaged in work for the sake of heaven to be knowledgeable in what they do. As our sages said (Berakhot 33a): Knowledge is important for the Bible in one sentence mentions God twice as the God of knowledge (I Sam. 2:3, "For the Lord is a God of knowledge").

Your honor must know that only a minor phase of the problem can be corrected through the method you suggest, through help from the government. The fundamental problem derives from more basic causes. The decline has come about not because the sages failed to protest against the heretics, who are undermining our Holy Land spiritually and materially, but because all they did was to protest, and no more.

If I should try to set forth even a small part of the thoughts evoked by a straightforward confrontation of this—paper will not suffice me. But I shall present some comments before a noble person like yourself; may the Lord bless you.

As I see it, the reason that everything done to strengthen Judaism and the position of the Jewish community in all its aspects is unsuccessful, is because of the neglect of the spiritual dimension, a total neglect in heart and mind. Everyone is trying to improve the "unenlightened piety," as though it were possible to keep alive the body without the soul. I am prepared to say that even Ḥasidism, whose entire raison d'être was to illumine every heart and mind with the divine light in its richness and splendor, has changed its character. It now follows the way of conventional piety so that there is no difference between it and the non-ḥasidic community. For this reason has love gone from the heart and all faces are stern, and reveal anger and depression, and it is for this reason that all is in a state of decline.

All these practical steps your honor has suggested will find their place. At times it will be in order to wage a vigorous defense against the worst offenses of the mixed multitude that has arisen in our time, on the eve of the coming of the messiah, but this will not bring us victory. What is most important is that we organize for the purpose of spreading the divine light in the world by wisdom, understanding and knowledge; to establish *yeshivot* in the diaspora and especially here in Ereẓ Israel where divine matters will be studied regularly, with a pure and lucid rationality; to take in hand the practical problems of the *yishuv*, establishing institutions, not merely for fundraising throughout the world, but for business and vocational training, under the supervision of people who know the Lord, praised be He, and truly love Him. As soon as we raise this banner, the power of evil in the Holy Land will be weakened and the esteem for the godly will be enhanced. As we increase these efforts, enlightenment will spread, and many of the defectors from our people will return in penitence, and the abuses will be ended.

As for the *ḥalukah* [stipends from charitable funds for families of Torah scholars], we shall certainly do our part to help that the transgressors of our religion not receive a portion. It seems to me that this principle has not been violated heretofore, thank God. But the work that must be done is not based on this. We suffer more from those who despise *ḥalukah* than anything we may suffer from those who depend on it. What is crucial is that we ignite the inner light by an increased study of Ḥasidism, and all those studies which focus on the hidden meaning of the Torah, to enhance piety as well as general enlightenment, that the divine light be made more manifest in the world. Then our reforms will prove efficacious.

Because of my preoccupation, I cannot elaborate any more at this time. I will close with warm greetings, as befits your precious self, and one who sends you best wishes from the Holy Land for success in your Torah endeavors. (*Iggerot haRe'ayah* I, 132)

SELECTIONS

1. The more clearly one studies the character of individual human souls, the more baffled one becomes over the great difference between personalities . . . It is, however, precisely through their differentiations that they are all united toward one objective, to contribute toward the perfection of the world, each person according to his special talent. Surely one must marvel at the higher wisdom wherein by an inner, mysterious power known only to God, these opposites are integrated and related one to the other, so that through the fusion of all the diverse minds and physiognomies, there emerges a unified structure of consummate harmony. (*Olat Re'ayah*, p. 388)

2. A chaotic world stands before us as long as we have not attained to that degree of higher perfection of uniting all life forces and all their diverse tendencies. As long as each one exalts himself, claiming, I am sovereign, I and none other—there cannot be peace in our midst . . . All our endeavors must be directed toward disclosing the light of general harmony, which derives not from suppressing any power, any thought, any tendency, but by bringing each of them within the vast ocean of infinite light, where all things find their unity, where all is ennobled, all is exalted, all is hallowed. (*ibid.*, p. 588)

3. Nothing remains the same; everything blooms, everything ascends, everything steadily increases in light and truth. The enlightened spirit does not become discouraged even when he discerns that the line of ascendance is circuitous, including both advance and decline, a forward movement but also fierce retreats, for even the retreats abound in the potential of future progress. (*Olat Re'ayah* II, p. 484)

4. Each body of thought has its own logic and all ideas are tied to each other by a systematic relatedness . . . There is no such thing as a vain or useless thought . . . since each emanates from the same source in the divine wisdom. If there are thoughts that appear futile or empty, the futility and the emptiness are only in the outer garb in which these thoughts are enwrapped. But if we probe into all their inwardness, we shall find that they, too, offer us the sustenance of life . . . and as man grows in the scale of perfection, he draws upon all ideas, his own and those of others, for the kernal of abiding truth. He is made more perfect through them, and they through him. (*Orot haKodesh* I, p. 17)

5. There is one who sings the song of his own life, and in himself he finds everything, his full spiritual sufficiency. There is another who sings the song of his people. He leaves the circle of his private existence, for he does not find it broad enough . . . He aspires for the heights and he attaches himself with tender love to the whole of Israel, he sings her songs, grieves in her afflictions, and delights in her hopes. He ponders lofty and pure thoughts concerning her past and her future, and probes lovingly and wisely the content of her inner essence. Then there is one whose spirit extends beyond the boundary of Israel, to sing the song of man . . . He is drawn to man's universal vocation and he hopes for his highest perfection. And this is the life source from which he draws his thoughts and probings, his yearnings and his visions. But there is one who rises even higher, uniting himself with the whole existence, with all creatures, with all worlds. With all of them he sings his song. It is of one such as this that tradition has said that whoever sings a portion of song each day is assured of the life of the world-to-come. (*Orot haKodesh* II, p. 458)

6. The highest level of holiness is expressed in silence. It is the holiness of existence as seen in its wholeness, in which the individual transcends his own particularity, and lives life in its universality, in the life of all being. He is the light of the universe, the basis of its being, and the vitalizing energy of its ongoing life. It is for his sake that the universe is sustained, but he is as nothing in his own eyes.

He is not withdrawn from the world. He is immersed in life and his life is the holy of the holy, it is life at its highest. His heartbeat, the blood coursing in his veins, his inner longing, the gaze of his eyes—they all register and they all proclaim a life of truth, a life of divine heroism.

If a person who has risen to the holiness of silence should lower himself to a particularized form of divine service, in prayer, Torah study, to the limited problems of morality, he will suffer and feel oppressed. He will feel as though his soul, which embraces all existence, is being pressed as though with prongs, to surrender her to the lowland where everything exists within a prescribed measure, to the narrowness of a particular path, when all paths are open to him, all abounding in light, all abounding in life's treasures. (*Orot haKodesh* II, p. 307)

7. Whenever a person raises himself through good deeds, through a higher stirring of his yearning for godliness, for wisdom, justice, beauty, and equity, he perfects thereby the spiritual disposition of all existence. All people become better in their inwardness through the ascendancy of the good in any of them . . . Such virtue in any one person is due to spread among the general populace, to stir each one, according to his capacity, toward merit, and thus all existence thereby becomes ennobled and more exalted. (*Orot haKodesh* III, pp. 314f.)

8. The Holy One, praised be He, bestowed a mercy on His world by not confining His endowments to one place, one person, one people, one land, one generation or one world, but His endowments are diffused, and the quest for perfection, which is the most idealistic striving of our nature, directs us to seek the higher unity which must finally come in the world. In that day—God will be one and His name one (*Orot Yisrael* 5:2)

9. I love everybody. It is impossible for me not to love all people, all nations. With all the depth of my being, I desire to see them grow toward beauty, toward perfection. My love for the Jewish people is with more ardor, more depth. But my inner desire reaches out with a mighty love toward all. There is veritably no need for me to force this feeling of love. It flows directly from the holy depth of wisdom, from the divine soul.

It is no accident, but of the very essence of my being, that I find delight in the pursuit of the divine mysteries in unrestrained freedom. This is my primary purpose. All my other goals, the practical and the rational, are only peripheral to my real self. I must find my happiness within my inner self, unconcerned whether people agree with me, or by what is happening to my own career. The more I shall recognize my own identity, and the more I will permit myself to be original, and to stand on my own feet with an inner conviction which is based on knowledge, perception, feeling and song, the more will the light of God shine on me, and the more will my potentialities develop to serve as a blessing to myself, and to the world.

The refinements to which I subject myself, my thoughts, my imagination, my morals, and my emotions, will also serve as general refinements for the whole world. A person must say, 'The whole world was created for my sake.' (*Arpele Tohar*, p. 22)

10. Concerning the other faiths. . . the aim of the enlightenment which emanates from Judaism is not to absorb or destroy them, as we do

not aim at the destruction of the world's different nationalities, but to perfect them and to stimulate them toward higher development so that they may free themselves of their dross, and then they will automatically be joined to the root of Israel. . . This applies even to pagan faiths, and certainly to those faiths which are in part based on the light of Israel's Torah. (*Iggerot* I, 112)

11. . . . We must begin by creating a literature, new-old in its orientation, that will not turn its back on the old, but that will fortify itself with the new in order to know all the profound good in the old, and how the new always supplements it and perfects it. . . . Songs throbbing with life, abounding with divine vitality will emerge, and a new, illuminating culture will arise and prosper. . . . The old will be renewed, and the new will be invested with holiness, and together they will become torches shining their light over Zion, and Zion will then draw to herself the noblest of her children who will also be her builders. (*Iggerot* I, 164)

12. We have abandoned the soul of the Torah . . . Whoever speaks of this to the shepherds of our people is deemed presumptuous and mad. The hour calls for a mighty act of penitence . . . We must be radical. With minor compromises we shall correct nothing. . . Orthodoxy, in waging . . . battles with negations, contents itself with vain imaginings . . . Whoever is strong of heart, who wields a vigorous pen, and whose soul is touched by the divine spirit, must go forth to the battlefield and cry out, "Give us light." (*Iggerot* II, 481)

13. Conventional theology assumes that the different religions must necessarily oppose each other . . . But on reaching full maturity the human spirit aspires to rise above every manner of conflict and opposition, and a person then recognizes all expressions of the spiritual life as an organic whole . . . When the light of Judaism becomes manifest in the world, and overcomes with decisive resoluteness its obscurities, resulting from the failure truly to know itself, there will at once be revealed to the world the precious attribute of unity, which harmonizes all forces as a unitary phenomenon, at the same time leaving untouched the distinctive essence of each. The spiritual world in all its expressions will then be integrated into an organic whole, so that even this realm which abounds in the conflict of the different religions will be pervaded by peace and light. There will remain a decided difference in the qualities of the different faiths and in the values of one as compared with another. From the entire ensemble there will automatically become manifest the central essence which is at the heart of all faiths. (*Talelei Orot* pp. 17f.)

LOVE

1. The heart must be filled with love for all beings.

2. The love of all creation comes first, then comes the love for all mankind, and then follows the love for the Jewish people, in which all other loves are included, since it is the destiny of the Jews to serve toward the perfection of all things. All these loves are to be expressed in practical action, by pursuing the welfare of those we are bidden to love, and to seek their advancement. But the highest of all loves is the love of God, which is love in its fullest maturing. This love is not intended for any derivative ends; when it fills the human heart, this itself spells man's greatest happiness.

3. The flame of the holy fire of the love of God is always burning in the human heart. It is this which warms the human spirit and illumines life; the delights it yields are endless, there is no measure by which to assess it. And how cruel is man toward himself, that he allows himself to be sunk in the dark abyss of life, troubles himself with petty considerations, while he erases from his mind this which spells true life, which is the basis for all that gives meaning to life. It is for this reason that he does not share in it, and walks this world bound by the heavy burden of his material existence, without light to illumine his way. But all this is contrary to the nature of life; indeed it is contrary to the nature of all existence. The grace of God's love, a boon from on high, is destined to break out from its confinements, and the holiness of life will hew a path toward this delight, so as to enable it to appear in its full splendor and might. "No eye has seen what God alone will do for those who wait for Him" (Isa. 64:3).

4. The love for people must be alive in heart and soul, a love for all people and a love for all nations, expressing itself in a desire for their spiritual and material advancement; hatred may direct itself only toward the evil and the filth in the world. One cannot reach the exalted position of being able to recite the verse from the morning prayer (I Chron. 16:8): "Praise the Lord, invoke His name, declare His works among the nations," without experiencing the deep, inner love stirring one to a solicitousness for all nations, to improve their material state, to promote their happiness. This disposition qualifies the Jewish people to experience the spirit of the messiah.

Whenever in our classic tradition we encounter allusions to hatred, clearly the reference is to the phenomenon of evil, which has disrupted by force the unity of many nations at the present time, and certainly in ancient times when the world was in a much lower moral state. But we must realize that the life process, its inherent light and holiness, never leaves the divine image, with which each person and each nation has been endowed, each according to its level of qualification, and this nucleus of holiness will uplift all. It is because of this perspective on life that we are concerned for the fullest progress to prevail in the world, for the ascent of justice, merged with beauty and vitality, for the perfection of all creation, commencing with man, in all the particular groupings through which he functions. This is the essence which lies at the heart of the Jewish outlook, that, by the grace of God, we are now reviving on a practical and spiritual plane.

5. Though our love for people must be all-inclusive, embracing the wicked as well, this in no way blunts our hatred for evil itself; on the contrary it strengthens it. For it is not because of the dimension of evil which clings to a person that we include him in our love, but because of the good in him, which our love tells us is to be found everywhere. And since we detach the dimension of the good to love him for it, our hatred for evil becomes unblunted and absolute.

6. It is proper to hate a currupt person only for his defects, but insofar as he is endowed with a divine image it is in order to love him. We must also realize that the precious dimension of his worth is a more authentic expression of his nature, than the lower characteristics which developed in him through circumstances.

7. Much effort is needed to broaden the love for people to the proper level, at which it must pervade life to its fullest depth. This must be done in opposition to the superficial view, which suggests itself initially on the basis of inadequate study of the Torah and of conventional morality, and where it would seem as though there is a contradiction to such love, or, at least, indifference to it. The highest level of love for people is the love due the individual person, it must embrace every single individual, regardless of differences in views on religion, or differences of race or climate. It is essential to understand the mentalities of different nations and groupings, to study their characteristics and life-styles, in order to know how to base our human love on foundations that will readily translate themselves into action. It is only a person rich in love for people, and a love for each individual person who can reach the love for his own nation in its noblest dimension, spiritually and practically. The narrow-mindedness which leads one to view whatever is outside a particular nation, even what is outside the Jewish people, as ugly and

defiling, is a phase of the frightful darkness that undermines altogether every effort to reach that state of spiritual development whose dawn is awaited by every sensitive spirit. (*Musar Avikha,* pp. 92–96, sections 1, 2, 4, 5, 8, 9, 10)

AFTERWORD

The Mystical Fraternity

The Jewish mystical tradition is splintered into many fragments. It sometimes invites us to the beatitude of cultivating closeness to God in a direct, lucid idiom, unencumbered by any strangeness of rite or symbol. Sometimes its quest is obscured by strange imagery, by complicated and esoteric conceptual structures within which it sets the path for man's journey toward God. But it is possible to discern amidst this divergence a common thrust which is sustained by a transcending reality. The Infinite and the finite do meet, the God who abides in mystery, whom finite minds cannot comprehend, meets his finite creatures halfway through a process of reducing His manifestations which adapts the divine light to the receptive vessels of a mortal.

The plant turns toward the sun, the root pushes its way deeper into the earth, the child reaches out toward the mother's breast. These and other parallel phenomena are part of a rhythm that pulsates through all being. The soul which is a dimension of the divine in all of us is astir with longing for union with the divine source whence all life emerges. Liberated from distractions which blunt this quest, the soul lifts us above the self we are by customary involvements, and it ushers us into the mysterious realm of the divine on the other side of the boundary which marks our finitude. It is the testimony of all mystics that the boundary is crossed from the other side as well, that the God we seek is also the God who seeks us, and that a channel of grace is thus established through a linking of the human and the divine.

Mystics vary in the intensity of their experience. Some who have felt deeply enough, on whom the light has shone with particular profusion, have sought to share their light with their fellow-men. Some have left documents of their experience, enabling others to feel vicariously what they have felt and to be charged with sensibilities that will make them receptive for a like encounter. Some mystics, so impressed with the uniqueness of their experience, have proclaimed themselves as the exclusive custodians of the only path by which man may journey toward God, as the sole guides to salvation. A confrontation of the universality of the human quest for God and the discernment of the transcendent reality that shines through this diversity helps us to rise above such particularism. The Talmud acknowledged that there were prophets and seers among people of other faiths. The gift of prophecy was not an exclusive grace bestowed on one person or one people.

This does not mean that all mystical systems are alike. None of them gives us absolute truth, because the receptive vessel of the human mind is limited and can receive only a fragment of the light that shines on it. According to Jewish tradition, even Moses could not break out of the barrier of finitude, and could not penetrate the fiftieth "gate of discernment." But all of them give us *some* truth, though they differ among themselves in the levels of truth they embody. And the quest is unfinished; God continues to reveal Himself to sensitive souls reaching out to Him in sincerity and in truth. We are the heirs of all these mystical treasures, and it is for us to probe them as one probes the precious rare ore extracted from the earth, to separate the genuine treasure from spurious substances that may cling to it.

Jewish mysticism is an episode in the larger treasure of mystical experience, and it has characteristics that are its own, which set it apart from other mystical systems. Differences in culture and in religious tradition find echoes in the form in which the mystic shapes the fruits of his vision. Sometimes the mystical systems interact. We have noted that a Christian adaptation of the Kabbalah gained a following among mystically inclined Christians during the latter part of the Middle Ages. The belief in reincarnation which appears to have originated among oriental mystics was adapted and became integrated with kabbalistic and hasidic teachings. But even where these mystical traditions remained in a seeming autonomy, they were inwardly akin. Their divergence of form remains transparent of an underlying commonality of inspiration and purpose. Amidst all their divergence, all mystical systems bear the same eloquent testimony, that man is by nature a seeker after his roots, which are set in heaven rather than in earth. Man is restless in alienation from God, and he cannot find peace until he finds God.

Whether they are aware of it or not, all mystics constitute a fraternity of seekers after God. They offer testimony that rites, creeds, laws and customs, which serve to introduce us to the knowledge of God and to fashion a bridge on which we may move to serving Him, are only a means to an end. The end is the encounter with God as a personal experience. When the mediating agents have introduced the lovers to each other, their work has been accomplished. When the lover and His beloved have met, words and gestures have become unnecessary.

Bibliography

The books cited here will be helpful in clarifying the nature of general mysticism as well as that of Jewish mysticism. Texts from which the selections in this book are quoted are mentioned in the sections where they appear and are not repeated here.

Abelson, J., *Jewish Mysticism* (London, 1913).
Agus, Jacob, *The Banner of Jerusalem* (New York, 1946).
Arberry, A.J., *Sufism* (London, 1969).

Band, Arnold J. (tr.), *Nahman of Bratslav—The Tales* (New York, 1978).
Ben Amos, Dan and Mintz, Jerome R., *In Praise of the Baal Shem Tov* (Bloomington, 1970).
Bennett, Charles A., *A Philosophical Study of Mysticism* (New Haven, 1931).
Blau, Joseph L., *The Christian Interpretation of the Cabbala in the Renaissance* (New York, 1944).
Blumenthal, David R., *Understanding Jewish Mysticism—The Merkabah Tradition and the Zoharic Tradition* (New York, 1978).

Bokser, Ben Zion, *From the World of the Cabbalah* (New York, 1954).
idem, *Abraham Isaac Kook* (New York, 1978).
Bridges, Hal, *American Mysticism* (New York, 1970).
Buber, Martin, *The Tales of Rabbi Nachman* (New York, 1956).
idem, *Hasidism and Modern Man* (New York, 1958).
idem, *The Origin and Meaning of Hasidism* (New York, 1960).
idem, *Tales of the Hasidim*, 2 vols. (New York, 1974).
Butler, Dom Cuthbert, *Western Mysticism* (New York, 1966).

Cumont, Franz, *Astrology and Religion Among the Greeks and Romans* (New York, 1960).

Danto, Arthur C., *Mysticism and Morality* (New York, 1972).
Dasgupta, S.N., *Hindu Mysticism* (New York, 1959).
Dresner, Samuel, *The Zaddik* (New York, 1960).

Franck, Adolph, *The Kabbalah* (tr. from the French by I. Sossnitz; New York, 1926).
Fremantle, Anne, *The Protestant Mystics* (Boston, 1965).
Friedman, Maurice, *Touchstones of Reality* (New York, 1972).

Ghiselin, Brewster, *The Creative Process* (New York, 1955).
Green, Arthur, *Tormented Master: A Life of Rabbi Nachman of Bratslav* (Alabama, 1978).

Heschel, Abraham Joshua, *Man is not Alone* (New York, 1951).
idem, *The Sabbath* (New York, 1951).
idem, *God in Search of Man* (New York, 1955).
idem, *A Passion for Truth* (New York, 1973).

Inge, William Randolph, *Mysticism in Religion* (London, 1969).

Jacobs, Louis (tr.), *The Palm Tree of Deborah* by Moses Cordovero (London, 1960).
idem, (tr.), *Tract on Ecstasy* by Dov Baer of Lubavitch (London, 1963).
idem, *Seeker of Unity* (New York, 1966).
idem, *Hasidic Prayer* (New York, 1973).
Jones, Rufus M., *Studies in Mystical Religion* (London, 1909).

Kramer, Simon G., *God and Man in the Sefer Hasidim* (New York, 1966).

Langer, Jiri, *Nine Gates to the Hasidic Mysteries* (New York, 1961).

Levin, Meyer, *Classic Hasidic Tales* (New York, 1951).

Meltzer, David, *The Secret Garden* (New York, 1976).
Mindel, Nisan (tr.), *Likutei Amarim* (*Tanya*) by Shneur Zalman of Lyady (New York, 1969).

Newman, Louis I., *The Hasidic Anthology* (New York, 1934).

Otto, Rudolph, *Mysticism East and West* (New York, 1962).

Rabinowicz, Harry M., *The World of Hasidism* (London, 1970).
Rabinowitsch, Wolf Zeev, *Lithuanian Hasidism* (London, 1970).

Schaya, Leo, *The Universal Meaning of the Kabbalah* (tr. from the French by Nancy Pearson; Baltimore, 1973).
Schochet, Jacob Immanuel (tr.), *Iggeret haKodesh* by Shneur Zalman of Lyady (New York, 1968).
Scholem, Gershom G., *Major Trends in Jewish Mysticism* (New York, 1954).
idem, *Jewish Gnosticism, Merkabah Mysticism and Talmudic Tradition* (New York, 1968).
idem, *On the Kabbalah and Its Symbolism* (New York, 1970).
idem, *The Messianic Idea in Judaism* (New York, 1971).
idem, *Shabbatai Sevi* (New York, 1973).
idem, *Kabbalah* (New York, 1974).
Singer, Shalom Alhanan, *Medieval Jewish Mysticism Book of the Pious* (Northbrook, 1971).
Spencer, Sidney, *Mysticism in World Religion* (New York, 1963).
Sperling H. and Simon, M. (tr.) *The Zohar*, 5 vols. (London, 1931–1934).
Steinsaltz, Adin, *The Thirteen Petalled Rose* (New York, 1980).
Sterning, Knut, *The Book of Formation* (London, 1923).
Suzuki, D.T., *Mysticism Christian Buddhist* (New York, 1962).

Underhill, Evelyn, *Mysticism* (Cleveland, 1965).

Waite, Arthur Edward, *The Holy Kabbalah* (London, 19[illegible]).
Weiner, Herbert, *9 1/2 Mystics* (New York, 1969).
Werblowsky, R. J. Z., *Joseph Karo* (Oxford, 1962).
Wiesel, Elie, *Souls on Fire* (New York, 1972).